Chinese Stories of Drug Addiction

Addiction to illicit drugs is a pressing social concern across greater China, where there are likely several million drug addicts at present. This research breaks new ground by examining Chinese people's stories of drug addiction.

Chinese Stories of Drug Addiction systematically evaluates how drug addiction is represented and constructed in a series of contemporary life stories and filmic stories from mainland China, Taiwan and Hong Kong. These stories recount experiences leading up to and during drug addiction, as well as experiences during drug rehabilitation and recovery. Through analysis of these contemporary life stories and filmic stories, the book presents a comprehensive picture of how Chinese people from both inside the experience of drug addiction and outside of it make sense of a social practice that is deemed to be highly transgressive in Chinese culture. It employs a blended discourse analytic and narrative analytic approach to show how salient cultural, political and institutional discourses shape these Chinese stories and experiences. Complementing existing humanities research, which documents the historical narrative of drug addiction in China at the expense of the contemporary narrative, the book also provides health and allied professionals with a rich insight into how Chinese people from different geographical locations and walks of life make sense of the experience of drug addiction.

Moving beyond historical narrative to examine contemporary stories, *Chinese Stories of Drug Addiction* offers a valuable contribution to the fields of Chinese studies and personal health and wellbeing, as well as being of practical use to health professionals.

Guy Ramsay is a senior lecturer in Chinese studies at The University of Queensland, Australia. In 2013, he published *Mental Illness, Dementia and Family in China* (Routledge).

Routledge/Asian Studies Association of Australia (ASAA) East Asia Series

Edited by Morris Low

Editorial Board: Professor Geremie Barmé (Australian National University), Emeritus Professor Colin Mackerras (Griffith University), Professor Vera Mackie (University of Wollongong) and Professor Sonia Ryang (University of Iowa)

This series represents a showcase for the latest cutting-edge research in the field of East Asian studies, from both established scholars and rising academics. It will include studies from every part of the East Asian region (including China, Japan, North and South Korea and Taiwan) as well as comparative studies dealing with more than one country. Topics covered may be contemporary or historical, and relate to any of the humanities or social sciences. The series is an invaluable source of information and challenging perspectives for advanced students and researchers alike.

Routledge is pleased to invite proposals for new books in the series. In the first instance, any interested authors should contact:

> Associate Professor Morris Low
> School of History, Philosophy, Religion and Classics
> University of Queensland
> Brisbane, QLD 4072, Australia

Routledge/Asian Studies Association of Australia (ASAA) East Asia Series

1 **Gender in Japan**
   Power and public policy
   Vera Mackie

2 **The Chaebol and Labour in Korea**
   The development of management strategy in Hyundai
   Seung Ho Kwon and Michael O'Donnell

3 **Rethinking Identity in Modern Japan**
   Nationalism as aesthetics
   Yumiko Iida

4 **The Manchurian Crisis and Japanese Society, 1931–33**
   Sandra Wilson

5 **Korea's Development Under Park Chung Hee**
Rapid industrialization, 1961–1979
Hyung-A Kim

6 **Japan and National Anthropology**
A critique
Sonia Ryang

7 **Homoerotic Sensibilities in Late Imperial China**
Wu Cuncun

8 **Postmodern, Feminist and Postcolonial Currents in Contemporary Japanese Culture**
A reading of Murakami Haruki, Yoshimoto Banana, Yoshimoto Takaaki and Karatani Kōjin
Murakami Fuminobu

9 **Japan on Display**
Photography and the emperor
Morris Low

10 **Technology and the Culture of Progress in Meiji Japan**
David G. Wittner

11 **Women's History and Local Community in Postwar Japan**
Curtis Anderson Gayle

12 **Defending Rights in Contemporary China**
Jonathan Benney

13 **Re-reading the Salaryman in Japan**
Crafting masculinities
Romit Dasgupta

14 **Mental Illness, Dementia and Family in China**
Guy Ramsay

15 **Japan's New Left Movements**
Legacies for civil society
Takemasa Ando

16 **Chinese Stories of Drug Addiction**
Beyond the opium dens
Guy Ramsay

Chinese Stories of Drug Addiction
Beyond the opium dens

Guy Ramsay

LONDON AND NEW YORK

First published 2016 by Routledge

2 Park Square, Milton Park, Abingdon, Oxfordshire OX14 4RN
711 Third Avenue, New York, NY 10017

Routledge is an imprint of the Taylor & Francis Group, an Informa business

First issued in paperback 2018

Copyright © 2016 Guy Ramsay

The right of Guy Ramsay to be identified as author of this work has been asserted by him in accordance with sections 77 and 78 of the Copyright, Designs and Patents Act 1988.

All rights reserved. No part of this book may be reprinted or reproduced or utilised in any form or by any electronic, mechanical, or other means, now known or hereafter invented, including photocopying and recording, or in any information storage or retrieval system, without permission in writing from the publishers.

Notice:
Product or corporate names may be trademarks or registered trademarks, and are used only for identification and explanation without intent to infringe.

British Library Cataloguing in Publication Data
A catalogue record for this book is available from the British Library

Library of Congress Cataloging-in-Publication Data
A catalog record for this book has been requested

ISBN: 978-1-138-94629-3 (hbk)
ISBN: 978-1-138-60899-3 (pbk)

Typeset in Times New Roman
by Apex CoVantage, LLC

This book is dedicated with love to Mum and Lily.

Contents

	Acknowledgements	xi
1	Introduction	1
2	Gendered exemplars: life stories of drug addiction and recovery	21
3	Institutional schema: life stories of drug addiction and rehabilitation	49
4	Marginalisation and palliation: filmic stories of drug addiction, rehabilitation and recovery	73
5	Conclusion	111
	Index	129

Acknowledgements

I wish to thank the following people and organisations for their kind assistance in the development and writing of this book: Rebecca Carter, Helen Creese, Daphne Hsieh, Wendy Jiang, Leong Ko, Yenney Lai, Yin Bing Leung, Haiyan Liang, Shirley Liu, Morris Low, Ying-hsiu Lu, Wai Wai Lui, John McNair, Karen Molnar, Alex Pan, Annie Pohlman, Rosie Roberts, Lara Vanderstaay, Yingxian Wang, Carol Wical, Shirley Wu; and the Centre for Critical and Cultural Studies at The University of Queensland, the University of Queensland Library, and the reviewers of the manuscript.

1 Introduction

Despite a global war against illicit drug use and trafficking, which has been carried out over many decades, drug addiction remains a pressing social concern in countries throughout the world. China is no exception. Drug addiction blighted twentieth-century Chinese society until it was virtually eliminated from mainland China in the early 1950s, following the Communist victory in 1949 (Dikötter, Laamann & Zhou 2004; Liang & Lu 2013; Zheng 2005; Zhou 1999, 2000b). The phenomenon, however, re-emerged in mainland China alongside the program of reform and opening up [改革开放] that was initiated in 1978, following the death of Mao Zedong some two years earlier (Biddulph & Xie 2011; Dikötter, Laamann & Zhou 2004; Liang & Lu 2013; Luo *et al.* 2014; Zheng 2005; Zhou 1999, 2000b). Drug addiction in the Chinese communities of nearby Taiwan and Hong Kong was an enduring concern during the Japanese and British colonial periods of the nineteenth and twentieth centuries, and persists to the present-day under local rule (Chou, Hung & Liao 2007; Chu 2008; Hsu 2014; Li 2013; Traver 1992).

Chinese Stories of Drug Addiction: Beyond the Opium Dens explores the phenomenon of drug addiction in mainland China, Taiwan and Hong Kong. The book moves beyond the opium dens of the Chinese historical narrative to examine contemporary stories told by Chinese people suffering from drug addiction as well as contemporary stories told by others about Chinese people suffering from drug addiction. The stories examined in the book include real life accounts of drug addiction written by Chinese people in rehabilitation or recovery, and filmic accounts of drug addiction presented in contemporary mainland Chinese, Taiwanese and Hong Kong film and television productions. The book utilises the perspectives and approaches of discourse analysis and narrative analysis to analyse the representation and construction of drug addiction from these different authorial positions, located both inside and outside the experience of addiction. In so doing, the book explains how salient discourses – cultural, political and institutional – shape these Chinese stories of drug addiction.

2 *Introduction*

Drug addiction in greater China

Clinical research profiles the typical Chinese drug addict as a young (under 35 years of age), single male, who lacks formal education and is either unemployed or self-employed (Chou, Hung & Liao 2007; Gao 2011; Liang & Lu 2013; Lu, Miethe & Liang 2009; Lu & Wang 2008; Luo *et al.* 2014; McCoy *et al.* 1997). Minority nationality groups [少数民族] are overrepresented in mainland China, a consequence of their close proximity to the southwestern and western borders with the drug-producing centres of Burma, Laos, Pakistan and Afghanistan (Lu, Miethe & Liang 2009; Lu & Wang 2008; McCoy *et al.* 1997; Trevaskes 2013; Zheng, 2005). Recent United Nations Office on Drugs and Crime (UNODC) percentages on the annual prevalence of illicit drug use among 15–64 year-olds place opiates (natural opium products) and opioids (synthetic products that behave like opiates) at 0.5% in mainland China, 0.4% in Taiwan, and 0.4% in Hong Kong (UNODC 2011). These figures resemble that for Australia (0.6%) but are well below that for the United States (6.47%) (UNODC 2011). The use of amphetamines registers at 0.6% for Taiwan and 0.4% for Hong Kong, with no data for mainland China (UNODC 2011). Their use is more common in the United States (1.5%) and Australia (2.7%) (UNODC 2011).

These data point to the continuing popularity of opiates, opioids and amphetamines amongst illicit drugs users in mainland China, Taiwan and Hong Kong. Nevertheless, recent UNODC figures for people in treatment for drug addiction show that opioids, such as heroin, constitute the leading illicit drug of addiction in mainland China, Taiwan and Hong Kong (79.7%, 73.1% and 57.9%, respectively), followed by amphetamines in mainland China and Taiwan (19.1% and 22.1%, respectively) and ketamine in Hong Kong (27.4%) (UNODC 2011). More people in Hong Kong are being treated for addiction to the dissociative drug, ketamine, than for addiction to the stimulants, amphetamine and methamphetamine (8.7%) (UNODC 2011). This prominence of ketamine addiction in Hong Kong is borne out in the Hong Kong life stories and filmic stories of drug addiction that are analysed in Chapters 3 and 4 of this book. Biddulph (2013), Lee, Hsu and Tsay (2013), Levin (2015), Li (2013), Luo *et al.* (2014) and the UNODC (2013) also point to an emerging ketamine problem in mainland China and Taiwan at present.

Historically, opiate addiction was a major social and political concern in China in the centuries leading up to the Communist takeover of mainland China in 1949. Opium had been grown and used for medicinal purposes in China since the Tang dynasty of the seventh to tenth centuries (Baumler 2007; Lu, Miethe & Liang 2009; Zheng 2005). It began to be used as an aphrodisiac by the elites during the middle period of the Ming rule[1] (Lu, Miethe & Liang 2009; Zheng 2005). Over time, opium was assigned a 'luxury . . . and feminine, if not explicitly sexual' status that it continued to hold through to the Qing rule of the seventeenth to twentieth centuries (Zheng 2005, p. 17).

The smoking of opium (often laced with tobacco as 'madak') was introduced by the Dutch in the sixteenth century and remained largely confined to southeast China, the hub for maritime trade, through the seventeenth and eighteenth centuries (Baumler 2007; Dikötter, Laamann & Zhou 2004; Lu, Miethe & Liang 2009; Zheng 2005; Zhou 1999). During the early part of the nineteenth century, opium smoking started to extend beyond the southeast coast, leading to the popularisation of its recreational use across China, often in specialised premises known as opium dens [鸦片馆 or 鸦片窟] (Baumler 2007; Dikötter, Laamann & Zhou 2004; Zheng 2005; Zhou 1999). Unlike heroin today, at this time, opium served as 'one of the chief factors of social inclusion rather than exclusion' (Dikötter, Laamann & Zhou 2004, p. 46). As a consequence, by the mid-nineteenth century, opium was 'used across the social scale, from the imperial household down to the poor rickshaw puller' (Dikötter, Laamann & Zhou 2004, p. 47). This crossing of class lines, Zheng (2005, p. 4) claims, sparked agitation for the prohibition of opium: 'When the rich smoked it, it was cultured and a status symbol; when the poor began to inhale, opium smoking became degrading and ultimately criminal.'

At the turn of the twentieth century, the number of opium users in China numbered around 2.5% of the population (Dikötter, Laamann & Zhou 2004). Before too long, around one in four Chinese men were regularly using opium and its derivatives (Lu, Fang & Wang 2008; Lu, Miethe & Liang 2009).[2] Drug addicts were turning to opium derivatives such as morphine and heroin, in part due to the lower cost of parenteral administration and the increasing popularisation of the use of syringes (Baumler 2007; Brook & Wakabayashi 2000; Dikötter, Laamann & Zhou 2004; Eykholt 2000; Zheng 2005). At the time, the use of morphine, like the use of the syringe, represented 'a "modern" statement' that 'conferred status, respect and prestige' on the user (Dikötter, Laamann & Zhou 2004, p. 152). As a consequence of this, Dikötter, Laamann and Zhou (2004, p. 186) state: 'the punctured skins of narcotic users became a cultural marker of addiction' in Republican era China (1912–1949).

A robust, well-organised and widely supported movement against the use of opium and its derivatives emerged during the late imperial and early Republican periods (Baumler 2007; Dikötter, Laamann & Zhou 2004; Zhou 1999). During these periods, the notion of drug addiction as a social vice gained social and political currency, being lexicalised in the expression yin [瘾] (Baumler 2007; Dikötter, Laamann & Zhou 2004).[3] Fears about opium addiction escalated, Dikötter, Laamann and Zhou (2004) contend, even though its recreational use probably caused few problems for most users. The development of the anti-opium discourse in large part can be attributed to a political agenda that sought to ferment nationalistic sentiment (Baumler 2007; Dikötter, Laamann & Zhou 2004; Wyman 2000; Zhou 1999, 2000b). This agenda successfully linked opium to the decline of China, as epitomised by the loss of the nineteenth century wars with Britain and Japan and the subsequent occupation of Chinese territory by foreign

4   *Introduction*

powers, which continued through the Republican period (Baumler 2007; Zheng 2005; Zhou 1999). Opium addiction thus came to represent both 'the epitome of imperialist power' and 'the principal cause of "racial" decline and "moral" turpitude' in China (Dikötter, Laamann & Zhou 2004, p. 109). The strength of this discourse is demonstrated by its continuing resonance in present-day China (Liang & Lu 2013; Zheng 2005). This occurs even though the origin of this discourse, somewhat ironically, can be traced back to foreign missionaries (Baumler 2007; Dikötter, Laamann & Zhou 2004).

The anti-opium movement ostensibly had some success during the Republican period in that opiate use was criminalised (Baumler 2007; Dikötter, Laamann & Zhou 2004).[4] Criminal sanctions included incarceration and even execution (Baumler 2007; Dikötter, Laamann & Zhou 2004; Zhou 1999, 2000b). The effectiveness of the anti-opium laws and movements, in the end, was limited by the political instability and the fracturing of Chinese sovereignty during the Republican period, a result of warlordism, foreign occupation and the civil war between the Nationalists and the Communists (Baumler 2007; Lu, Miethe & Liang 2009). At this time, the colonial governments of nearby Taiwan and Hong Kong held monopolies over the legal production and supply of opium to local residents (Baumler 2007; Hsu 2014; Kobayashi 2000; Li 2013; Munn 2000; Traver 1992; Wakabayashi 2000). The Japanese rulers used their monopoly to significantly curb the use of opium in Taiwan, by gradually reducing supply and potency (Brook & Wakabayashi 2000; Chu 2008; Hsu 2014; Li 2013).[5] The British rulers, on the other hand, used their monopoly to maximise government revenue,[6] by permitting the use of opium in Hong Kong while proscribing the use of competing drugs, such as morphine and heroin (Traver 1992). After World War II, opium was supplanted by heroin in Taiwan and Hong Kong, due to opium's criminalisation and heroin's relative ease of use (Traver 1992).

When the Communists took control of mainland China in 1949, around 5% of the population were opium users (Lu, Fang & Wang 2008; Lu, Miethe & Liang 2009). Within a few years, drug addiction virtually had been eliminated from mainland China (Biddulph & Xie 2011; Dikötter, Laamann & Zhou 2004; Liang & Lu 2013; Zhou 1999, 2000b). Mainland China remained drug-free throughout Mao Zedong's rule, due to the 'unprecedented state hegemony' that stemmed from the Communist Party's 'attempts to establish effective social control in China' (Zhou 1999, p. 108). Opium suppression, once again, became linked to a nationalistic agenda that, now, was being advanced by the government of the People's Republic of China (Liang & Lu 2013; Zhou 1999). Drug addiction, nevertheless, returned with mainland China's opening up to the outside world post-1978 (Biddulph & Xie 2011; Dikötter, Laamann & Zhou 2004; Liang & Lu 2013; Luo *et al.* 2014; Zheng 2005; Zhou 1999, 2000b). Drug addiction continues to escalate on the mainland to the present-day, despite the vigorous hardline anti-drug campaigns of the 1980s and 1990s, such as the 'six evils' [六害], and the highly punitive legal

Introduction 5

sanctions instituted by the state and its public security apparatus (Biddulph 2013; Biddulph & Xie 2011; Liang & Lu 2013; Lu, Miethe & Liang 2009; Lu & Wang 2008; Trevaskes 2013; Yang *et al.* 2014; Zhou 1999, 2000a, 2000b). Moreover, this escalation continues despite drug addiction being cast by the state, drawing on a discourse of old, as 'a very unpatriotic action that has allowed drugs, which had caused so much humiliation to China, to reappear' (Zhou 1999, p. 125. See also Liang & Lu 2013).

Analysing stories of drug addiction

The previous section summarises the existing humanities and social science research that has documented the historical narrative of drug addiction in China and the impact that this has had on the governing national narratives of the Republican and Communist eras. *Chinese Stories of Drug Addiction: Beyond the Opium Dens* turns attention to contemporary stories[7] told by Chinese individuals located inside and outside of the experience of drug addiction. The book aims to identify how salient cultural, political and institutional discourses are engaged or contested in these stories (Anderson, Swan & Lane 2010; Aston 2009; Gibson, Acquah & Robinson 2004; Hänninen & Koski-Jännes 1999; Lilienfeld 1999; Redfield & Brodie 2002; Warhol 2002; Weinberg 2000). As such, the book considers any story to be a representation and reformulation of a life experience, here, drug addiction, which is impacted and shaped by the contexts within which the story is being told (Babrow, Kline & Rawlins 2005; Elliott 2005; Garden 2010; Hawkins 1999; Lieblich, Tuval-Mashiach & Zilber 1998; Ramsay 2013; Riessman 1993; Shapiro 2011; Thomas 2010).

These contexts may be situational or discursive. The stories under study are situated as commercially published texts, both written and filmic, composed for a wider public audience. This distinguishes them from stories told in the course of everyday conversation or stories told in an interview, which can be tailored to suit a particular, identifiable interlocutor and setting within which the conversation or interview is taking place (Thornborrow & Coates 2005). The audience for the stories under study is more indeterminate and general, with the setting of production essentially institutional in one form or another. In this circumstance, discourse or the 'normative beliefs or ways of viewing the world that are both constituted by as well as reflected in language use' attracts particular analytic interest (Ramsay 2008, p. 40). The published story of drug addiction, as an occasion of language in use, 'is assumed to be interdependent with social life, such that its analysis necessarily intersects with meanings, activities, and systems outside of itself' (Schiffrin 1994, p. 31). In the stories under study, these 'meanings, activities and systems' encompass the cultural, namely, 'understandings, norms, values and scripts that the storytellers have acquired through being members of a Chinese community' (Ramsay 2013, p. 3). They also include the political, namely, governing beliefs

6   Introduction

and national narratives such as those identified by the cultural history research discussed in the previous section; and the institutional, namely, 'a pre-existing systemic order or organisational structure, or the agenda promoted by such entities' which inevitably delineates and prescribes the understandings and protocols pertaining to a social practice or phenomenon, such as drug addiction (Ramsay 2008, p. 48). In determining how cultural, political and institutional discourses shape the Chinese stories of drug addiction, the book focuses analytically on three narrative processes deemed to be quintessential to storytelling, namely, the temporal sequencing of events, the claiming and refashioning of identities, and language use (Ramsay 2013).

The temporal sequencing of a series of events is a defining attribute of any narrative (Labov and Waletzky 1997; Ricoeur 1984). Stories selectively foreground and reconstruct past, present and future happenings in seemingly coherent and functionally significant ways (Bakhtin 1981; Bamberg, De Fina & Schiffrin 2007; Brockmeier & Carbaugh 2001; Polanyi 1989; Riessman 1993). Within stories, relationships are implied or explicitly drawn between the past and the present, the present and the future, as well as the past and the future (Clandinin & Connelly 2000; Daiute & Lightfoot 2004; Ramsay 2013; Riessman 2004). The forms that these relationships take, be they causal, limiting, facilitative or preclusive, and the differential emphases given to each temporal component, assign meaning that may be discursively shaped (Babrow, Kline & Rawlins 2005; Frank 1995; Garro 2000, 2001; Gergen 2004; Ramsay 2013).

Western stories, for example tend to present drug addiction as a 'biographical disruption' rather than a seamless accompaniment of the person's being, which at times finds expression and at other times does not (Gibson, Acquah & Robinson 2004, p. 614). This may be a consequence of the biomedicalisation of addiction in the West (Anderson, Swan & Lane 2010), given that physical and mental illnesses commonly are presented as unforeseen intrusions into an expected life course (Bury 1982, 2001). Nevertheless, while the onset of an illness may be portrayed as temporally sudden, Western accounts of drug addiction tend to describe a progression over time, a slow 'descent' with the endpoint being the 'sedimentation of drug-using routines in everyday life' (Gibson, Acquah & Robinson 2004, p. 610). At this point, these stories often lay emphasis on the 'search' for the 'next "fix"' (Wiseman 1994, p. 261), encasing the narrative in temporal notions of 'waiting and expectancy' (p. 263). Eventually the drug addict experiences a discernible 'turning point' (Aston 2009; Hersey 2005; McIntosh & McKeganey 2000), that is, a 'point at which the decision to give up drugs is made and/or consolidated' (Taïeb *et al.* 2008, p. 996). This marks 'the beginning of the end of addiction' in the story (Taïeb *et al.* 2008, p. 996) and the inexorable movement toward non-addiction in recovery (Aubry 2008). While many Western stories feature this overall 'linear' narrative trajectory of drug addiction (Hirschman 1995; Murdoch 1999; Smith 2001), some stories exhibit 'a more irregular, recursive pattern' (Murdoch 1999,

Introduction 7

p. 2121). In such stories, the non-addicted and the addicted selves temporally coexist, being variably engaged throughout the course of the day-to-day existence of the active drug user (Keep & Randall 1999; Murdoch 1999). In these stories, the movement toward non-addiction in recovery generally occurs when the conflict between non-addicted and addicted selves becomes unmanageable (Baker 2000; McIntosh & McKeganey 2000).

Thus, while arranging life events in a seemingly coherent temporal and causal sequence, stories also create, affirm and refashion identities or senses of self (Charon 2006; Cheshire & Ziebland 2005; Harter, Japp & Beck 2005; Hydén & Örulv 2009; Kirmayer 2000; Woods 2011). These identities may be temporally situated, formulated around a self from before or a future self whom one aspires to be (Ramsay 2013). They also may draw on, and so accede to, normative prescriptions as to what it means to be a man, a mother or a drug addict; or they may challenge and subvert these prescriptions (Baker 2000; Gibson, Acquah & Robinson 2004). The identities that are formulated through storytelling not only define selves but imply or stipulate attachments to others (Brockmeier & Carbaugh 2001; Brody 2003; Charon 2006; Woods 2011). This connects the individual, through her or his story, to a community, subculture or cultural group, which may be real or imagined (Hunt 2000; Ramsay 2013; Thornborrow & Coates 2005).

Western stories of drug addiction can equate addiction to an absence of self (Infantino 1999; Keep & Randall 1999; Melley 2002). The drug addict is deemed to hold 'a jaded indifference to [her or his] own subjective state of being' (Weinberg 2000, p. 610). More commonly, however, Western stories of drug addiction assign a distinct identity to the drug addict (Aston, 2009; Hirschman 1995; McIntosh & McKeganey 2000; Shapiro 2003). This addict identity, for the most part, is exceedingly negative (Gibson, Acquah & Robinson 2004; Murdoch 1999; Muzak 2008; Shapiro 2003; Warhol 2002). Hughes (2007, p. 674) observes that drug addicts 'constitute and maintain' this identity through their accounts of the 'practices of addiction', such as their routine pursuit of the next 'fix', the rituals they perform when using illicit drugs, and their pursuit and nurturing of the usually unwholesome social connections that are required to carry out these activities (see also Gibson, Acquah & Robinson 2004). In these stories, the addict identity stands in contrast to a non-addict identity that generally takes shape during recovery from drug addiction, but can coexist with the addict identity during active drug use, for example, where a parent is raising young children and only uses illicit drugs in their absence (McIntosh & McKeganey 2000; Murdoch 1999). The addicted self is characterised as inherently bad and the non-addicted self is characterised as inherently good in Western stories of drug addiction (Addenbrooke 2011; Baker 2000; Gibson, Acquah & Robinson 2004; Hammersley & Reid 2002; Hänninen & Koski-Jännes 1999; Harding 1986; Hirschman 1992; Hughes 2007; McIntosh & McKeganey 2000; Muzak 2008; Weinberg 2000). The former is typically arrogant, deceitful, uncaring, irresponsible and weak, while the latter

8   *Introduction*

is kind, authentic, aware, loving, caring, reasoned, self-controlled and responsible (Hänninen & Koski-Jännes 1999; Weinberg 2000). A 'turning point' (see earlier in this section) commonly marks the 'transformation' from the addicted self to the non-addicted self (Baker 2000, p. 863; McIntosh & McKeganey 2000, p. 1508). This transformation entails discarding the addict identity and constructing a new identity; discarding the addict identity and reinstating an identity from before drug addiction; or yielding to the non-addict identity where both addict and non-addict identities coexist in active drug use but their fundamental conflict has become unmanageable (Baker 2000; McIntosh & McKeganey 2000; Murdoch 1999). Regardless of the means by which the non-addict identity is formulated in Western stories of drug addiction, it remains vital to the process of recovery (Aubry 2008; Baker 2000).

Both addict and non-addict identities tend to be gendered in Western stories of drug addiction (Addenbrooke 2011; Aston 2009; Baker 2000; Friedling 1996; Hirschman 1995; Muzak 2007, 2008). Hersey (2005, p. 482) observes that women addicts commonly are presented as 'victims' who have been 'driven' to drug addiction by relationship problems. Men, on the other hand, simply 'choose' to abuse illicit drugs (Hersey 2005, p. 482). Women addicts also embody 'the double alterity' of being both a drug addict and a woman (Infantino 1999, p. 93). Moreover, they frequently 'violat[e] normative femininity' by neglecting or debasing their role as mother or wife (Muzak 2008, p. 106. See also Addenbrooke 2011; Hirschman 1995). As a consequence, recovery from drug addiction is symbolised in some Western stories by a 'Mother-child reunion' (Friedling 1996, p. 115), whereby a woman recaptures, albeit sometimes figuratively, a normatively gendered identity that had been destroyed by her drug addiction (Addenbrooke 2011; Friedling 1996). By contrast, Hänninen and Koski-Jännes (1999, p. 1847) point out that the non-addict identity that is formulated in recovery from drug addiction often can contravene gender norms. In many Western stories of drug addiction, 'men who have developed as individualists meet the challenge of relating to others while women, who have defined their identity in relation to others, meet the challenge of developing individual agency' (Hänninen & Koski-Jännes 1999, p. 1847). Aston (2009, p. 624) adds that, in developing such agency, women may reject 'the machinist terms and conditions of prevailing [Western] addiction and addiction treatment ideologies historically grounded in the exaltation of male rationality and transcendence of the feminine' and instead create 'alternative or counter addict identities more congruent with their political beliefs and more inclusive of their gender-specific needs'. The empowerment that this bestows on these women in recovery from drug addiction stands in contrast to the victimhood that had characterised their experience of active drug use (Hersey 2005).

Biomedicine constitutes another salient influence on the formulation of identity in Western stories of drug addiction (Anderson, Swan & Lane 2010;

Aston 2009; Davies 1997b; Franzwa 1999; Gibson, Acquah & Robinson 2004; Hirschman 1992; Lilienfeld 1999; Muzak 2007, 2008; Shapiro 2003; Taïeb *et al.* 2008; Warhol 2002; Weinberg 2000). Anderson, Swan and Lane (2010, p. 481) observe that 'the medicalization of drug addiction began to occur [in the West] as the power and authority of science, rationality, and medicine increased, and the power and authority of religion and religious leaders decreased, during industrialization'. They cite 'four broad biological orientations to explaining drug addiction. They include constitutional, genetic, psychopathological, and neuroscience or brain-based theories and approaches' (Anderson, Swan & Lane 2010, p. 482). Genetic and neuroscience or brain-based explanations currently dominate (Anderson, Swan & Lane 2010. See also Muzak 2007, 2008). Bio-medicalising drug addiction can subjectively empower the drug addict by offering 'the "gift" of a new identity' (Aston 2009, p. 619). This 'illness identity' can absolve, at least in part, the moral censure associated with being a drug addict in the West (Franzwa 1999; Muzak 2008). This particularly is the case for 'white middle-class' people who 'don't have socioeconomic excuses for their condition' (Muzak 2007, p. 262) and who 'must be ill, since such behavior is inconsistent with their virtuous, hard-working natures' (Franzwa 1999, p. 26). For non-white 'minorities' and the poor in the West there is less ready access to the illness identity in drug addiction (Franzwa 1999; Hersey 2005; Muzak 2007). For these people, drug addiction usually is considered to be a 'vice' or a 'character defect' (Muzak 2007, pp. 256–257. See also Shapiro 2003). Thus, while members of the white middle-class 'deserve treatment for their illness', minorities and the poor 'deserve punishment for their sins' (Franzwa 1999, p. 26). The hope of remedy that the illness identity provides (Muzak 2007; Weinberg 2000), therefore, remains the province of the privileged in the West (Franzwa 1999; Muzak 2007).

Notwithstanding this, biomedicine necessarily binds those who have access to the illness identity to an 'institutional matrix' of health professionals, treatment regimens and expectations of compliance and submission (Järvinen & Andersen 2009, p. 875. See also Gibson, Acquah & Robinson 2004; Melley 2002; Muzak 2007; Taïeb *et al.* 2008; Weinberg 2000). In such institutional settings, addict and non-addict identities must be formulated to 'match the working logic of the treatment system' (Järvinen & Andersen 2009, p. 865. See also Aubry 2008; Taïeb *et al.* 2008; Weinberg 2000). In the West, this treatment system usually is grounded in the abstinence paradigm promoted by Narcotics Anonymous or in the harm-minimisation paradigm embraced by most clinical health services (Biddulph & Xie 2011; Järvinen & Andersen 2009). A person's compliance with this treatment system connects him or her to a therapeutic community that includes others in recovery from drug addiction (Weinberg 2000). Membership of this community is contingent on on-going compliance, such that those who 'relapse' are cast out from this (supportive) community and have to return to the

10 *Introduction*

(harmful) addict community (Weinberg 2000, p. 609).[8] Attachments to the addict community, in turn, are sustained by 'a profoundly *shared* understanding of the shame associated with drug-taking' and the perverted comfort found in 'mutually assured distrust and shame' (original emphasis) (Hughes 2007, p. 684).

Discourse can shape the form of language used in any text, including narratives (Ramsay 1997, 2008, 2013). The biomedical institution, for example can provide a vocabulary and a way of reasoning for explaining a social practice or phenomenon, such as drug addiction (Gee 1999; MacDonald 2002; Selander *et al.* 1997). This discourse of the biomedical institution, in turn, may 'colonise' lay accounts of the social practice or phenomenon (Barry *et al.* 2001; Ramsay 2009). As a consequence, a storyteller can assert and legitimise claims to an illness identity and so, profit from the benefits that this may bring, such as amelioration of personal blame or release from familial and cultural responsibilities (Lafrance 2007; Mathieson & Stam 1995; Ramsay 2013). Likewise, cultural and political discourse can provide a vocabulary and a suite of cogent metaphors that possess distinct and clear meanings that are well understood within a community (Berger 1997; Carney 2004; Fox 2006; Kleinman 1988; Ramsay 2013). This language can be employed by storytellers, when explaining a perplexing and confounding social practice or phenomenon, to 'offer solace in the face of the unknown' (Ramsay 2013, p. 5).

The vocabulary characterising Western stories of drug addiction signifies the good versus bad dichotomy noted earlier in this chapter. Active drug users are cast as 'dirty', while people in recovery are 'clean' (Baker 2000; Gibson, Acquah & Robinson 2004; Weinberg 2000). Active drug users (wantonly) 'use' and 'consume' (Margolis 2002; Shapiro 2003), while people in recovery (conscientiously) 'work' a program (Weinberg 2000). Active drug users are 'imprisoned' by addiction, while people in recovery are 'free' (Aubry 2008; Davies 1997a; Melley 2002; Muzak 2008). The life of the active drug user is 'inauthentic', while the life of the person in recovery is 'genuine' (McIntosh & McKeganey 2000). The use of such language may be formulaic, originating from the institutionally based recovery community to which the person belongs (Hersey 2005; Järvinen & Andersen 2009; Taïeb *et al.* 2008). The figurative language commonly employed in Western stories of drug addiction also commonly positions active drug users as social and cultural 'outsiders' who inhabit the lower strata of society. In a spatial sense, active drug users are considered to have 'gone out', while people who abstain are 'in' recovery or 'in' the program (Hammersley & Reid 2002; Weinberg 2000). In a directional sense, illicit drug users 'descend' into addiction (Muzak 2008; Norton 1999; Weinberg 2000), continue to sink to 'rock bottom' (Hersey 2005; McIntosh & McKeganey 2000), and then 'ascen[d] from the depths' during recovery from drug addiction (Weinberg 2000, p. 613). This ascension frequently is constituted as a 'battle'. Well documented in Western illness stories (Hawkins 1999; Lupton 2003; Sontag 1989), the battle metaphor resonates with a politicised 'war

Introduction 11

on drugs' (Viano 2002); the biomedicalisation of drug addiction as illness; and the cultural 'othering' of illicit drug users as 'enemy' (Friedling 1996; Hammersley & Reid 2002; Keep & Randall 1999; Melley 2002; Shapiro 2003; Viano 2002; Weinberg 2000; Wiseman 1994). This metaphor also assigns familiar meaning to a social practice and phenomenon that is not well understood by the wider community (Davies 1997b; Green & Kupferberg 2000; Keep & Randall 1999) and for which there exists a high degree of aetiological ambiguity in the West (Davies 1997b; Hughes 2007; Lilienfeld 1999; Taïeb *et al.* 2008).

Analytic approach of the book

Humanities and social science research on contemporary stories of drug addiction to date has centred on Western accounts. While humanities research has examined the Chinese historical narrative of drug addiction in great detail (see earlier in this chapter), no work has examined contemporary Chinese stories of drug addiction. This book examines how salient cultural, political and institutional discourses shape temporality, subjectivity and language use in Chinese stories of drug addiction. Drug addiction is defined in the book as 'a chronic condition in which compulsive drug-taking behavior persists despite serious negative consequences' (Taïeb *et al.* 2008, p. 990. See also Davies 1997b; Muzak 2007). The book considers drug addiction to be not just a state of being but also 'a way of thinking' and 'a way of talking', that is, a discursive 'construct' (Davies 1997a, p. 9). As such, the stories of drug addiction that are analysed in the book are believed to both 'inform' the Chinese community about drug addiction as well as 'perform' drug addiction for the Chinese community (Davies 1997a).

The book analyses contemporary life stories and filmic[9] stories as complementary forms of narrative that proffer insider and outsider perspectives on drug addiction (Ramsay 2013; Taïeb *et al.* 2008; Viano 2002). Voice is given in these stories to both the ' "private" and "individual" spheres' of drug addiction (Zhou 1999, p. 5) as well as the dominant metanarrative of drug addiction circulating in the community (Hersey 2005; Hirschman 1992, 1995). The analysis of temporality, subjectivity and language use in the stories is 'necessarily interpretative' at many levels (Ramsay 2013, p. 6), including the level of the storyteller, the level of the researcher and, in cross-linguistic studies such as this, the level of translation. The analysis also requires interpreting what is said and what is unsaid in the stories (Hersey 2005; Ramsay 2013). Transparency is crafted in such an analytic endeavour through specification of the analytic steps; through inclusion of bilingual (original Chinese + English translation or gloss) illustrative examples that are taken from the stories; and through detailing the circumstances of publication or production of the stories (Ramsay 2013). This strengthens the coherence and plausibility of analytic conclusions drawn in the book (Ramsay 2013).

12   *Introduction*

Chapter summaries

The introductory chapter has laid out the context and rationale for the book and framed its principle research question, namely, how do salient cultural, political and institutional discourses shape temporality, subjectivity and language use in contemporary Chinese stories of drug addiction? The chapter has discussed the existing humanities research on drug addiction in greater China (cultural histories) and reviewed the existing humanities and social science research on stories of drug addiction (overwhelmingly Western). The chapter has provided a working definition of drug addiction and laid out the analytical approach to be employed in subsequent chapters.

Chapter 2 of the book analyses how cultural, political and institutional discourses shape two book-length first-person life stories of drug addiction and recovery from mainland China. *Heaven and Hell* [地狱天堂] tells a Chinese man's story and *Struggle Spirit* [灵魂交锋] tells a Chinese woman's story. Particular attention is given in the analysis to the issue of gender, due to the different genders of the respective storytellers; as well as the issue of 'exemplarity', due to the official status, in Communist mainland China, of the books' publishing houses (Bakken 2000, p. 1). The chapter ascertains who is afforded and who is denied the status of moral exemplar in these contemporary life stories, which deal with such a highly morally transgressive phenomenon as drug addiction.

Chapter 3 turns its attention to life stories that are told by Chinese people who reside in, or still are actively engaged with, the specialist drug rehabilitation facilities where they have undertaken programs to overcome their drug addiction. These contemporary life stories are from three Chinese communities that have distinct political systems and histories, namely Communist mainland China, recently democratic Taiwan, and the former British colony of Hong Kong. Within each geographical community, stories from well-known drug rehabilitation facilities are subject to analysis, as in Chapter 2. The drug rehabilitation facilities comprise the secular Daytop [戴托普] facility in mainland China, the Christian Operation Dawn [晨曦會] facilities in Taiwan, the secular Society for the Aid and Rehabilitation of Drug Abusers (SARDA) [香港戒毒會] facilities in Hong Kong, along with the Christian Zheng Sheng College [基督教正生書院] facility in Hong Kong. The chapter identifies the ways in which the life stories of drug addiction that are told in each of these institutions align with or depart from the 'preferred' story of the institution (Ramsay 2013, p. 13). The chapter also points out the ways in which these stories negotiate the broader cultural and political forces in play in their local geographical settings.

Chapters 2 and 3 examine Chinese life stories of drug addiction, rehabilitation and recovery. Chapter 4, by contrast, examines fictional or quasi-documentary stories of drug addiction, rehabilitation and recovery, as told in six contemporary film and television productions from mainland China, Taiwan and Hong Kong. There are two films from mainland China, *Quitting* [昨天] and *The War of Two* [两个人的战争]; two films from Taiwan, *Help Me Eros* [幫幫我愛神] and *Jump Ashin!* [翻滾吧! 阿信]; and two television serial dramas from Hong Kong, *He Is Not Lonely* [他不寂寞] and *Happily Sharing, Seventeen Years of Age* [開心 share 十七歲]. The filmic stories that generally are told from outside the experience of drug addiction usefully complement the Chapter 2 and 3 life stories that are told from within this experience. The stories are analysed as in Chapters 2 and 3. Based on this analysis, the chapter considers the extent to which these stories engage the prevailing cultural meta-narrative of drug addiction that circulates in Chinese communities, 'aspects of which may remain hidden from view in life stories told by those inside the experience' (Ramsay 2013, p.61). The chapter also explores how these stories utilise the key narrative processes of temporality, subjectivity and language use, in order to discursively marginalise or palliate the Chinese drug addict.

Chapter 5 concludes *Chinese Stories of Drug Addiction: Beyond the Opium Dens*. The chapter summarises how salient cultural, political and institutional discourses shape the life stories and filmic stories of drug addiction that are analysed in Chapters 2–4. The summary draws attention to the interrelationships and interconnections between the key narrative processes that contribute to sense-making in these stories: the temporal and causal ordering of life events, the claiming and refashioning of identities, and language use. The chapter considers the issues pertaining to morality, gender, exemplarity, stigma, disempowerment, marginalisation, palliation and institutional schema, which arise through the analysis of the life stories and filmic stories that is undertaken in Chapters 2–4. It compares these findings with those from the research into Western stories of drug addiction, as outlined in this introductory chapter. Chapter 5 contemplates the clinical applications of the book's findings, where professional services are provided to Chinese clients who are drug-addicted. It also reflects on the methodological strengths and limitations of the book, in particular, the merit of comparatively analysing the complementary data sources of life stories and filmic stories. The chapter concludes by calling attention to the contribution that the book makes to the existing humanities research into drug addiction in greater China, which, to date, has focused on the historical narrative.

Notes

1 In 1997, the mainland Chinese government announced that it had evidence that the Ming emperor Wanli [万历] had been an opium addict (Zheng 2005).
2 Gao (2011) states that few women used illicit drugs in Republican era China. Baumler (2007) and Brook and Wakabayashi (2000), however, record quite significant numbers of women opium users, in particular, in coastal metropolitan areas such as Shanghai. In Republican era China, opiate addiction was more commonly encountered amongst prostitutes, thieves and officials and less commonly encountered amongst labourers and farmers (Lu, Miethe & Liang 2009).

14   *Introduction*

3 Earlier anti-opium discourse from the 1800s had emphasised the impact of opium addiction on an *individual's* physical and moral health (Baumler 2007; Zhou 1999). Such discourse likely was appropriated from foreign missionaries (Baumler 2007; Dikötter, Laamann & Zhou 2004).

4 Lu, Miethe and Liang (2009, p. 40) state that 'The first edict banning opium issued by an emperor [of China] was published in 1729.' Opium trade was legal in China from 1858–1906 (Baumler 2007; Brook & Wakabayashi 2000; Munn 2000; Zhou 1999).

5 Meanwhile, Japan was 'flooding' its occupied territories in mainland China with opiates in order to accelerate its expansionist agenda (Traver 1992, p. 313. See also Baumler 2007).

6 Traver (1992) reports that, in 1918, local opium revenue accounted for almost half of the total revenue of the Hong Kong government. Around this time, approximately one in four Chinese adults in Hong Kong were using opium (Traver 1992).

7 As per Garro and Mattingly (2000a, 2000b), Ramsay (2013), Squire (2005) and Thornborrow and Coates (2005), 'narrative' and 'story' are used interchangeably throughout the book.

8 Muzak (2008, p. 102) claims that the states of drug addiction and non-addiction in recovery readily lend themselves to community formation, due to Western 'cultural constructs of drug addiction as a tangible and distinct condition that signifies as an obviously serious problem' that warrants social connection and support.

9 Viano (2002, p. 139) interestingly observes that 'The representation of drugs was one of the first objectives that early filmmakers pursued with cinema in its prelinguistic infancy', the world's 'first-known' film *Chinese Opium Den*, made in the 1890s, portraying Chinese opium addicts.

References

Addenbrooke, M. 2011. *Survivors of addiction: narratives of recovery*. New York, NY: Routledge.

Anderson, T., Swan, H. and Lane, D. C. 2010. Institutional fads and the medicalization of drug addiction. *Sociology Compass*, 4 (7), 476–494.

Aston, S. 2009. Identities under construction: women hailed as addicts. *Health: An Interdisciplinary Journal for the Social Study of Health, Illness and Medicine*, 13 (6), 611–628.

Aubry, T. 2008. Selfless cravings: addiction and recovery in David Foster Wallace's *Infinite Jest*. In J. Prosser (ed.) *American fiction of the 1990s: reflections of history and culture* (pp. 206–219). London: Routledge.

Babrow, A. S., Kline, K. N. and Rawlins, W. K. 2005. Narrating problems and problematizing narratives: linking problematic integration and narrative theory in telling stories about our health. In L. M. Harter, P. M. Japp and C. S. Beck (eds) *Narratives, health, and healing: communication theory, research, and practice* (pp. 31–52). Mahwah, NJ: L. Erlbaum Associates.

Baker, P. L. 2000. I didn't know: discoveries and identity transformation of women addicts in treatment. *Journal of Drug Issues*, 30 (4), 863–880.

Bakhtin, M. M. 1981. *The dialogic imagination: four essays*. Austin, TX: University of Texas Press.

Bakken, B. 2000. *The exemplary society: human improvement, social control, and the dangers of modernity in China*. Oxford: Oxford University Press.

Bamberg, M., De Fina, A. and Schiffrin, D. 2007. Introduction to the volume. In M. Bamberg, A. De Fina and D. Schiffrin (eds) *Selves and identities in narrative and discourse* (pp. 1–8). Amsterdam: John Benjamins.

Barry, C. A., Stevenson, F. A., Britten, N., Barber, N. and Bradley, C. P. 2001. Giving voice to the lifeworld. More humane, more effective medical care? A qualitative study of

Introduction   15

doctor-patient communication in general practice. *Social Science and Medicine*, 53 (4), 487–505.

Baumler, A. 2007. *The Chinese and opium under the Republic: worse than floods and wild beasts*. New York, NY: SUNY Press.

Berger, A.A. 1997. *Narratives in popular culture, media, and everyday life*. Thousand Oaks, CA: Sage.

Biddulph, S. 2013. Compulsory drug rehabilitation in China. In F. Rahman and N. Crofts (eds) *Drug law reform in East and Southeast Asia* (pp. 233–244). Lanham, MD: Lexington.

Biddulph, S. and Xie, C. 2011. Regulating drug dependency in China: the 2008 PRC Drug Prohibition Law. *British Journal of Criminology*, 51, 978–996.

Brockmeier, J. and Carbaugh, D. 2001. Introduction. In J. Brockmeier and D. Carbaugh (eds) *Narrative and identity: studies in autobiography, self and culture* (pp. 1–24). Amsterdam: John Benjamins.

Brody, H. 2003. *Stories of sickness*. Oxford: Oxford University Press.

Brook, T. and Wakabayashi, B.T. 2000. Introduction: opium's history in China. In T. Brook and B.T. Wakabayashi (eds) *Opium regimes: China, Britain, and Japan, 1839–1952* (pp. 1–27). Berkeley: University of California Press.

Bury, M. 1982. Chronic illness as biographical disruption. *Sociology of Health and Illness*, 4 (2), 167–182.

Bury, M. 2001. Illness narratives: fact or fiction? *Sociology of Health and Illness*, 23 (3), 263–285.

Carney, S. 2004. Transcendent stories and counternarratives in holocaust survivor life histories: searching for meaning in video-testimony archives. In C. Daiute and C. Lightfoot (eds) *Narrative analysis: studying the development of individuals in society* (pp. 201–222). Thousand Oaks, CA: Sage.

Charon, R. 2006. *Narrative medicine: honoring the stories of illness*. Oxford: Oxford University Press.

Cheshire, J. and Ziebland, S. 2005. Narrative as a resource in accounts of the experience of illness. In J. Thornborrow and J. Coates (eds) *The sociolinguistics of narrative* (pp. 17–40). Amsterdam: John Benjamins.

Chou, T.C., Hung, Y.J. and Liao, F.C. 2007. A study on factors affecting the abstention of drug abuse in private rehabilitation institutes in Taiwan – Operation Dawn Taiwan as an example. *Flinders Journal of Law Reform*, 10 (3), 737–758.

Chu, N.S. 2008. Eradication of opium smoking in Taiwan during the Japanese colonial period (1895–1945). *Acta Neurologica Taiwanica*, 17 (1), 66–73.

Clandinin, D.J. and Connelly, F.M. 2000. *Narrative inquiry: experience and story in qualitative research*. San Francisco, CA: Jossey-Bass Inc.

Daiute, C. and Lightfoot, C. 2004. Editors' introduction: theory and craft in narrative inquiry. In C. Daiute and C. Lightfoot (eds) *Narrative analysis: studying the development of individuals in society* (pp. vii–xviii). Thousand Oaks, CA: Sage.

Davies, J.B. 1997a. *Drugspeak: the analysis of drug discourse*. Amsterdam: Harwood Academic.

Davies, J.B. 1997b. *The myth of addiction*. Amsterdam: Harwood Academic.

Dikötter, F., Laamann, L. and Zhou, X. 2004. *Narcotic culture: a history of drugs in China*. London: C. Hurst.

Elliott, J. 2005. *Using narrative in social research: qualitative and quantitative approaches*. Thousand Oaks, CA: Sage.

Eykholt, M.S. 2000. Resistance to opium as a social evil in wartime China. In T. Brook and B.T. Wakabayashi (eds) *Opium regimes: China, Britain, and Japan, 1839–1952* (pp. 360–379). Berkeley: University of California Press.

16   *Introduction*

Fox, C. 2006. Stories within stories: dissolving the boundaries in narrative research and analysis. In S. Trahar (ed.) *Narrative research on learning: comparative and international perspectives* (pp. 47–60). Didcot, Oxford: Symposium Books.

Frank, A. W. 1995. *The wounded storyteller: body, illness, and ethics.* Chicago: University of Chicago Press.

Franzwa, G. 1999. Aristotle and the language of addiction. In J. Lilienfeld and J. Oxford (eds) *The languages of addiction* (pp. 15–28). New York, NY: St. Martin's Press.

Friedling, M. 1996. Feminisms and the Jewish mother syndrome: identity, autobiography, and the rhetoric of addiction. *Discourse*, 19 (1), 105–130.

Gao, H. 2011. *Women and heroin addiction in China's changing society.* New York, NY: Routledge.

Garden, R. 2010. Telling stories about illness and disability: the limits and lessons of narrative. *Perspectives in Biology and Medicine*, 53 (1), 121–135.

Garro, L. C. 2000. Cultural knowledge as resource in illness narratives: remembering through accounts of illness. In C. Mattingly and L. C. Garro (eds) *Narrative and the cultural construction of illness and healing* (pp. 70–87). Berkeley: University of California Press.

Garro, L. C. 2001. The remembered past in a culturally meaningful life: remembering as cultural, social, and cognitive process. In C. C. Moore and H. F. Mathews (eds) *The psychology of cultural experience* (pp. 105–147). Cambridge: Cambridge University Press.

Garro, L. C. and Mattingly, C. 2000a. Narrative as construct and as construction. In C. Mattingly and L. C. Garro (eds) *Narrative and the cultural construction of illness and healing* (pp. 1–49). Berkeley: University of California Press.

Garro, L. C. and Mattingly, C. 2000b. Narrative turns. In C. Mattingly and L. C. Garro (eds) *Narrative and the cultural construction of illness and healing* (pp. 259–270). Berkeley: University of California Press.

Gee, J. P. 1999. *An introduction to discourse analysis: theory and method.* New York, NY: Routledge.

Gergen, M. 2004. Once upon a time: a narratologist's tale. In C. Daiute and C. Lightfoot (eds) *Narrative analysis: studying the development of individuals in society* (pp. 267–286). Thousand Oaks, CA: Sage.

Gibson, B., Acquah, S. and Robinson, P. G. 2004. Entangled identities and psychotropic substance use. *Sociology of Health and Illness*, 26 (5), 597–616.

Green, D. and Kupferberg, I. 2000. Detailed and succinct self-portraits of addicts in broadcast stories. *Discourse Studies*, 2 (3), 305–322.

Hammersley, R. and Reid, M. 2002. Why the pervasive addiction myth is still believed. *Addiction Research and Theory*, 10 (1), 7–30.

Hänninen, V. and Koski-Jännes, A. 1999. Narratives of recovery from addictive behaviours. *Addiction*, 94 (12), 1837–1848.

Harding, G. 1986. Constructing addiction as a moral failing. *Sociology of Health and Illness*, 8 (1), 75–85.

Harter, L. M., Japp, P. M. and Beck, C. S. 2005. Vital problematics of narrative theorizing about health and healing. In L. M. Harter, P. M. Japp and C. S. Beck (eds) *Narratives, health, and healing: communication theory, research, and practice* (pp. 7–30). Mahwah, NJ: L. Erlbaum Associates.

Hawkins, A. H. 1999. *Reconstructing illness: studies in pathography* (2nd ed.). West Lafayette, IN: Purdue University Press.

Hersey, C. 2005. Script(ing) treatment: representations of recovery from addiction in Hollywood film. *Contemporary Drug Problems*, 32, 467–493.

Hirschman, E. C. 1992. Mundane addiction: the cinematic depiction of cocaine consumption. *Advances in Consumer Research*, 19, 424–428.

Hirschman, E. C. 1995. The cinematic depiction of drug addiction: a semiotic account. *Semiotica*, 104 (1/2), 119–164.

Hsu, H. B. 2014. The taste of opium: science, monopoly, and the Japanese colonization in Taiwan, 1895–1945. *Past and Present*, 222 (suppl. 9), 227–246.

Hughes, K. 2007. Migrating identities: the relational constitution of drug use and addiction. *Sociology of Heath and Illness*, 29 (5), 673–691.

Hunt, L. M. 2000. Strategic suffering: illness narratives as social empowerment among Mexican cancer patients. In C. Mattingly and L. C. Garro (eds) *Narrative and the cultural construction of illness and healing* (pp. 88–107). Berkeley: University of California Press.

Hydén, L. C. and Örulv, L. 2009. Narrative and identity in Alzheimer's disease: a case study. *Journal of Aging Studies*, 23, 205–214.

Infantino, S. C. 1999. Female addiction and sacrifice: literary tradition or user's manual? In J. Lilienfeld and J. Oxford (eds) *The languages of addiction* (pp. 91–102). New York, NY: St. Martin's Press.

Järvinen, M. and Andersen, D. 2009. Creating problematic identities: the making of the chronic addict. *Substance Use and Misuse*, 44, 865–885.

Keep, C. and Randall, D. 1999. Addiction, empire, and narrative in Arthur Conan Doyle's *The Sign of the Four*. *Novel*, 32 (2), 207–221.

Kirmayer, L. J. 2000. Broken narratives: clinical encounters and the poetics of illness experience. In C. Mattingly and L. C. Garro (eds) *Narrative and the cultural construction of illness and healing* (pp. 153–180). Berkeley: University of California Press.

Kleinman, A. 1988. *The illness narratives: suffering, healing, and the human condition.* New York, NY: Basic Books.

Kobayashi, M. 2000. Drug operations by resident Japanese in Tianjin. In T. Brook and B. T. Wakabayashi (eds) *Opium regimes: China, Britain, and Japan*, 1839–1952 (pp. 152–166). Berkeley: University of California Press.

Labov, W. and Waletzky, J. 1997. Narrative analysis: oral versions of personal experience. *Journal of Narrative and Life History*, 7 (1–4), 3–38.

Lafrance, M. 2007. A bitter pill: a discursive analysis of women's medicalized accounts of depression. *Journal of Health Psychology*, 12 (1), 127–140.

Lee, S. F., Hsu, J. and Tsay, W. I. 2013. The trend of drug abuse in Taiwan during the years 1999 to 2011. *Journal of Food and Drug Analysis*, 21, 390–396.

Levin, D. 2015, January 24. Despite a crackdown, use of illegal drugs in China continues unabated. *The New York Times*. Retrieved from www.nytimes.com/2015/01/25/world/despite-a-crackdown-use-of-illegal-drugs-in-china-continues-unabated.html 24 February 2015.

Li, J. H. 2013. From gradual prohibition to harm reduction: the experience of drug policy and law reform in Taiwan. In F. Rahman and N. Crofts (eds) *Drug law reform in East and Southeast Asia* (pp. 199–210). Lanham, MD: Lexington.

Liang, B. and Lu, H. 2013. Discourses of drug problems and drug control in China: reports in the *People's Daily*, 1946–2009. *China Information*, 27 (3), 301–326.

Lieblich, A., Tuval-Mashiach, R. and Zilber, T. 1998. *Narrative research: reading, analysis and interpretation*. Thousand Oaks, CA: Sage.

Lilienfeld, J. 1999. Introduction. In J. Lilienfeld and J. Oxford (eds) *The languages of addiction* (pp. xiii–xxvii). New York, NY: St. Martin's Press.

Lu, H., Miethe, T. D. and Liang, B. 2009. *China's drug practices and policies: regulating controlled substances in a global context*. Farnham, UK: Ashgate.

18 *Introduction*

Lu, L., Fang, Y. and Wang, X. 2008. Drug abuse in China: past, present and future. *Cellular and Molecular Neurobiology*, 28, 479–490.

Lu, L. and Wang, X. 2008. Drug addiction in China. *Annals of the New York Academy of Sciences*, 1141, 304–317.

Luo, T., Wang, J., Li, Y., Wang, X., Tan, L., Deng, Q., Thakoor, J. P. D. and Hao, W. 2014. Stigmatization of people with drug dependence in China: a community-based study in Hunan province. *Drug and Alcohol Dependence*, 134, 285–289.

Lupton, D. 2003. *Medicine as culture: illness, disease and the body in Western societies*. Thousand Oaks, CA: Sage.

MacDonald, M. N. 2002. Pedagogy, pathology and ideology: the production, transmission and reproduction of medical discourse. *Discourse and Society*, 13 (4), 447–467.

Margolis. S. 2002. Addiction and the ends of desire. In J. F. Brodie and M. Redfield (eds) *High anxieties: cultural studies in addiction* (pp. 19–37). Berkeley: University of California Press.

Mathieson, C. M. and Stam, H. J. 1995. Renegotiating identity: cancer narratives. *Sociology of Health and Illness*, 17 (3), 283–306.

McCoy, C. B., Lai, S., Metsch, L. R., Wang, X., Li, C., Yang, M. and Li, Y. 1997. No pain no gain, establishing the Kunming, China, drug rehabilitation center. *Journal of Drug Issues*, 27 (1), 73–85.

McIntosh, J. and McKeganey, N. 2000. Addicts' narratives of recovery from drug use: constructing a non-addict identity. *Social Science and Medicine*, 50, 1501–1510.

Melley, T. 2002. A terminal case: William Burroughs and the logic of addiction. In J. F. Brodie and M. Redfield (eds) *High anxieties: cultural studies in addiction* (pp. 38–60). Berkeley: University of California Press.

Munn, C. 2000. The Hong Kong opium revenue, 1845–1885. In T. Brook and B. T. Wakabayashi (eds) *Opium regimes: China, Britain, and Japan, 1839–1952* (pp. 105–126). Berkeley: University of California Press.

Murdoch, R. O. 1999. Working and "drugging" in the city: economics and substance use in a sample of working addicts. *Substance Use and Misuse*, 34 (14), 2115–2133.

Muzak, J. 2007. "They say the disease is responsible": social identity and the disease concept of drug addiction. In V. Raoul, C. Canam, A. D. Henderson and C. Paterson (eds), *Unfitting stories: narrative approaches to disease, disability, and trauma* (pp. 255–264). Waterloo, ON: Wilfrid Laurier University Press.

Muzak, J. 2008. "Addiction got me what I needed": depression and drug addiction in Elizabeth Wurtzel's memoirs. In H. Clark (ed.) *Depression and narrative: telling the dark* (pp. 97–109). Albany, NY: SUNY Press.

Norton, S. M. 1999. "To keep from shaking to pieces": addiction and bearing reality in "Sonny's Blues". In J. Lilienfeld and J. Oxford (eds) *The languages of addiction* (pp. 175–192). New York, NY: St. Martin's Press.

Polanyi, L. 1989. *Telling the American story: a structural and cultural analysis of conversational storytelling*. Cambridge, MA: MIT Press.

Ramsay, G. 1997. *Beijing review newstext: a comparative cross-cultural analysis of lexico-semantic and discourse structural features*. Unpublished doctoral dissertation. St Lucia, QLD: The University of Queensland.

Ramsay, G. 2008. *Shaping minds: a discourse analysis of Chinese-language community mental health literature*. Amsterdam: John Benjamins.

Ramsay, G. 2009. Chinese mental illness narratives: controlling the spirit. *Communication and Medicine*, 6 (2), 189–198.

Ramsay, G. 2013. *Mental illness, dementia and family in China*. London: Routledge.

Redfield, M. and Brodie, J. F. 2002. Introduction. In J. F. Brodie and M. Redfield (eds) *High anxieties: cultural studies in addiction* (pp. 1–15). Berkeley: University of California Press.

Ricoeur, P. 1984. *Time and narrative*. Chicago: University of Chicago Press.

Riessman, C. K. 1993. *Narrative analysis*. Newbury Park, CA: Sage.

Riessman, C. K. 2004. A thrice-told tale: new readings of an old story. In B. Hurwitz, T. Greenhalgh and V. Skultans (eds) *Narrative research in health and illness* (pp. 309–324). Malden, MA: BMJ Books.

Schiffrin, D. 1994. *Approaches to discourse*. Oxford: Blackwell.

Selander, S., Troein, M., Finnegan, Jr, J. and. Råstam, L. 1997. The discursive formation of health: a study of printed health education material used in primary care. *Patient Education and Counselling*, 31, 181–189.

Shapiro, H. 2003. *Shooting stars: drugs, Hollywood and the movies*. London: Serpent's Tail.

Shapiro, J. 2011. Illness narratives: reliability, authenticity and the empathic witness. *Medical Humanities*, 37 (2), 68–72.

Smith, R. M. 2001. Addiction and recovery in Denis Johnson's *Jesus' Son. Critique*, 42 (2), 180–191.

Sontag, S. 1989. *Illness as metaphor and AIDS and its metaphors*. New York, NY: Picador.

Squire, C. 2005. Reading narratives. *Group Analysis*, 38 (1), 91–107.

Taïeb, O., Révah-Lévy, A., Moro, M. R. and Baubet, T. 2008. Is Ricoeur's notion of narrative identity useful in understanding recovery in drug addicts? *Qualitative Health Research*, 18 (7), 990–1000.

Thomas, C. 2010. Negotiating the contested terrain of narrative methods in illness contexts. *Sociology of Health and Illness*, 32 (4), 647–660.

Thornborrow, J. and Coates, J. 2005. The sociolinguistics of narrative: identity, performance, culture. In J. Thornborrow and J. Coates (eds) *The sociolinguistics of narrative* (pp. 1–16). Amsterdam: John Benjamins.

Traver, H. 1992. Opium to heroin: restrictive opium legislation and the rise of heroin consumption in Hong Kong. *Journal of Policy History*, 4 (3), 307–324.

Trevaskes, S. 2013. Drug policy in China. In F. Rahman and N. Crofts (eds) *Drug law reform in East and Southeast Asia* (pp. 221–232). Lanham, MD: Lexington.

UNODC. 2011. *World drug report 2011*. New York, NY: United Nations.

UNODC. 2013. *World drug report 2013*. New York, NY: United Nations.

Viano, M. 2002. An intoxicated screen: reflections on film and drugs. In J. F. Brodie and M. Redfield (eds) *High anxieties: cultural studies in addiction* (pp. 134–158). Berkeley: University of California Press.

Wakabayashi, B. T. 2000. From peril to profit: opium in late-Edo to Meiji eyes. In T. Brook and B. T. Wakabayashi (eds) *Opium regimes: China, Britain, and Japan, 1839–1952* (pp. 55–78). Berkeley: University of California Press.

Warhol, R. R. 2002. The rhetoric of addiction: from Victorian novels to AA. In J. F. Brodie and M. Redfield (eds) *High anxieties: cultural studies in addiction* (pp. 97–108). Berkeley: University of California Press.

Weinberg, D. 2000. "Out there": the ecology of addiction in drug abuse treatment discourse. *Social Problems*, 47 (4), 606–621.

Wiseman, S. 1994. Addiction and the avant-garde: heroin addiction and narrative in Alexander Trocchi's *Cain's Book*. In S. Vice (ed.) *Beyond the pleasure dome: writing and addiction from the Romantics* (pp. 256–266). Sheffield: Sheffield Academic Press.

20 *Introduction*

Woods, A. 2011. The limits of narrative: provocations for the medical humanities. *Medical Humanities*, 37 (2), 73–78.

Wyman, J. 2000. Opium and the state in late-Qing Sichuan. In T. Brook and B.T. Wakabayashi (eds) *Opium regimes: China, Britain, and Japan, 1839–1952* (pp. 212–227). Berkeley: University of California Press.

Yang, M., Zhou, L., Hao, W. and Xiao, S.Y. 2014. Drug policy in China: progress and challenges. *The Lancet*, 383 (9916), 509.

Zheng, Y. 2005. *The social life of opium in China*. Cambridge, UK: Cambridge University Press.

Zhou, Y. 1999. *Anti-drug crusades in twentieth-century China: nationalism, history, and state building*. Lanham, MD: Rowman and Littlefield.

Zhou, Y. 2000a. *China's anti-drug campaign in the reform era*. Singapore: World Scientific and Singapore University Press.

Zhou, Y. 2000b. Nationalism, identity, and state-building: the antidrug crusade in the People's Republic, 1949–1952. In T. Brook and B.T. Wakabayashi (eds) *Opium regimes: China, Britain, and Japan, 1839–1952* (pp. 380–404). Berkeley: University of California Press.

2 Gendered exemplars

Life stories of drug addiction and recovery

This chapter analyses two life stories of drug addiction and recovery, one told by a mainland Chinese man and the other told by a mainland Chinese woman. Each life story is book length and comprises first-person accounts of life from before drug use, during drug use and addiction, and post-addiction, as remembered years into recovery. The accounts are analysed in line with the narrative-cum-discourse analytic approach laid out in Chapter 1. First, a synopsis of the life story is provided. This is followed by analysis of how salient cultural, political and institutional discourses shape temporality, subjectivity and language use in the story. The chapter compares the analytic findings for the man's life story and the woman's life story. It also compares the analytic findings for both life stories with the findings for Western counterpart stories, as summarised in Chapter 1.

The analysis draws attention to two prominent issues that manifest in the life stories: gender and 'exemplarity' (Bakken 2000, p. 1). The issue of gender arises from analysing a man's account and a woman's account of drug addiction and recovery. The issue of exemplarity stems from the nature of the publishing houses that published the books in which the two life stories are recounted. Both publishing houses are state-sanctioned presses that are closely aligned to the mainland Chinese government. Bakken (2000, p. 1) states that, in mainland China, 'People's morality and their physical, mental, and behavioural qualities [have] become important for the sake of state power and the nation.' As a consequence, the narrating of exemplars [榜样] serves an important political didactic purpose (Bakken 2000; Brady 2008).

Exemplary stories

Ever since the mainland Chinese government instituted the program of reform and opening up to the outside world in 1978, the government and Chinese Communist Party authorities have continued to place great importance on the 'moral education' of the general public (Bakken 2000, p. 169). Many members of the

22   *Gendered exemplars*

government and the Party hold the view that it is inevitable that the overwhelmingly positive economic reform program will have some deleterious effects on the greater 'public morality' of the nation (Bakken 2000, p. 20). A clear example can be found in the dramatic increase in the use and trafficking of illicit drugs across mainland China, in particular opiates, opioids and amphetamines. These forms of social vice and criminality had been virtually eliminated from mainland China during the Mao rule from 1949–1976 (see Chapter 1).

One way that the mainland Chinese authorities have sought to counter this 'so-called "spiritual slide"' [精神滑坡] in contemporary society is through the narrating of moral exemplars (Bakken 2000, p. 20). By no means unique to the reform era, these 'model figures' embody the good citizen, soldier or official of the times (Brady 2008, p. 75). Nowadays, moral exemplars 'no longer have to be perfect', as long as they can play a 'role in educating the Chinese public' about proper conduct in contemporary society (Brady 2008, pp. 75–76). Present-day exemplars, for example should display the highly valued personal qualities of honesty, selflessness, discipline, everydayness, family-centeredness, industry and clean living (Bakken 2000; Brady 2008). They also should strive to maintain sound physical and mental health (Brady 2008).[1] These qualities represent a blend of traditional Confucian and contemporary Communist values (Bakken 2000; Brady 2002, 2009, 2012; Niquet 2012). They are qualities that the mainland Chinese authorities expect all good citizens to aspire to (Brady 2002, 2008). The authorities ensure that the masses are well versed in these moral exemplars, by integrating them into the education system and featuring them in a range of contemporary popular media, such as books, newspapers, television programs and public billboards (Bakken 2000; Brady 2009). In this way, the authorities can hope 'to build a new, modern set of values for Chinese society', and achieve a level of 'spiritual civilization' [精神文明] that can 'match China's modern material civilization' [物质文明], namely, 'economic development and infrastructure' (Brady 2009, p. 448).

Books that are published by the state-sanctioned presses in mainland China would be expected to espouse these 'spiritual' values that are promoted by the authorities of the time. The well-developed propaganda apparatus of the contemporary mainland Chinese state ensures that this occurs (Brady 2008). As a consequence, moral exemplars who embody these values should feature in the two books to be analysed in this chapter. This is because both books are published by state-sanctioned presses. The ensuing analysis, therefore, will explore how exemplarity can manifest in life stories that deal with such a highly morally transgressive phenomenon as drug addiction. The analysis will seek to ascertain who is afforded the status of moral exemplar in the stories. It will do so by identifying how the storytellers discursively utilise the key narrative processes of temporality, subjectivity and language use, in order to assert or deny moral exemplarity in their life stories.

Mainland Chinese man's life story of drug addiction and recovery

Heaven and Hell: A Drug User's Tragic Tale [地狱天堂: 一个吸毒者的血泪诉说] tells the life story of Wen Lianping [文连平], his initiation into illicit drug use in his late twenties and his subsequent addiction to opium and recovery from opium addiction. His story takes place in mainland China during the late 1980s through to the early 2000s. Wen's first-person account is transcribed by Wang Yunxiang [王云香], the accredited author of *Heaven and Hell*. The book is 310 pages in length and was published in 2004 by the Mass Press [群众出版社], which is the publishing house of mainland China's Public Security Bureau [公安部] (Mass Press 2008). The press publishes works that contribute to the endeavours of China's public security and police forces (Mass Press 2008). As a consequence, these works would be expected to acknowledge and endorse the positive role that the mainland Chinese public security and police forces play in society, in addition to the laws and policies that they uphold.

Wen's life story begins in Guangzhou in southern China, where he routinely goes to purchase modern commodities that he sells-on, for a handsome profit, back in his hometown of Xian in China's mid-west. By chance, Wen runs into a trusted childhood friend, who is a member of a highly successful group of business associates. Wen wishes to join this group in order to increase his now modest income. The members of this group enjoy smoking opium and, as part of Wen's initiation into the group, he is offered opium. Wen initially hesitates and then accepts the challenge, even though he is quite uninformed and naïve about illicit drugs like opium. He has a very bad reaction to his first use of opium, which requires a day to recover from, much to the bemusement and amusement of the group members. They question Wen's suitability to join the group, which humiliates him and his childhood friend who had introduced him to the group. Wen resolves to master the use of opium on his return to Xian and, as a consequence, regain his and his childhood friend's 'face'.

Back home in Xian, Wen buys and consumes copious amounts of opium until he is able to 'tame' [驯服][2] the serious negative side-effects that he initially had experienced in Guangzhou (Wang 2004, p. 52). On Wen's next trip to Guangzhou, he meets with the group of business associates again, where he defiantly and valiantly shows off his newfound flair [他们几个面前逞得了英雄] (Wang 2004, p. 52). He does this while sharing large quantities of high-quality opium with them, which he had purchased in the backstreets of Xian. The business associates are suitably impressed and enthusiastically accept Wen into their group [入伙] (Wang 2004, p. 61). Consequently, Wen's and his childhood friend's 'face' [面子] is regained and Wen's income dramatically rises (Wang 2004, p. 61). With time, Wen develops a strong sense of brotherhood with the group members, one that 'even surpasses brotherly affection' [我们情同兄弟, 甚至胜过手足之情的兄弟]

24 *Gendered exemplars*

(Wang 2004, p. 64). This feeling, however, is not a product of their joint business endeavours, but a product of their unbridled recreational use of opium.

Continuing to use opium when back at home, drugs slowly and 'silently take away' Wen's 'essential strength' [毒品正在把我的整个精壮不声不响地拿走] (Wang 2004, p. 29). He is not troubled by using illicit drugs at home [那时我的内心没有明显的矛盾斗争] (Wang 2004, p. 40). In fact, he begins to question why opium is illegal in China. Nevertheless, Wen keeps his drug use secret from his wife, Aiyu [艾玉], because he fears that she, like most people in China, would have an exaggerated fear of opium [大烟不值得可怕] (Wang 2004, p. 22). Soon, opium comes to 'plunder' his 'reasoning' [毒品首先在我身上要掠夺的 . . . 是作为人最可贵的理性], compromising his value as a human being (Wang 2004, p. 66). Wen's idleness and loss of interest in his family life predictably trouble his wife, who soon catches him using opium. She is extremely angry and exhorts him to stop using illicit drugs. Wen is ashamed, losing face [无地自容] as well as the respect and the 'trust' of his wife [她会看不起我, 我在她面前说话会没有威信] (Wang 2004, p. 69). He cries, yet does not know why he cries. He promises not to use opium again, yet immediately qualifies this in his mind as not using opium when at home.

It is not long before Wen begins using illicit drugs at home again. His wife, who was once the centre of his existence, is now cold and distant. Wen has asked her not to tell the neighbours about their 'plight' [矛盾] (Wang 2004, p. 80). He had lived in the tenement, where he, his wife and son reside, all of his life, yet he now feels curiously estranged from his local surroundings [送走二十六个春秋之后, 竟然像生人一样不认识这地方了] (Wang 2004, p. 77). He rarely speaks to his wife or to his neighbours, an 'irrational physical compulsion' [没有理性的肉体的强迫] driving him to seek solace in the opium 'viper' [毒蛇] (Wang 2004, p. 79). Wen is addicted. He feels 'numb' [麻木] and 'insentient [没有知觉] (Wang 2004, p. 81). He experiences both 'absolute freedom and rampant tyranny' [绝对的自由, 并且横行霸道] (Wang 2004, p. 82).

Wen becomes annoyed that his wife continues to hound him to quit using opium, at times aggressively so. He does not believe that his opium use could impact his family in any way. He feels wronged that she does not attend to him anymore and suspects that she despises him. He had originally married Aiyu because of her dutiful care for him and his widowed father. Wen starts to openly use opium in her presence and no longer cares that she may leave him. They share a 'corpse-like' existence together [尸体一样对付着生活] (Wang 2004, p. 88). Meanwhile, Wen is able to maintain his successful business and he uses the profits to fund his drug addiction. He initially finds company in the fellow illicit drug users who frequent his home in order to share his large opium stash. Subsequently, he only can find company in the rats that infest his home. They, too, have become addicted to opium, thanks to the second-hand smoke that persistently clouds the dwelling. Wen's illicit drug use eventually comes to the attention of the local police and he is arrested. He feels great shame in being paraded in front of his neighbours as he is taken to detention. Wen spends a week in detention where he continues to use opium. It is smuggled in to him by his younger brother during visitations. Wen has 'become a loyal slave to opium' [我成了大烟的忠实奴隶], yet he distances himself from other drug addicts who are 'idle' [游手好闲无所事事], 'without legitimate work or money' [没有正当工作 . . . 没钱], and driven to 'steal and rob' [去偷去抢] (Wang 2004, pp. 112–113).

After Wen's release from detention, a kind police officer helps him by introducing him to a doctor of Traditional Chinese Medicine (TCM), who specialises in drug detoxification. Wen tells his wife this news, only to find out that she now is using opium as well. In the story, the wife is haughty and unrepentant in front of Wen: she has 'triumphed' over Wen [我的失败成了她的勋章 . . . 艾玉赢了. 艾玉是个胜者] (Wang 2004, p. 121). Wen suggests that they both detoxify according to the TCM doctor's regimen, but Aiyu angrily refuses. Instead, they both choose to use opium at home, becoming 'wooden people' [木人一样] (Wang 2004, p. 132). In their drug-induced mutuality, a bond between the couple is re-established and Wen, once again, speaks positively about his wife. With this, home life becomes pleasant, each partner freely using opium when she or he chooses to do so, and sharing opium and food with drug-using friends, echoing a modest 'Communist' lifestyle of 'distribution according to need' [我的家在那段吸毒的日子里, 实行的是共产主义政策: 按需分配] (Wang 2004, p. 134).

Wen reflects on his drug-using behaviour when he visits Sun Yat-sen's [孙中山] monument in Nanjing, while on vacation with Aiyu. Sun is the founding father of the Republic of China and is equally respected by Republican and Communist authorities. Wen immediately feels ashamed in the presence of this great man, who so readily gains 'the admiration of another man' [一个男人对另一个男人的佩服] (Wang 2004, p. 144). Wen believes that Sun holds him in contempt [先生冷峻地把脸别过去没有看我] (Wang 2004, p. 144). On his return to Xian, Wen observes a 'disheveled madman' [痴傻的人 . . . 蓬头垢面] on the street (Wang 2004, p. 146): could he become like this man? Soon, Wen does become like this man. Seriously addicted to opium, Wen stops working and uses opium alone at home, twenty-four hours a day. He does not wash or leave the home and rarely eats. He becomes wholly disconnected from his past life: all his 'memories' are gone [我的大脑的记忆, 真的成了一片空白] (Wang 2004, p. 152). He no longer lives as a human being, except for his use of opium: apart from human beings, 'no other creatures' in this world 'smoke opium' [惟一能够拿出来可以证明我还是个人的证据 . . . 正好是 . . . 那个毒品 . . . 我还是个人. 因为别的动物据我所知, 它们并不吸食大烟] (Wang 2004, p. 153).

Wen unintentionally leads his younger sister into opium addiction as well. He gives her opium in order to ameliorate the distressing symptoms of a chronic respiratory complaint. Opium, however, was 'plotting and setting a trap' for her [毒品在阴谋和陷阱中] (Wang 2004, p. 164). It becomes clear that there is 'no

26   *Gendered exemplars*

limit to drugs' frightful malice' [无法涵盖毒品可怕的恶毒] (Wang 2004, p. 170). Wen's younger sister dies from the lung disease, because the symptoms had been masked by her opium use. Wen is distraught, blaming himself and opium for her death [我在吸毒的路上，从一开始就把自己和一切亲人捆绑到葬送生命的路途上去了] (Wang 2004, p. 193). Nevertheless, he uses opium as he watches over her body in the hospital morgue and at her funeral. From this point on, Wen's home becomes his 'tomb' [世界上尚有另一种比真正的坟墓更加可怕更加富有实际意义的坟墓，那就是当时我的家] (Wang 2004, p. 201). He 'loses all human integrity', including 'dignity, personality, honour' and 'even shame and embarrassment' [我把做人的一切都丢失了，尊严、人格、光荣…连羞愧和难为情] (Wang 2004, p. 202). He lives totally alone in his grimy, ramshackle home. His wife has left to live at her natal home. Wen's only companions are the opium-addicted rats that infest his home.

The arrest of his younger brother for drug possession constitutes the turning point for Wen to seek recovery from his drug addiction. He visits his mother's grave, confessing his wrongdoings and promising to quit illicit drugs. He then recites a verse from a poem by Chairman Mao: 'This land so rich in beauty' ['江山如此多娇'], the words 'most accurately expressing Wen's boundlessly aroused state of mind at this time' [那句诗最准确地抒发了我当时无限激动的心怀] (Wang 2004, p. 209). Wen immediately sets off for Xinjiang, in China's frontier northwest, to re-enter 'the world in which people live' [置身于这个人类栖居的世界中] (Wang 2004, pp. 211–212). Wen is inspired by the 'tenacity' [顽强] of the Xinjiang landscape (Wang 2004, p. 212). In Xinjiang, he lodges with a strict and serious old woman, a former People's Liberation Army soldier who helps him to detoxify and quit using illicit drugs. By means of a 'solemn' five-day therapeutic 'ritual' [庄严的'仪式'] that is carried out in an all-white, scantly furnished room, opium's 'spiritual base camp' within Wen 'crumbles' [毒品在人精神方面的根据地…土崩瓦解了] (Wang 2004, pp. 219–220). Wen totally obeys the old woman: 'obedience' [服从] is his new 'mission' [天职] (Wang 2004, p. 222). The old woman, who he calls Aunty [大妈], is the 'queen' [女王], and he is 'her servant' [她的仆人] (Wang 2004, p. 221). Her 'military plan' [军事方案] succeeds where other's had failed like 'the routed Nationalist troops' [跟国民党溃逃的军队差不多] (Wang 2004, p. 222). Aunty had helped him to reclaim his 'body' [身体] and 'self' [自己] as well as his 'past' [从前] and 'future' [未来] (Wang 2004, p. 224).

Wen praises Aunty's actions as those that 'only a mother can do' [只有母亲才能做得到] (Wang 2004, p. 227). Aunty dismisses any sacrifice that she has made in helping Wen quit illicit drugs as 'inconsequential', 'so long as' he 'has quit drugs' permanently [她说只要我把毒戒了，她受这点苦不算什么] (Wang 2004, p. 227). Wen's life in recovery from drug addiction is not easy. The 'many hands' [千万只手] of opium continue to 'torment' [折磨] him, seeking his 'satisfaction' [迫使我来满足它们] (Wang 2004, p. 229). Wen, however, resolutely 'persists' in his 'struggle' for 'liberation from the hands of drugs' [坚持、坚持、再坚持. 和每一分钟时间作斗争 . . . 从毒品手下解放出来] (Wang 2004, p. 230). At an epiphanous moment in his life story, Wen races a fine steed across the wild frontier lands of Xinjiang. It is here that he feels that his 'self is restored' [我恢复了 自己], in both 'flesh' [肉体] and 'soul' [心灵] (Wang 2004, p. 235). The 'former vitality inside' his 'body', which 'had been tormented to death by drugs, had completely reignited' [我身体里过去很活跃, 后来被毒品折磨得死亡了的东西, 全部都点燃了] (Wang 2004, p. 235). He 'loudly proclaims' to the frontier lands: 'I have returned!——I——have——returned——!' [我放开喉咙 . . . 大喊起来: '我回来了——我——回——来——了——'] (Wang 2004, p. 235).

Wen is content living with Aunty in Xinjiang, and socialising with her family, friends and the local Uyghur minority people. He enjoys and appreciates the simple pleasures in life, something that he had 'never experienced before' [我怎么从来没有仔细观察细心体会过, 这样一个小小的场面也如此动人] (Wang 2004, pp. 238–239). He gradually feels that he is becoming a 'normal person' [正常人] and living a 'normal life' [正常的生活] (Wang 2004, pp. 244–245). With this, Wen decides to return to his wife and son in Xian and 'start again from the very beginning' [从头开始]: Xian is where he 'fell down' so that is where he should 'climb back up' [回到自己的家里去, 在哪儿跌倒的, 就在哪儿爬起来!] (Wang 2004, pp. 254, 256). On his return to Xian, he is appalled and angry to find that his wife is still using opium. He had thought that she was in recovery too. Aiyu appears 'dirty and unkempt, not the slightest bit like a woman' [蓬头垢面, 没有一点女人的样子] (Wang 2004, 263). Wen wants her to 'be restored to the previously clean, honourable, clever and virtuous wife' who he had loved before [还原成从前的那个她, 一个干净体面聪明贤淑的我的所爱, 我的妻子] (Wang 2004, p. 263). He threatens divorce if she does not quit using opium. He fears that she will 'drag him back' into using opium [把我也拖进来] (Wang 2004, p. 265). Aiyu refuses to quit, 'choosing', rather, to divorce Wen [艾玉在戒毒和离婚的选择上, 她选择了离婚] (Wang 2004, p. 266).

Wen's 'will is as impregnable as the Great Wall of China' [意志像万里长城一样, 任何力量都无法把我摧毁] (Wang 2004, p. 266). Memory of the Xinjiang Aunty keeps it this way. He successively establishes a number of modestly successful individual business enterprises and cares for his son at home. Gradually, he is 'accepted' [接纳] back into society (Wang 2004, p. 275). This confirms his belief in the 'glorious truth of naïve materialism eternally radiated by humanity' [人类永恒的放射着朴素唯物主义光辉的真理] (Wang 2004, p. 275). While Wen is 'transforming' himself [自我改造], his former wife is arrested for, and then convicted of, drug trafficking (Wang 2004, p. 283). Wen suffers great loss of face over this, lamenting that 'several generations must pay before the whiff of drugs has been totally wiped clean from our lives' [需要几代人的付出. 才能从我们的生活中把毒品的那股烟清除干净] (Wang 2004, pp. 287–288). He persists in his recovery, nevertheless, under the 'care' [关心] of his neighbours, friends and the

28 *Gendered exemplars*

local neighbourhood committee [街道居委会] (Wang 2004, p. 288). He believes that his ex-wife had 'gotten what she had deserved' [罪有应得. 自作自受] (Wang 2004, pp. 291–292). Yet, he regrets that his young son must now bear the social consequences of being marked as 'inferior' due to his mother's crimes [父母作奸犯科, 子女必须低人一等...我八岁的儿子...必须要背着母亲的黑锅生活在这个世界上] (Wang 2004, pp. 292–293).

Wen concludes his life story by reflecting on the 'new order' [新秩序] of sorts, which has developed in his life (Wang 2004, p. 296). He has come to terms with his ex-wife being in jail and the recent death of his younger brother from a comorbid illness that was caused by his drug addiction. Wen also had been interviewed by the local Xian media about his life as a drug addict and now counsels families and conducts presentations in drug rehabilitation centres on how to quit illicit drugs. His achievements are publicly acknowledged: 'a prodigal son returned home is worth more than gold' [浪子回头金不换] (Wang 2004, p. 299). Wen returns to the old neighbourhood where he had grown up, got married and used illicit drugs. It has been razed and remodeled beyond recognition. Yet, Wen can still sense 'the ashen-faced' people who have lost their lives to opium addiction there, as they say their 'last goodbye to the world where they had once lived' [已经死去了的他们...向这个曾经生活过的世界, 用那副被大烟熏成青灰色的面孔, 作着最后的告别] (Wang 2004, p. 310).

Analysis

In *Heaven and Hell*, Wen tells a story that does not understate or mask the deep tragedy and extreme unpleasantness of his life as a drug addict. He, nevertheless, is able to place sufficient distance between himself and the events that transpire during his life as a drug addict, or provide cogent counterbalances to these events, such that he retains a semblance of 'moral face' [脸] throughout his life story (Kleinman *et al.* 2011, pp. 12, 245). The plausibility of Wen's essential morality is enhanced in *Heaven and Hell* by the apparent impermanence of his drug addiction; his largely seamless performance of Chinese masculinity; his use of language that carries familiar political overtones of accomplishment, fortitude and virtue; and his meritorious conduct as a socialist citizen.

Drug addiction constitutes a discrete and finite period in Wen's life story. He lives a 'normal' [正常] life before using opium and returns to such a life after quitting opium. His life as a drug addict is an impermanent 'biographical disruption' lasting for three years (Gibson, Acquah & Robinson 2004, p. 614). If it were able to be 'cut out' from his life story [把吸毒的三年时间剪掉], Wen's pre-drug-using life and post-drug-using life could be patched together reasonably seamlessly, although with some obvious discontinuities: he now is divorced, his former wife is incarcerated, and his younger sister and younger brother are both dead (Wang 2004, p. 228). Wen's pre-drug-using past features prominently in his life story at all times. This life from before drug addiction exemplifies highly valued merits of family life in mainland China at that time: a happily married couple with one healthy son; a dutiful wife, who tends to the home and takes care of the child and the elderly widowed father-in-law; an individual-entrepreneur [个体户] husband, whose enterprise is quite successful; a very modest family home, with basic yet sufficient furnishings [小康水平][3]; a supportive extended family; a friendly and pleasant local neighbourhood; and fond memories of family life as a child (in the very same home). This characterised Wen's life from before drug use. Memories of this sustain him in drug addiction, and many of these past-lived merits – the incarcerated ex-wife and the dead siblings being the notable exceptions – re-emerge in his life in recovery from drug addiction. Wen re-establishes a number of individual enterprises with modest success; he maintains a modest home for his son and himself; his surviving extended family remains supportive; his local community are friendly and supportive, once they are convinced he is well 'reformed' [已经改了, 改了就好]; and he is sustained in his recovery by his fond memories of the Xinjiang Aunty and his birth parents (Wang 2004, p. 299). As a consequence, the 'new order' [新秩序] in Wen's life in recovery from drug addiction is belied by a temporal continuity, whereby a wholly moral self from before drug addiction resurfaces in recovery.

Wen maintains a semblance of moral face *during* drug addiction as well. In the story, he is respectful of elders and the public authorities. He does not exploit others or engage in criminality, even when times are financially tough. He continues to care for his family and friends, although the care that he gives his little sister merely hastens her death. In addition, when still capable of managing his business ventures, Wen is open with his employees about his drug addiction and takes every opportunity to 'warn them off' illicit drug use [我特别郑重地提醒他们 . . . 毒品是天下最惹不起的恶汉] (Wang 2004, p. 176). The reasons for Wen's illicit drug use also allow him to maintain a semblance of moral face in *Heaven and Hell*. In the story, his drug addiction is not caused by any intrinsic mental or physical flaw. He does not suffer from any illness, as his little sister did. Nor is he genetically programmed to be a drug addict, although the morbidity of drug addiction in his family might suggest otherwise. Wen does not entertain a biomedical aetiological explanation for his drug addiction, most probably because such an explanation would markedly and permanently taint him and his family, as it regularly does in mental illness in Chinese culture (Ramsay 2008, 2013). Instead, Wen suggests that he became addicted to illicit drugs because, first, he sought to make more money by joining a group of successful business associates. Second, he wanted to gain the respect of these business associates after having shamed himself in their presence. Third, he wished to restore the face of his close childhood friend, who had introduced him to the business associates. Thus, Wen is not ill, troubled or sullied, but simply a naïve everyday man, who makes a grave 'mistake' [错了就错了, 人生一世谁没有做错事] in a misguided attempt

30 *Gendered exemplars*

to regain honour and become more prosperous (Wang 2004, p. 299). At that time, political discourse promoted the virtue of the pursuit of prosperity [致富光荣].

Wen's essential morality is made more plausible due to his consistent performance of normative masculinity in Chinese culture in *Heaven and Hell*. Wen unambiguously asserts his masculine identity in the story: 'I am a man' [我是个男子汉] (Wang 2004, p. 197). He performs this masculine identity through his business achievements; through his deep respect for venerated male national leaders; and through his displays of male bonding. Achievement in the business sphere traditionally was devalued in Confucian culture. Louie (2002, 2015), however, states that business acumen now constitutes an important component of Chinese masculinity, specifically *wen* ('literary') [文] masculinity. Wen is a successful individual entrepreneur, with an ambition for even greater success. He maintains this success for some time while using illicit drugs and quickly regains this success on his recovery from drug addiction. Wen's masculinity also is demonstrated by his high regard for the venerated male leaders of China: Sun Yat-sen, the founding father of the Republic of China, and Mao Zedong, the founding father of the People's Republic of China. He believes that men of their calibre deserve the admiration of other men. Wen's masculine esteem for great men in *Heaven and Hell* is matched by his displays of male-bonding. Hetero-normative fraternity [手足情谊] has been a key facet of Chinese manhood since traditional times (Huang 2007; Louie 2002; Lu 2012; Song 2003). In Chinese chivalry tales of old, heroic men enact their masculinity through male-bonding practices such as 'sharing a bed and eating together . . . 食则同桌, 寝则同床' (Lu 2012, p. 41). In traditional times, Chinese men also would smoke copious amounts of opium in front of other men in opium dens, for the purposes of 'homosocial recreation' (Brook & Wakabayashi 2000, p. 8) and 'male display' (Baumler 2007, p. 37). In *Heaven and Hell*, Wen masters opium smoking as part of an initiation ritual, the successful 'performance' [表演给他们] of which 'admits' him into a business fraternity [接纳我入伙] (Wang 2004, pp. 53, 60). Wen also masters opium smoking in order to restore the face of his trusted and loyal male childhood friend. The fraternal relationship between Wen and his childhood mate is cast as 'surpassing that of blood-brothers' [我们胜似亲兄弟那样], having been forged amidst 'mutual hardship and camaraderie' [共过患难, 同舟共济] while growing up during the troubled years of the Cultural Revolution (1966–1976) and the early open-door reform period (Wang 2004, p. 2).

Wen's masculine traits, his respect for authority and the law, together with his righteous moral concern and care for his father, his younger siblings and his son, discursively position him as an essentially moral man [男子汉], despite the aberration of his drug addiction. Wen's discursive position as an essentially moral man, furthermore, stands in contrast to the subjective position of his wife and other illicit drug users in *Heaven and Hell*. His wife, Aiyu, starts out as the embodiment of normative Chinese womanhood: she is supportive, dutiful, virtuous, attractive and filial. However, she coldly ignores Wen when he starts using opium, apart from pestering him to quit, and she does not visit him when he is in jail, much to his annoyance. Wen's family, in contrast, remains very supportive of him at all times. Eventually, Aiyu starts using opium, it seems, as a 'spiteful' [轻蔑], 'malicious' [恶毒] and 'arrogant' [骄傲] act of 'retaliation' against Wen [对我实施报复] (Wang 2004, pp. 120–121). When drug-addicted, she once again appears supportive of Wen by tending to his basic needs. However, she angrily refuses to quit opium when Wen does and, instead, chooses to divorce Wen and leave their son in his care. With this, Aiyu's normative femininity and her attractive physical appearance as a woman wholly dissolve in the story. Soon after, Aiyu commits what Wen considers to be her most heinous transgression: she becomes a common criminal and is arrested by the police and jailed for drug trafficking. This transgression, Wen believes, stains their son for life. As a result, Aiyu abrogates her responsibilities as a mother and a wife, in contravention of normative womanhood in Chinese culture (Cai 2005; Croll 1995; Guo 2010; Roberts 2010). As a contrast, the Xinjiang Aunty conscientiously and successfully enacts normative Chinese womanhood in the face of adversity. She selflessly cares for Wen around the clock for days on end while he is undergoing drug detoxification, as if she were his own mother [尽了一位母亲的责任, 做了只有母亲才能做得到的事情] (Wang 2004, p. 227).

Other illicit drug users in *Heaven and Hell* also stand in contrast to Wen's discursive position as an essentially moral man. His male drug buddies, who initially frequent his house, are no-hopers and hangers-on. They never quit using illicit drugs, often traffic in illicit drugs and, by the conclusion of the story, many of them are dead. Wen's younger brother chooses to wallow in 'pessimism' [弟弟是个悲观厌世的人], rather than 'be full of hope' like Wen [他和我不一样, 我在任何时候都充满着希望] (Wang 2004, p. 297). He dies of a comorbid illness caused by his drug addiction. Wen's younger sister forsakes her kind and caring disabled husband for opium. She dies from a chronic lung complaint, whose symptoms had been masked by her opium use. On the other hand, Wen's fundamental moral righteousness, together with a largely seamless performance of Chinese manhood, enables him to overcome his drug addiction and return to everyday society as a 'normal person' [正常人] living a 'normal life' [正常的生活]. In the story, his restored moral status is acknowledged by members of his local community, when they accept him as their neighbour. It also is acknowledged by the broader society, by way of his continuing social welfare and media engagements in Xian.

Wen's life as a drug addict in *Heaven and Hell* is cast in the language of absence: there is an absence of light, an absence of sound, an absence of life, and an absence of freedom. The drug days [那个日子] are 'dark' [黑暗; 黑洞洞; 深黑] and 'silent' [沉默; 没有声音] (Wang 2004, pp. 4–40). The addict is 'dead' [死亡; 尸体; 萎萎缩缩; 木人; 末日] or 'entombed' [埋葬; 坟墓; 坑井] (Wang 2004, pp. 9–235). The only form of being ever conferred on the drug addict is

32 *Gendered exemplars*

one of a 'slave' or 'prisoner' [奴隶; 捆绑; 属于毒品; 控制; 囚徒] (Wang 2004, pp. 29–170). Illicit drugs, meanwhile, are personified. They are 'villains' [恶汉] or 'colonists brandishing weapons' [挥舞着大刀长枪的殖民者] (Wang 2004, pp. 150, 176). They 'plot' [策划阴谋], 'plunder' [掠夺], 'invade' [侵入] and 'wait' [等待]; and they should be 'obeyed' [服从] and 'satisfied' [满足] (Wang 2004, pp. 53–261). They have 'black hands' [黑手] that 'steal' [偷偷拿走], 'torment' [折磨], 'smear' [涂抹], 'snatch away' [夺走] and 'embrace' [怀抱]; and they have 'voices' [声音] that 'laugh' [哈哈大笑] (Wang 2004, pp. 71–297). The personified drugs are recast as an enemy and, accordingly, Wen's recovery from drug addiction becomes a battle. Illicit drugs need to be 'conquered' [战胜] (Wang 2004, p. 303). Wen's body, which figuratively is dead or enslaved, becomes a 'battleground' [一场体内的战争; 战场; 根据地]; a place where 'troops' [军队] wage war in keeping with a 'military plan' [军事方案] (Wang 2004, pp. 12–222). The Xinjiang Aunty, a People's Liberation Army veteran, is victorious in her campaign: she helps 'liberate' [解放] Wen from the clutches of opium. For his part, Wen must 'persist' [坚持] in a 'long-term struggle' [作斗争] against a relapse of drug addiction. He accomplishes this by figuratively transforming his formerly drug-addicted body into an 'obedient' and 'innocent' 'child' [比一个孩子都要听话; 孩提时代纯真] (Wang, pp. 221, 225). As a result, linguistically, Wen travels a full circle in *Heaven and Hell*, from a 'naughty', 'lost' 'child' [孩子一样淘气; 迷了路的孩子], who was just 'learning to walk' [学步孩子] when he first tried opium, to the innocent and obedient child who he enters into recovery from drug addiction (Wang 2004, pp. 17–38).

In sum, cultural, political and institutional discourses shape temporality, subjectivity and language use in *Heaven and Hell* in ways that cast Wen as an essentially moral and meritorious man. This is achieved by shaping the narrative processes in ways that observe and uphold: (i) Chinese cultural norms, values and scripts, in particular, normative gender in Chinese culture; (ii) the broader political agenda of the mainland Chinese government; and (iii) the mission of the Public Security Bureau whose publishing house published the book. From the cultural perspective, Wen is an essentially moral and righteous man because of his family-centeredness, his respect for authority and the law, and his largely seamless performance of Chinese manhood. Wen looks after his widowed father and his younger siblings, even when he is addicted to opium. He also takes care of his young son, when his wife abandons him. Wen does not partake in crime and acknowledges and consents to the wishes of those in authority. In addition, Wen places high regard on hetero-normative fraternity and displays *wen* traits in accordance with the ideal Chinese man. This makes his morality sounder and more plausible. At the same time, those around Wen are cast either as moral human beings by conforming to normative cultural scripts, for example the Xinjiang Aunty; or as immoral human beings by contravening these scripts, for example, Aiyu and other illicit drug users in the story. As a consequence, Chinese cultural norms, values and scripts are observed and upheld in *Heaven and Hell*, in particular, normative gender in Chinese culture.

From a political perspective, Wen displays some of the key attributes of the 'ideal' (Kleinman *et al.* 2011, p. 9) or 'exemplary' (Bakken 2000, p. 1) socialist citizen. He is committed in his struggle and battle against illicit drugs; he has unswerving respect for public authorities and esteemed national leaders; he shows stamina and fortitude in overcoming drug addiction; he is an everyday man who returns to everyday society; and he works hard and gives back to society when he recovers from drug addiction. This constitutes meritorious conduct for a socialist citizen in contemporary mainland China (Bakken 2000; Kleinman *et al.* 2011; Roberts 2014). At the same time, Wen's life story satisfies the mainland Chinese political agenda, by recounting the degradation that characterises a social vice like drug addiction, and doing so in a way that endorses contemporary political rhetoric and values, such as long-term struggle and battle. Contemporary Chinese political discourse speaks of the 'people's war against drugs' (人民禁毒战争) (Liang & Lu 2013, p. 315. See also Biddulph 2013; Biddulph & Xie 2011; Levin 2015; Trevaskes 2013; Zhou 2000a, 2000b). Such discourse draws on the language of the anti-Japanese war and the civil war, which continues to shape current government pronouncements on the conflict with regional neighbours over the sovereignty of off-shore territory.

From an institutional perspective, Wen is as an appropriate (male) role-model for public security authorities to use for public drug education in mainland China. This is because Wen maintains an everydayness and a semblance of morality throughout the course of his story. In addition to this, Wen can be characterised as exemplary in political terms (the model socialist citizen) as well as in cultural terms (the moral man). At the same time, Wen's story largely endorses the institutional mission of China's public security authorities: criminalising drug addiction and eliminating illicit drugs from mainland Chinese society (see Chapter 1). In his story, failure to abstain from illicit drugs eventually leads to criminality or death. Moreover, the police are cast as benevolent and supportive in the story, as is the local neighbourhood committee that supports the Chinese public security authorities in their day-to-day law enforcement activities (Biddulph 2013; Biddulph & Xie 2011; Zhou 1999).

Similar to Western accounts of drug addiction and recovery (see Chapter 1), life as a drug addict is bad and life in recovery is good in *Heaven and Hell*. As a man, Wen actively pursues illicit drugs: he is not a passive victim (Hersey 2005). Once addicted, however, he is enslaved. Recovery from drug addiction is heralded by the distinct turning point that characterises Western counterpart stories (Aston 2009; Hersey 2005; McIntosh & McKeganey 2000; Taïeb *et al.* 2008). Tellingly, the turning point for Wen is the arrest of his younger brother for illicit drug possession, and not the death of his younger sister from an illness that was masked by her illicit drug use. Also similar to Western counterparts, drug

34 *Gendered exemplars*

addiction and recovery are cast as a battle in *Heaven and Hell* (Viano 2002). In contrast to Western accounts of drug addiction and recovery, no discernible addict identity emerges in Wen's life story. Wen's essentially good self merely temporarily goes astray, due to misguided senses of male honour and fraternity. Moreover, Wen does not seek refuge in an illness identity: this could permanently taint him and his family, as is common in mental illness in Chinese culture (Ramsay 2008, 2013).

Mainland Chinese woman's life story of drug addiction and recovery

Struggle Spirit[4] [灵魂交锋: 作家与吸毒女300天心灵对话实录] tells the life story of Wang Tongtong's [王彤彤] more than ten years of heroin use and addiction and her subsequent recovery from heroin addiction, during the 1990s and early 2000s in mainland China. The book is 294 pages in length and was published in 2009 by Xinhua Press [新华出版社], which is the publishing house of China's official news agency, Xinhua News Agency [新华社] (Xinhua Press 2013). The press publishes 'social science books' [社科类图书] that address 'current affairs, news, cultural, educational, economic and lifestyle' [时政、新闻、文教、经济、生活] issues in mainland China (Xinhua Press 2013). As an affiliate of the mainland Chinese government's official news agency, works published by Xinhua Press would be expected to espouse the viewpoint of the state.

Wang's first-person account of drug addiction and recovery is presented in *Struggle Spirit* by way of a series of emails that she had sent to an author of human interest books, Chen Beidi [陈贝帝], throughout March to December 2008. These emails are reproduced verbatim in *Struggle Spirit*, with each email approximately one to three pages in length. Wang originally had sent the emails to Chen, because he had authored a number of works that deal with illicit drug use and addiction in mainland China. Chen subsequently convinced Wang to publish her emails in a co-authored book, *Struggle Spirit*, along with his email replies that reflect on Wang's account in light of knowledge that he had gained from his earlier writings and his considerable knowledge of Chinese and Western philosophy. *Struggle Spirit* also contains reproductions of short paragraph-long cell phone text communications between Wang and Chen throughout March to December 2008. These communications do not recount Wang's life story, but discuss what Wang or Chen had been doing at that moment of time. The text messages also included their debates on philosophical or theoretical issues raised by Chen in his email replies, and advice from Chen to Wang, for example on how to get her life story of drug addiction and recovery in print, or how to deal with media appearances. The emails and cell phone texts are reproduced in the book in their chronological order of sending.

The following synopsis and analysis of Wang's life story of drug addiction and recovery only draw on Wang's email communications as data. The synopsis and analysis do not draw on any of Chen's communications or Wang's cell phone texts. This is because the content of these communications is ancillary to Wang's life story. Wang's life story covers the period from her childhood in the 1960s and 1970s up to her contact with Chen in 2008. She had grown up in Wenzhou in eastern China in a family of two parents and two children: her older brother and herself. Wang is much loved by her brother and her 'upright and kind-hearted' [正直善良] parents, who selflessly 'would attribute their achievements, gained through great effort, to cultivation by the Party and the people' [他们曾经所努力的成就都会归功于党和人民的栽培] (Chen & Wang 2009, pp. 17, 62). Her parents are quite well-off and well-respected in the local community [在社会上也是有头有脸的人] (Chen & Wang 2009, p. 62). The mother 'is criticised and struggled against' [被批斗了] during the Cultural Revolution, forcing Wang and her older brother to go and live in the countryside with their maternal grandmother's family (Chen & Wang 2009, p. 65). This separation does not overly impact Wang negatively and she subsequently achieves very good results at school.

Wang's father dies when she is eighteen years old. This impacts her greatly, as she had spent a lot of time with her father as a child, when her mother, who was an actor, was out performing. Not long after, Wang marries a small business owner and gives birth to a daughter. She raises her daughter and supports her husband in his business endeavours, first a restaurant and then a small nightclub. During this time, she 'befriends and comes to know many different kinds of people in society' [由于职业上的缘故, 结交和认识了不少社会上各色各样的人物] (Chen & Wang 2009, p. 51). She 'also comes to know many so-called fashionable things, such as drugs' [也知道了很多所谓时髦的东西, 比如毒品] (Chen & Wang 2009, p. 51). Wang and her husband, nevertheless, have no interest in using illicit drugs [不会去碰毒品] (Chen & Wang 2009, p. 52). She believes that, 'at that time, he, probably even into his next life, would not have anticipated that I, who was aloof, arrogant and viewed bad conduct as dirty, would sometime in the future find company in drugs' [他当时可能下辈子都不会想到清高、傲气、视不良行为为粪土的我有朝一日会和毒品为伴] (Chen & Wang 2009, p. 52).

By the time her daughter is a young school-aged girl, Wang has grown tired of her husband [只是我不怎么喜欢他] (Chen & Wang 2009, p. 52). She is 'not like those kinds of people who are content with just having a child and carrying on with life' [不像有些人那样有了孩子感情就平淡了, 将就过日子] (Chen & Wang 2009, p. 52). As a result, she becomes 'quite cold and indifferent' to her husband [我就对他比较冷淡] (Chen & Wang 2009, p. 52). She behaves in a way that 'is probably most intolerable for men' [对男人来说可能是最受不了的事], by 'ignoring him' and refusing him intimacy [不理他, 不让他接近] (Chen & Wang 2009, p. 52). In addition, she behaves duplicitously in 'seeming, to outsiders, to be a tender and virtuous wife' [我这外人看似温柔贤惠的女人], while being 'as cold as ice' [冷若冰霜] to her husband (Chen & Wang 2009, p. 52).

36 *Gendered exemplars*

Ultimately, Wang sees no use for a husband now that she has a daughter [有女儿的日子老公是多余的], so she decides to leave him.

Wang is not overly affected by the failure of her relationship with her husband [我从没想过自暴自弃或放纵自流] (Chen & Wang 2009, p. 53). She does not consider herself to be 'the kind of woman whose world collapses if she doesn't have a man' [那种没有男人天就塌了的女人] (Chen & Wang 2009, p. 53). She happily spends more time with women friends. As it happens, some friends of one of Wang's closest women friends use illicit drugs. One day, while visiting this close friend, Wang asks the drug-using friends if she can try heroin. At the time, she considers that using heroin is just 'like child's play' [像小孩过家家] (Chen & Wang 2009, p. 53). Thereafter, Wang uses heroin 'on occasion' for a number of years [偶尔吸一下], until one day she suddenly realises that she has 'fallen into the morass of drugs' [陷到了毒品的泥沼中去了] (Chen & Wang 2009, pp. 57–58). She has become addicted to heroin. While Wang 'lacks the strength to struggle against the power of the white devil' [白魔的力量让当时的我无力挣扎], she manages to retain a sense of 'shame and contempt' [廉耻和卑鄙] and 'the most basic morals and conscience of human conduct' [做人最起码的道德和良知] during drug addiction (Chen & Wang 2009, p. 103). She, for example 'does not commit crime or engage in salacious behaviour in order to fund' her 'drug habit' [不会为了毒资而去做所谓的'偷鸡摸狗'的事情] (Chen & Wang 2009, p. 103). As a result, Wang reports that she has two selves when she is addicted to heroin: a 'drug self' and an 'essential self' [有毒的我和那个本我] (Chen & Wang 2009, p. 103). These identities are 'indistinguishably entangled together' [在一起纠缠不清] (Chen & Wang 2009, p. 103). Ultimately, her drug self subdues her essential self, leaving Wang to feel an intense sense of personal and social 'humiliation' [屈辱] when addicted to heroin (Chen & Wang 2009, p. 106). Wang's daughter, thankfully, is spared this humiliation, as she is in boarding school. Wang's mother, on the other hand, stands by Wang and supports her throughout her heroin addiction, until the mother unexpectedly contracts cancer and dies. At this point of Wang's life story, her 'childhood dreams and past glory have faded amidst the wisps of white smoke' [孩时的梦想、曾经的辉煌已在一缕缕白烟中淡去] (Chen & Wang 2009, p. 115). She has become a '"heroin sister", who lacks willpower, disregards the feelings of her family, and has no conscience' [自己也不过是个没有意志、漠视亲情、失去良知的 '白粉妹'] (Chen & Wang 2009, p. 115). She has 'forsaken all sense of responsibility for' her family [对家人也失去了责任 . . . 责任已离我而去] (Chen & Wang 2009, p. 116).

In time, Wang is arrested by the police for soliciting illicit drugs. She is sentenced to six months compulsory drug rehabilitation in a government penal facility [强制戒毒所] (Chen & Wang 2009, p. 120). Currently, there are more than one million officially registered drug addicts in mainland China, although '[u]nofficial estimates put the number . . . in the region of millions' (Liang & Lu 2013, p. 302. See also Biddulph & Xie 2011; Levin 2015; Luo *et al.* 2014; Trevaskes 2013). The

2008 *Anti-Drug Law of the People's Republic of China* stipulates that repeat drug offenders undergo one to three years of compulsory drug rehabilitation in one of several hundred government-approved drug treatment facilities across mainland China (Biddulph & Xie 2011; Gao 2011; Liang & Lu 2013; Lu & Wang 2008; Luo *et al.* 2014; Yang *et al.* 2014). Formerly, repeat drug offenders were sentenced to long-term detention in government re-education-through-labour [劳教] facilities, which number around 200 across mainland China (Biddulph & Xie 2011; Gao 2011; Lu & Wang 2008; Luo *et al.* 2014; Tang *et al.* 2006; Yang *et al.* 2014). Biddulph (2013), Biddulph and Xie (2011) and Yang *et al.* (2014) note that most of the present-day compulsory drug rehabilitation facilities simply are retitled former re-education-through-labour facilities. Yang *et al.* (2014, p. 509) observe 'little difference' in the day-to-day practices of the former and the latter. Conditions in both facilities are very rudimentary, with strict discipline imposed (Gao 2011; Zhou 1999).

Wang avoids re-education-through-labour but is incarcerated in a compulsory drug rehabilitation facility. Life for Wang in the penal facility is strict and regimented. She is extremely unhappy, because she resents the fact that the authorities are forcing her to quit heroin: she feels that she could do it herself if she wanted to [我要戒自己会戒的，不需要政府和警察来给我这种压力和枷锁] (Chen & Wang 2009, p. 121). Moreover, she feels quite out of place in the facility, claiming that fellow inmates and staff are astonished that she could be a drug addict [不管是戒毒人员还是队长都曾说过同样的话：彤彤，你怎么也会吸毒，你一点也不像个吸毒者] (Chen & Wang 2009, p. 123). Wang maintains an 'aloof and arrogant' [清高、傲气] demeanour while in the facility (Chen & Wang 2009, p. 123). She believes that her higher level of 'education' [文化] and 'intention' [内涵] 'made people' in the facility 'feel that' her 'overall quality was quite good' [让人感觉我的整体素质相当不错] (Chen & Wang 2009, p. 124). As a consequence, Wang is given the task of reporting inmate production statistics to officials as well as being promoted to inmate 'group leader' [大组长] (Chen & Wang 2009, p. 124). These 'both are much admired positions' [两者都是一个让人羡慕的工种], which leads her to rapidly 'ingratiate' herself with her fellow inmates [奉承我的戒毒人员也不少] (Chen & Wang 2009, p. 124). Wang takes care to treat everyone equally [大家都一样，不分三流九等], but some of her fellow inmates resent her authority. They physically attack her and a melee immediately erupts between her attackers and her supporters. Afterward, Wang nobly insists on taking responsibility for the incident herself.

On completion of her six-month stint in penal drug rehabilitation, Wang wants to 'start all over again' in her life [一切重新开始] (Chen & Wang 2009, p. 134). She stays with her family for a few months and then rents a place in Wenzhou, where she plans to study English. One day, Wang catches up with a former fellow inmate of the drug rehabilitation facility, who pressures her to try some heroin. She initially hesitates but then capitulates. Wang uses more heroin the following

38   *Gendered exemplars*

day, when the police unexpectedly arrive and ask her to do a urine test. She suspects that her former fellow inmate has set her up. She believes that the former fellow inmate has been let off by the police for her own infraction, in return for giving up the names of other illicit drug users, such as Wang. This, Wang claims, would allow the police to meet their monthly arrest 'quota' [我成了警察和吸毒者的指标] (Chen & Wang 2009, p. 145). Wang, in turn, does not inform on the former fellow inmate to the arresting police. She 'despises' such behaviour and her 'principles of human conduct prevent' her 'from becoming self-contemptuous' [我也做不到把她作为一个'指标', 我鄙视这样的人, 我做人的原则不允许我成为自己鄙视的人] (Chen & Wang 2009, p. 145).

Wang now is classified as 'a repeat-recidivist "heroin sister"' [一个多次戒不了毒的'白粉妹'] (Chen & Wang 2009, p. 148). Her 'prospects and future are forever branded with a dark shadow' and her 'political file contains an indelible stain' [前途和未来永远烙上了阴影 . . . 政治档案就有了怎么也抹不去的污点] (Chen & Wang 2009, p. 148). She feels as if she 'has fallen into a deep abyss' [跌入万丈深渊] (Chen & Wang 2009, p. 149). She is sentenced to two years in a re-education-through-labour facility, in accordance with the pre-2008 sanctions for repeat drug offenders (see earlier in this section). She is far from a model inmate in the facility. She is 'aloof and arrogant' [清高傲气], 'supercilious' [目空一切], 'rebellious' [反叛], 'obstinate' [顽固] and 'opinionated' [自以为是] (Chen & Wang 2009, p. 156). Her production output is constantly low. Because of this, she is punished with demerit points, extra duties and extensions to her sentence. She briefly serves as group leader of her fellow inmates in the facility, a role that she had successfully carried out during compulsory drug rehabilitation. However, her insolence makes her 'the innermost enemy of the prison officers' [我就成了警官们内心的敌人] (Chen & Wang 2009, p. 170). They successfully conspire to send her to solitary confinement [反省室], so that she can reflect for a while on her uncompliant behaviour (Chen & Wang 2009, p. 174). This infuriates Wang, who refuses to allow them to remove the shackles that they had placed on her arms during her transfer to solitary confinement. She also begins a hunger strike. After six days, the shackles are forcibly removed by prison officers, and after another five days, her hunger strike is broken when prison officers and medical staff force-feed her through a nasogastric tube.

During the many weeks in solitary confinement, Wang secretly is looked after by fellow inmates who she had helped her out previously. They are women on the margins: a crippled inmate [一个双脚不会走路的劳教], a lesbian inmate, and several inmates suffering from HIV-AIDS who happen to be housed next to her (Chen & Wang 2009, p. 178). Their care and support strengthen Wang's resolve not to give in to the prison officers, who are seeking a written apology from her. She remains as steadfast as 'an underground Party member' [地下党人], preferring to 'die rather than compromise!' with the prison officers [我就是死了也决不向你们妥协的!] (Chen & Wang 2009, pp. 180, 184). The stand-off only is resolved when the governor [所长] of the re-education-through-labour facility, Deputy Director Guo [郭副], personally intervenes (Chen & Wang 2009, p. 159). He is the only person in authority who Wang respects and trusts. Wang initially had met him at the facility's open-day event. She had found him 'attentive' [他眼睛一直注视着我], 'respectful' [他很尊敬我], egalitarian [他就告诉我, 虽然我们身份不同, 但我们是平等的], 'rational' [郭副是个明理的所长] and 'a good leader' [郭副是个好领导], who has 'virtue and merit' [功德和修行] (Chen & Wang 2009, pp. 158–159, 161). During Wang's detention in the re-education-through-labour facility, he 'became' her 'slice of heaven' and 'big tree' [郭副在我的心里成了我的一片天, 成了我的大树] (Chen & Wang 2009, p. 165). In the story, she claims that he is solely responsible for her being able to 'forge a completely new self' [铸就了一个全新的我] in her recovery from drug addiction (Chen & Wang 2009, p. 211). If it were not for him, she would not have entertained any thought of a future life without heroin. In view of this, she continues to 'appreciate and respect Deputy Director Guo' [我欣赏郭副, 敬重郭副] and 'remains eternally grateful for his views on re-education' [他的教育理念至今让我心存感激] (Chen & Wang 2009, pp. 159, 213).

Wang is released from the re-education-through-labour facility after having served her full sentence and extension penalties. She initially lives with the now-released lesbian former inmate, who she had befriended in the facility, together with her girlfriend. Wang and the lesbian friend both get jobs in a real estate firm. Wang is successful in her new career. The lesbian friend and her partner, however, return to illicit drug use. Wang leaves the household, since she 'cannot be friends with a person who has no moral backbone!' [我不会和一个没有骨气的人交朋友!] (Chen & Wang 2009, p. 220). Wang resigns from the real estate firm to take up a sales job in a home decoration business, where she, once again, succeeds. In her new role, she motivates and encourages the young subordinates at the firm. Wang now feels 'reborn into a new life' [脱胎换骨生活] (Chen & Wang 2009, p. 223). She lives a celibate, 'independent life' [自力更生的生活], without a boyfriend and far away from her family (Chen & Wang 2009, p. 228). She, nevertheless, believes that 'a person who has used drugs and then broken away from drugs' [作为一个曾经吸毒现又断绝毒品的人] can never be a 'normal person' [正常人] (Chen & Wang 2009, pp. 232, 236).

In order to improve the situation for future generations of drug users, Wang resolves 'to set up a [drug] recovery school' [创办一所康复学校] that will teach an illicit drug user 'to be a genuinely respected, law-abiding citizen' [做一个真正受人尊敬的守法公民] (Chen & Wang 2009, p. 258). She also vows to try and change the existing social attitudes toward illicit drug users in mainland China, by convincing the general public that 'drug users are people with an illness' [吸毒者是病人], who 'require the understanding and support of all society' [需要全社会的理解、支持] (Chen & Wang 2009, p. 283). Wang, though, does not consider herself to be ill. China Central Television [中央电视台] provides her with

40 *Gendered exemplars*

the opportunity to improve the lot of illicit drug users in mainland China, when the broadcaster approaches her to tell her life story on the 'Xiao Cui Talk Show' [《小崔说事》], a popular national talk show in mainland China. *Struggle Spirit* concludes with Wang requesting help from Chen to make full use of this and other opportunities that had befallen her in her new life.

Analysis

In *Struggle Spirit*, Wang demonstrates her essential morality despite the chaos and tragedy of her drug addiction. Wang's claim to morality, however, is insufficient to afford her exemplar status in *Struggle Spirit*. This is because, in her account of her life from before, during and after drug addiction, she repeatedly contravenes normative womanhood in Chinese culture; assumes disparate, inconsistent and, at times, contradictory identities; and casts herself as an extraordinary, rather than every day, person. As a consequence, in contrast to *Heaven and Hell*, exemplarity is not afforded to the storyteller in *Struggle Spirit* but to her male mentor, Deputy Director Guo.

Wang's essential morality is demonstrated from childhood, when she is an obedient and scholarly daughter. She attributes these qualities to her parents, who she casts as upright and decent reform-period socialist citizens. Her parents love the Party and the Chinese state. Her mother is unjustly persecuted during the Cultural Revolution. The parents scrupulously acquire modest wealth during the open-door reform period. They also selflessly attribute their achievements to the support of the Party and the Chinese people. As an adult, Wang follows in her parents' moral footsteps in being conscientious and successful in all her career endeavours, and through her unswerving respect for the Party and the Chinese state. Even when drug-addicted, Wang does not resort to crime or sexual impropriety to fund her heroin habit. Similarly, Wang supports and leads her fellow inmates when she is incarcerated and she gives special attention to those who she believes are most in need, namely, the physically disabled, homosexuals and people with HIV-AIDS. As a leader of her fellow inmates, Wang behaves in an upright and principled manner in treating everyone equally and taking the blame for infractions that are committed by her fellow inmates. Moreover, Wang remains drug-free when discharged from the re-education-through-labour facility, unlike a former fellow inmate. She quickly finds employment, and is industrious and supportive of her subordinates in the workplace. She also is benevolent in planning to set up a drug rehabilitation school, where drug addicts can 'gain the most basic respect of moral human conduct' [得到做人最起码的那份尊严] (Chen & Wang 2009, p. 259).

The plausibility of Wang's claim to morality, however, is diminished by her transgressions against normative womanhood in Chinese culture. Before, during and after drug addiction, she is indulgent, assertive and belligerent and she abrogates her responsibilities as a Chinese wife and mother (Cai 2005; Croll

1995; Guo 2010; Roberts 2010). Wang disrespects her outwardly faithful and hardworking husband, when she suddenly grows tired of him after their daughter reaches school age. She then decides to divorce him. She tries heroin soon after, apparently, just for fun. She states that she never would have contemplated using illicit drugs when she was married to her husband. Wang abandons the care of her daughter to others, once she becomes addicted to heroin. In due course, she is arrested and incarcerated, first in a penal drug rehabilitation facility and then in a re-education-through-labour facility. This may blemish her daughter for life (see *Analysis* section for *Heaven and Hell*, earlier in the chapter). While incarcerated, Wang is uncooperative, rebellious and dismissive of prison officers [我对穿警服之人充满了仇视] (Chen & Wang 2009, p. 107). She retains her dislike for prison officers and the police after her release from prison [我恨所有穿警服的人] (Chen & Wang 2009, p. 243). Upon her release, she chooses to live an independent life, away from her natal family and her daughter. She shares a dwelling with lesbians and purposely eschews the company of men.[5]

The plausibility of Wang's claim to morality also is diminished by the disparate, inconsistent and, at times, contradictory identities that she assumes in *Struggle Spirit*. Wang initially is cast as a dutiful daughter and a devoted wife until, suddenly, she divorces her husband and assumes the identity of an independent woman. Once she starts using heroin, she successively takes on the identity of 'a drug-using woman' [自己是个吸毒女] and a 'heroin sister' [白粉妹] (Chen & Wang 2009, pp. 111–229). These addict identities connect her to a wider 'drug community' [吸毒群体; 吸毒人群] (Chen & Wang 2009, pp. 5, 30, 82). Wang, however, repeatedly distances herself from this community. She asserts that she is 'more cultured than the others' [我比别人多了一种文化] and does not engage in the criminal and salacious behaviours that they often do (Chen & Wang 2009, p. 124). She also labels them as 'ill people' [吸毒者是一个病人] or 'victims' [吸毒者本人也是一个受害者] whose 'minds are distorted' [心里扭曲的病人] (Chen & Wang 2009, pp. 16, 17, 44). She believes that they are 'very much in need of a skilled doctor' [最需要有一个良医] to help them during their 'long-term recuperation' [长期的疗养] from drug addiction (Chen & Wang 2009, pp. 23, 258). Wang, however, is not ill. She eschews the illness identity that she unhesitatingly assigns to other members of the drug community. In so doing, she evades the enduring and heritable stain that can attend the embracing of an illness identity in Chinese culture, in particular one that connotes mental illness (Ramsay 2008, 2013). The 'branded stain' that she acquires by assuming an addict identity [烙上污点的吸毒者], by contrast, is more readily contained and not passed on to her family members (Chen & Wang 2009, p. 271). The stain, nevertheless, continues to haunt her during her recovery from drug addiction. She claims that she fashions 'a completely new self' [一个全新的我] in recovery, yet her new self remains inexorably tied to her drug-using self from before [曾经有过吸毒经历的我; 曾经吸毒的我; 曾经吸毒现正处于康复期间的我; 曾经受毒品侵害

42 *Gendered exemplars*

的我] (Chen & Wang 2009, pp. 211, 213, 219, 236, 261). This undermines Wang's avowal of complete newness in recovery. This also means that, in contrast to Wen in *Heaven and Hell*, Wang 'can never again be a normal person' [我再也无法成为一个正常人了] (Chen & Wang 2009, p. 26).

Although Wang longs to be accepted as a 'normal person' [正常人] (Gao 2011), the language that she uses to describe herself in *Struggle Spirit* connotes exceptionality and extraordinariness. This stands in contrast to the everydayness that characterises Wen in *Heaven and Hell*. Wang variably presents herself as 'cultured' [多了一种文化], 'offbeat' [另类], 'alien' [外星人], a 'freak' [怪物], and a 'stand out' [我这个与众不同的人; 出头鸟] (Chen & Wang 2009, pp. 156, 170, 190). She also brands other drug addicts as victims of illness, but not herself (see immediately above). Nevertheless, like Wen, she casts her life as a drug addict as a battle. Her use of such language evokes the mainland Chinese government's 'people's war against drugs' (人民禁毒战争) (Liang & Lu 2013, p. 315), as well as the high regard that is placed on long-term struggle and battle in contemporary mainland Chinese political discourse. Because of heroin, she 'falls' [掉入; 陷到; 跌入; 坠落] into a 'quagmire' [泥潭], 'swamp' [泥沼] and 'deep abyss' [深渊] (Chen & Wang 2009, pp. 23, 43, 58, 149, 262). In order to escape from this predicament, she 'must declare war on drugs' [要向毒品宣战] and 'fight a protracted battle' [打上持久战] against an 'enemy' [敌人] who captures [成了毒品的'俘虏'], enslaves [做毒品的奴隶], 'controls' [控制], and 'violates' [侵害] (Chen & Wang 2009, pp. 6–261). Ultimately, she 'conquers' [战胜; 征服] heroin and is 'victorious' [得赢] in her recovery from drug addiction (Chen & Wang 2009, pp. 11, 38, 102, 107, 262).

Being an extraordinary, rather than every day, person – in addition to contravening normative womanhood in Chinese culture, and assuming disparate, inconsistent and, at times, contradictory identities – seemingly, preclude Wang from exemplarity in *Struggle Spirit*. Instead, exemplarity is afforded to her male mentor, Deputy Director Guo. Wang attributes all of her success in recovery from drug addiction to him [我的戒断毒瘾不是自己的功劳而是郭副的功德] (Chen & Wang 2009, p. 269). She casts him as wise, honest, kind and deserving of respect. Throughout her account, she points out his *wen* [文] ('literary') traits in accordance with the ideal Chinese man: he is educated and willing to share his knowledge with her (Cai 2005; Louie 2002). She also points out his *wu* [武] ('martial') traits in accordance with the ideal Chinese man: he is powerful yet even-handed when exercising his authority over her (Cai 2005; Louie 2002). Moreover, his masculinity is matched by his political merit. He is a high-level leader who, according to Wang, rationally and justly executes his role as governor of the re-education-through-labour facility, while upholding the will of the Party and the state. This positions him as a model socialist cadre (Bakken 2000). Tellingly, model socialist cadres in mainland Chinese political discourse tend to be middle-aged, father-like figures like Deputy Director Guo.

In sum, cultural, political and institutional discourses shape temporality, subjectivity and language use in *Struggle Spirit* in ways that maintain a semblance of moral face for Wang, but deny her the exemplar status afforded to Wen in *Heaven and Hell*. Wang stakes claims to morality throughout her life story, but, in the end, the plausibility of her claims are diminished because she regularly contravenes gender norms in Chinese culture; assumes disparate, inconsistent and, at times, contradictory identities; and casts herself as an extraordinary, rather than every day, person. By contrast, the exemplar in *Struggle Spirit*, Deputy Director Guo, is an upright and righteous man who consistently conforms to gender norms in Chinese culture. A discursive implication may be that only people who unfailingly observe cultural norms, values and scripts can be held up as an exemplar in stories of this type.

Wang displays political merit through her unswerving respect for the Party, the Chinese state and high-ranking cadres like Deputy Director Guo. She biomedicalises drug addiction, at least in reference to other people, in line with the language used in the 2008 *Anti-Drug Law of the People's Republic of China*[6] (Biddulph & Xie 2011). Chinese cultural stigma normally would countermand such biomedicalisation (Ramsay 2008, 2013). The 2008 law had come into effect in the same year that Wang had begun email communication with her co-author, Chen Beidi. Wang also displays political merit by discursively validating contemporary political rhetoric and values, in figuratively portraying drug addiction and recovery as a long-term struggle and battle, as Wen does in *Heaven and Hell*. Unlike Wen, however, she is disrespectful to prison officers and the police. Deputy Director Guo, by contrast, embodies the model socialist cadre in mainland China.

Wang's life story meets the institutional agenda by warning the general public of the dangers of illicit drug use, while delivering didactic advice to those who happen to succumb to drug addiction. Positive, didactic content would be a necessary feature of a book that is published by an official state publishing house, such as Xinhua Press (Bakken 2000; Brady 2008, 2009). As already noted, the exemplar in the story is not the storyteller, Wang, but her male mentor, Deputy Director Guo. Nevertheless, a didactic implication of Wang's life story is that, even if one is *not* exemplary, one can still succeed in recovery from drug addiction, provided that one finds an appropriate moral authority to serve as a mentor. That is to say, Wang's great achievement, as presented in *Struggle Spirit*, stems from her ability to successfully identify and build a relationship with a man who is exemplary and capable of guiding her into a drug-free life in recovery, which she maintains several years on.

Wang's life story of a mainland Chinese woman in drug addiction and recovery has similarities with Western counterparts (see Chapter 1), but with some notable qualifications. First, Wang casts drug addicts as victims (Hersey 2005) and suffering from illness (Aston 2009; Franzwa 1999; Muzak 2008). Such a characterisation is not widely held in mainland Chinese society (Luo *et al.* 2014), but

44 *Gendered exemplars*

is in line with existing state legislation (Biddulph 2013; Biddulph & Xie 2011). Wang's characterisation does not extend to herself, possibly due to an awareness of the stigma that can attend mental illness and related disorders in Chinese culture (Ramsay 2008, 2013). Second, Wang creates addict and non-addict identities in her life story, in line with many Western counterparts (Aston, 2009; Hirschman 1995; Hughes 2007; McIntosh & McKeganey 2000; Shapiro 2003). Wen did not do so in *Heaven and Hell*. This ultimately becomes problematic for Wang in her recovery from drug addiction, because her addict identity continues to haunt her emergent non-addict identity. Finally, Wang's life story, like many Western counterparts, affirms 'the double alterity' of being a drug addict and a woman (Infantino 1999, p. 93). Wang signifies this, in a disempowering way, by labelling herself as a 'drug-using woman' [自己是个吸毒女] and a 'heroin sister' [白粉妹].

Nevertheless, two features of Wang's life story, which run counter to many Western counterparts, may be construed as gender empowering. First, she experiences no 'mother-child reunion' on her recovery from drug addiction (Friedling 1996, p. 115). Second, she does not recapture a femininity that has been destroyed by drug addiction on her recovery from addiction (Addenbrooke 2011; Friedling 1996). However, these features of Wang's life story, in all likelihood, act to accentuate her flouting of normative gender in Chinese culture. Moreover, any sense of gender empowerment that Wang may gain by living an independent and drug-free life in recovery – as identified by Aston (2009) in Western counterpart stories – is extinguished by wholly attributing her achievement to her male mentor, Deputy Director Guo.

Conclusion

The chapter has identified how cultural, political and institutional discourses shape temporality, subjectivity and language use in two mainland Chinese life stories of drug addiction and recovery, one told by a man and the other told by a woman. Political and institutional imperatives likely drive the need for exemplarity in these accounts. This would meet the didactic purpose of publishing the life stories (Bakken 2000; Brady 2008, 2009). Gender norms in Chinese culture, however, appear to restrict exemplarity to men in both life stories. Both Wen in *Heaven and Hell* and Wang in *Struggle Spirit* assert a semblance of moral face throughout their accounts of drug addiction and recovery. This may be a minimal requirement, in their minds, that justifies their right to tell their story to others. Equally, this may reflect the importance of the maintenance of face in Chinese culture (Hinze 2002; Wong 2000; Yang & Kleinman 2008), even when one is recounting an experience that is considered to be extremely morally transgressive in Chinese culture (Kleinman *et al.* 2011; Lu & Wang 2008; Lu, Fang & Wang 2008). Nevertheless, despite the maintenance of a semblance of moral face in

Gendered exemplars   45

both accounts, only Wen meets the criteria for exemplarity, both in cultural terms (the moral man) and political terms (the model socialist citizen). He achieves this through his everydayness, his unswerving family-centeredness, his manliness and his unfailing respect for the law, public authorities and the Chinese national leadership. Wang, on the other hand, fails to meet these criteria. She is extraordinary; lives apart from her daughter and her natal family; is unfeminine; and is highly critical of the police and the prison officers of the re-education-through-labour facility where she is incarcerated.

Instead, exemplarity is afforded to a model high-ranking male cadre in Wang's life story. Wang attributes all her success in her recovery from drug addiction to his wisdom and guidance. Although Wen is facilitated in his recovery by the Xinjiang Aunty, he makes the critical decision to quit drugs of his own accord and, on his return home to Xian, singlehandedly remains drug-free, despite being abandoned by his wife. He does this by wholly and steadfastly reengaging his meritorious and masculine self from before drug addiction. As a result, he is able to return to society as a 'normal person' [正常人] (Gao 2011). This is something that Wang can never do: she is not an everyday woman; she is gender transgressive; she distrusts lower-ranking authorities; and she is unable to break free from her addict identity during her recovery from drug addiction. Instead, she relies on the enduring wisdom and guidance of her male mentor, Deputy Director Guo, in order to remain drug-free. An implication of this apparent gendering of exemplarity in these mainland Chinese life stories of drug addiction and recovery is that only men can be exemplary in stories of this type. Zhou (1999, p. 119) states that the mainland Chinese mass media typically depicts women drug addicts 'as the most shameless human beings on the earth'. Accordingly, it may be quite problematic to portray any woman drug user as exemplary in a mainland Chinese story of drug addiction and recovery. The stories of drug-addicted Chinese women that are analysed in the following chapters of this book should give credence to or place doubt on such a proposition. The next chapter examines Chinese life stories of drug addiction and rehabilitation.

Notes

1 Brady (2008, p. 29) notes that the Central Propaganda Department in mainland China plays 'a leadership role' in 'propaganda and thought work matters within the health sector', for example by 'manag[ing] public debate on politically sensitive health-related issues which have erupted in recent years, such as . . . drug addiction' (see also Brady 2012).

2 As stated in Chapter 1, throughout the analytic chapters of the book there are bilingual (original Chinese + English translation or gloss) illustrative examples that are taken from the life stories and filmic stories. The original Chinese extracts that are taken from the stories are enclosed in square brackets []. The English translations or glosses, which are the work of the author unless otherwise indicated, precede the square brackets. Direct translations from the Chinese text are enclosed by single quotation marks ('').

46 *Gendered exemplars*

3 Brady (2012, p. 66) states that the expression '小康' originates 'from the Liji or Book of Rites, one of the five classics of Confucianism. It is a metaphor for an idealized society where all have enough for their needs.' The expression is 'widely used . . . in contemporary political discourse in China' (Brady 2012, p. 66).
4 The published English-language title of the book.
5 Wang stresses in *Struggle Spirit* that she is not in any way sexually attracted to women.
6 Biddulph and Xie (2011, p. 980) claim that the use of such language in the 2008 law merely constitutes a 'gesture towards [the] health-oriented treatment approach' embraced by global agencies such as the United Nations. They argue that the law remains punitive and authoritative in practice (Biddulph & Xie 2011).

References

Addenbrooke, M. 2011. *Survivors of addiction: narratives of recovery*. New York, NY: Routledge.

Aston, S. 2009. Identities under construction: women hailed as addicts. *Health: An Interdisciplinary Journal for the Social Study of Health, Illness and Medicine*, 13 (6), 611–628.

Bakken, B. 2000. *The exemplary society: human improvement, social control, and the dangers of modernity in China*. Oxford: Oxford University Press.

Baumler, A. 2007. *The Chinese and opium under the Republic: worse than floods and wild beasts*. New York, NY: SUNY Press.

Biddulph, S. 2013. Compulsory drug rehabilitation in China. In F. Rahman and N. Crofts (eds) *Drug law reform in East and Southeast Asia* (pp. 233–244). Lanham, MD: Lexington.

Biddulph, S. and Xie, C. 2011. Regulating drug dependency in China: the 2008 PRC Drug Prohibition Law. *British Journal of Criminology*, 51, 978–996.

Brady, A. 2002. Regimenting the public mind: the modernization of propaganda in the PRC. *International Journal*, 57 (4), 563–578.

Brady, A. 2008. *Marketing dictatorship: propaganda and thought work in contemporary China*. Lanham, MD: Rowman & Littlefield.

Brady, A. 2009. Mass persuasion as a means of legitimation and China's popular authoritarianism. *American Behavioral Scientist*, 53 (3), 434–457.

Brady, A. 2012. State Confucianism, Chineseness, and tradition in CCP propaganda. In A. Brady (ed.) *China's thought management* (pp. 57–75). London: Routledge.

Brook, T. and Wakabayashi, B. T. 2000. Introduction: opium's history in China. In T. Brook and B. T. Wakabayashi (eds) *Opium regimes: China, Britain, and Japan, 1839–1952* (pp. 1–27). Berkeley: University of California Press.

Cai, R. 2005. Gender imaginations in *Crouching Tiger, Hidden Dragon* and the *Wuxia* world. *Positions: East Asia Cultures Critique*, 13 (2), 441–471.

Chen, B. and Wang, T. [陈贝帝, 王彤彤]. 2009. *Struggle spirit* [灵魂交锋: 作家与吸毒女 300 天心灵对话实录]. Beijing: Xinhua Press [新华出版社].

Croll, E. 1995. *Changing identities of Chinese women: rhetoric, experience and self perception in twentieth century China*. Hong Kong: Hong Kong University Press.

Franzwa, G. 1999. Aristotle and the language of addiction. In J. Lilienfeld and J. Oxford (eds) *The languages of addiction* (pp. 15–28). New York, NY: St. Martin's Press.

Friedling, M. 1996. Feminisms and the Jewish mother syndrome: identity, autobiography, and the rhetoric of addiction. *Discourse*, 19 (1), 105–130.

Gao, H. 2011. *Women and heroin addiction in China's changing society*. New York, NY: Routledge.

Gibson, B., Acquah, S. and Robinson, P.G. 2004. Entangled identities and psychotropic substance use. *Sociology of Health and Illness*, 26 (5), 597–616.

Guo, Y. 2010. China's celebrity mothers: female virtues, patriotism and social harmony. In L. Edwards and E. Jeffreys (eds) *Celebrity in China* (pp. 45–66). Hong Kong: Hong Kong University Press.

Hersey, C. 2005. Script(ing) treatment: representations of recovery from addiction in Hollywood film. *Contemporary Drug Problems*, 32, 467–493.

Hinze, C. 2002. *Re-thinking 'face': pursuing an emic-etic understanding of Chinese mian and lian and English face*. Unpublished doctoral dissertation. St Lucia, QLD: The University of Queensland.

Hirschman, E.C. 1995. The cinematic depiction of drug addiction: a semiotic account. *Semiotica*, 104 (1/2), 119–164.

Huang, M.W. 2007. Male friendship and *Jiangxue* (philosophical debates) in sixteenth-century China. *Nan Nü: Men, Women, and Gender in China*, 9 (1), 146–178.

Hughes, K. 2007. Migrating identities: the relational constitution of drug use and addiction. *Sociology of Heath and Illness*, 29 (5), 673–691.

Infantino, S.C. 1999. Female addiction and sacrifice: literary tradition or user's manual? In J. Lilienfeld and J. Oxford (eds) *The languages of addiction* (pp. 91–102). New York, NY: St. Martin's Press.

Kleinman, A., Yan, Y., Jun, J., Lee, S., Zhang, E., Pan, T., Wu, F. and Guo, J. 2011. *Deep China: the moral life of the person: what anthropology and psychiatry tell us about China today*. Berkeley: University of California Press.

Levin, D. 2015, January 24. Despite a crackdown, use of illegal drugs in China continues unabated. *The New York Times*. Retrieved from www.nytimes.com/2015/01/25/world/despite-a-crackdown-use-of-illegal-drugs-in-china-continues-unabated.html 24 February 2015.

Liang, B. and Lu, H. 2013. Discourses of drug problems and drug control in China: reports in the *People's Daily*, 1946–2009. *China Information*, 27 (3), 301–326.

Louie, K. 2002. *Theorising Chinese masculinity: society and gender in China*. Cambridge, UK: Cambridge University Press.

Louie, K. 2015. *Chinese masculinities in a globalizing world*. New York, NY: Routledge.

Lu, L., Fang, Y. and Wang, X. 2008. Drug abuse in China: past, present and future. *Cellular and Molecular Neurobiology*, 28, 479–490.

Lu, L. and Wang, X. 2008. Drug addiction in China. *Annals of the New York Academy of Sciences*, 1141, 304–317.

Lu, Y. 2012. *Heroic masculinity and male homosociality in Three Kingdoms and Le Morte Darthur*. Unpublished doctoral dissertation. St Lucia, QLD: The University of Queensland.

Luo, T., Wang, J., Li, Y., Wang, X., Tan, L., Deng, Q., Thakoor, J.P.D. and Hao, W. 2014. Stigmatization of people with drug dependence in China: a community-based study in Hunan province. *Drug and Alcohol Dependence*, 134, 285–289.

Mass Press [群众出版社]. 2008. *Agency overview* [本社概况]. Retrieved from www.qzcbs.com/intro.asp 5 August 2013.

McIntosh, J. and McKeganey, N. 2000. Addicts' narratives of recovery from drug use: constructing a non-addict identity. *Social Science and Medicine*, 50, 1501–1510.

Muzak, J. 2008. "Addiction got me what I needed": depression and drug addiction in Elizabeth Wurtzel's memoirs. In H. Clark (ed.) *Depression and narrative: telling the dark* (pp. 97–109). Albany, NY: SUNY Press.

Niquet, V. 2012. "Confu-talk": the use of Confucian concepts in contemporary Chinese foreign policy. In A. Brady (ed.) *China's thought management* (pp. 76–89). London: Routledge.

48   *Gendered exemplars*

Ramsay, G. 2008. *Shaping minds: a discourse analysis of Chinese-language community mental health literature.* Amsterdam: John Benjamins.

Ramsay, G. 2013. *Mental illness, dementia and family in China.* London: Routledge.

Roberts, R.A. 2010. *Maoist model theatre: the semiotics of gender and sexuality in the Chinese Cultural Revolution (1966–1976).* Leiden: Brill.

Roberts, R.A. 2014. The Confucian moral foundations of socialist model man: Lei Feng and the twenty four exemplars of filial behaviour. *New Zealand Journal of Asian Studies,* 16 (1), 23–38.

Shapiro, H. 2003. *Shooting stars: drugs, Hollywood and the movies.* London: Serpent's Tail.

Song, G. 2003. *The fragile scholar: power and masculinity in Chinese culture.* Hong Kong: Hong Kong University Press.

Taïeb, O., Révah-Lévy, A., Moro, M.R. and Baubet, T. 2008. Is Ricoeur's notion of narrative identity useful in understanding recovery in drug addicts? *Qualitative Health Research,* 18 (7), 990–1000.

Tang, Y.L., Zhao, D., Zhao, C. and Cubells, J.F. 2006. Opiate addiction in China: current situation and treatments. *Addiction,* 101, 657–665.

Trevaskes, S. 2013. Drug policy in China. In F. Rahman and N. Crofts (eds) *Drug law reform in East and Southeast Asia* (pp. 221–232). Lanham, MD: Lexington.

Viano, M. 2002. An intoxicated screen: reflections on film and drugs. In J.F. Brodie and M. Redfield (eds) *High anxieties: cultural studies in addiction* (pp. 134–158). Berkeley: University of California Press.

Wang, Y. [王云香]. 2004. *Heaven and hell: a drug user's tragic tale* [地狱天堂: 一个吸毒者的血泪诉说]. Beijing: Mass Press [群众出版社].

Wong, D. 2000. Stress factors and mental health of carers with relatives suffering from schizophrenia in Hong Kong: implications for culturally sensitive practices. *British Journal of Social Work,* 30, 365–382.

Xinhua Press [新华出版社]. 2013. *A brief introduction to Xinhua Press* [新华出版社简介]. Retrieved from http://press.xinhuanet.com/gywm/2006–12/08/content_24546.htm 18 November 2013.

Yang, L.H. and Kleinman, A. 2008. 'Face' and the embodiment of stigma in China: the cases of schizophrenia and AIDS. *Social Science and Medicine,* 67, 398–408.

Yang, M., Zhou, L., Hao, W. and Xiao, S.Y. 2014. Drug policy in China: progress and challenges. *The Lancet,* 383 (9916), 509.

Zhou, Y. 1999. *Anti-drug crusades in twentieth-century China: nationalism, history, and state building.* Lanham, MD: Rowman and Littlefield.

Zhou, Y. 2000a. *China's anti-drug campaign in the reform era.* Singapore: World Scientific and Singapore University Press.

Zhou, Y. 2000b. Nationalism, identity, and state-building: the antidrug crusade in the People's Republic, 1949–1952. In T. Brook and B.T. Wakabayashi (eds) *Opium regimes: China, Britain, and Japan, 1839–1952* (pp. 380–404). Berkeley: University of California Press.

3 Institutional schema

Life stories of drug addiction and rehabilitation

This chapter analyses life stories of drug addiction and rehabilitation from mainland China, Taiwan and Hong Kong. The stories analysed in this chapter differ from those analysed in Chapter 2 in that the storyteller[1] is residing in, or still actively engaged with, a specialist drug rehabilitation institution whose singular mission is drug rehabilitation. Moreover, the stories are short, rather than book-length accounts, and are drawn from Chinese communities with differing political systems and histories. One corpus of life stories is from mainland China, which has been under Communist rule since 1949. Another narrative corpus is from Taiwan, which has been self-governed, mostly by the Nationalist Party [國民黨], since the Communists took over on the mainland. The third narrative corpus is from Hong Kong, which was under British colonial rule for around 150 years until 1997, when it was returned to the People's Republic of China under the status of Special Administrative Region [特別行政區]. Although the three narrative corpora are from communities with distinct political systems and histories, the storytellers in each corpus are culturally Chinese (Ramsay 2013).

Some of the life stories are first-person written accounts, while others are first-person oral accounts [口述] that have been transcribed by second parties. They most likely are authentic accounts, given the nature of the host publications (see below) and the storyteller photographs and personal creations that often accompany the stories. The phenomena of ' "ghost-writing" or co-authorship', nevertheless, cannot be ruled out (Ramsay 2013, p. 13). Ghost-written or co-authored life stories, however, also would be shaped by the contexts within which the story is being told and, as a result, would remain useful objects of narrative and discourse analytic study (Ramsay 2013). The sheer number of life stories in each narrative corpus requires an adjustment to the analytic process followed in Chapter 2. Summarising each life story is not feasible. Instead, the chapter provides a synopsis of the 'common, shared experience' of drug addiction and rehabilitation that characterises each narrative corpus (Ramsay 2013, p. 14). This takes into account how 'each new life story' in a narrative corpus 'appears to confirm the main elements of the previous stories' (Elliott 2005, p. 40). The synopses are followed by

50 *Institutional schema*

analyses of how cultural, political and institutional discourses shape temporality, subjectivity and language use in the life stories.

'Preferred' stories of the institutions

The life stories that are analysed in Chapter 2 were published by state-sanctioned presses in mainland China. As a result, they assign and deny moral exemplarity, based on the gendered expression of 'spiritual' values that currently are espoused by the mainland Chinese authorities. The life stories that are analysed in this chapter, on the other hand, are written in, and often published by, the drug rehabilitation facilities where the Chinese drug addicts have undertaken programs to overcome their addiction. As a result, these stories likely present accounts of drug addiction and rehabilitation that accord with the 'preferred' stories of the institutions within which they are told (Ramsay 2013, p. 13). As noted in Chapter 1, by telling the stories in this way, storytellers can discursively legitimise their choice of intervention program, reinforce their connection with fellow members of the institutional community, and avail themselves of a repertoire of formulaic language in order to make sense of their drug addiction and a recovery that they now so desire.

The ensuing analysis, accordingly, will explore how the mainland Chinese, Taiwanese and Hong Kong storytellers utilise temporality, subjectivity and language use in their life stories of drug addiction and rehabilitation in ways that align with, or, possibly, depart from, the preferred story of the institution. The analysis also will consider how these stories of institutional origins negotiate the broader cultural and political forces in play in the local geographical setting, namely, mainland China, Taiwan and Hong Kong. The chapter will identify and discuss the commonalities and differences in analytic findings across the three narrative corpora, and compare these with the findings from analogous Western research.

Mainland Chinese life stories of drug addiction and rehabilitation

Out From the Margins [走出边缘] compiles the life stories of ten mainland Chinese people who reside in, or are still actively engaged with, the Daytop Drug Rehabilitation Village [戴托普戒毒康复村] in Kunming, Yunnan [昆明, 云南]. The Daytop organisation originated in the United States in the 1960s and maintains its home base there (Daytop 2012b). It adopts a 'therapeutic community' [治疗社区] model of drug rehabilitation, which is a personalized, holistic approach that involves all members of the rehabilitation facility in a range of activities (Daytop 2012a). These activities 'lead members to learn about themselves . . . through challenge and action, understanding and sharing common human experiences' (Daytop 2012a). Yunnan, where the sole mainland Chinese Daytop facility is located, is a border province in southwest China that is renowned for opiate and opioid use and trafficking (see Chapter 1). Daytop set up there in 1998 and is one of several government and privately run drug rehabilitation facilities that continue to operate in the area (Liang 2002; Tong 2013).

Out from the Margins was published in 2002 by the Yunnan People's Publishing House [云南人民出版社]. The press publishes a wide variety of books dealing with the humanities and sciences for a general readership, in particular books dealing with topics related to Yunnan (*Yunnan People's Publishing House* 2010). As noted earlier, opiate and opioid addiction is a prominent concern in Yunnan, at least historically. The ten first-person accounts of drug addiction and rehabilitation in *Out from the Margins* are transcribed by the accredited author of the volume, Liang Ping [梁苹]. Seven are life stories of Chinese men and three are life stories of Chinese women. Their ages range from twenty-four to forty-one years old, with most storytellers around thirty. Each story is about twenty pages in length, bar two that are thirty-odd pages.

All the life stories in *Out from the Margins* follow a similar narrative format. They begin with reflections on life as a child or teenager before illicit drug use. They move on to describe initiation into illicit drug use (opium or heroin), and life as a 'drug addict' [瘾君子; 隐君子] (Liang 2002, pp. 141, 151, 262, 264). The stories conclude with life after a lengthy and successful period in drug rehabilitation. Storytellers still may be residing in Daytop or may have left but retain a continuing association with the facility, for example by working there or periodically returning to be involved with community activities. All stories recount troubled childhood or teenage years, or life as a young adult. Some storytellers are not scholarly [我对读书不感兴趣], suffer 'bullying' at school [在学校常有人欺负我] or frequently 'truant from school' [成天逃学] (Liang 2002, pp. 41, 97, 173). Some engage in street hooliganism and violence [打群架], smuggling and other petty crime, or serious crime such as fraud or 'manslaughter' [过失杀人] (Liang 2002, p. 97). Others claim to have innate character flaws, because they are 'rebellious' [我的逆反心里], 'vain' [爱慕虚荣], profligate or 'felt a strong sense of inferiority' [我感到了一种强烈的自卑感] (Liang 2002, pp. 117, 123, 200–201). A smaller number tell of very poor relationships with parents [母亲基本没有文化, 她对我的管束是粗暴的; 父亲对我 . . . 是恨之入骨], suffering physical abuse in the home [挨打成了家常便饭], or having siblings or close friends who already were illicit drug users [我的一个弟弟和一个妹妹吸上了毒] (Liang 2002, pp. 125, 149, 214–217). The oldest storyteller describes the stress that he still suffers from, after having been sent down to the countryside as an 'educated youth' [知青] during the Cultural Revolution (Liang 2002, p. 118).[2] Thus, unlike the counterparts in Chapter 2, storytellers in *Out from the Margins* are cast as sullied or having a 'distorted value system' [价值观的扭曲] from the outset of their life stories (Liang 2002, p. 122). This leads them to 'deviate from the normal track' [偏离了正常的轨道] and into illicit drug use and addiction (Liang 2002, p. 117).

52 *Institutional schema*

The stories in *Out from the Margins* describe daily life as a drug addict as consumed by sourcing and using illicit drugs, and finding money to purchase the drugs, usually through nefarious or unlawful means. Since all the storytellers use opiates or opioids, they spend a great deal of time in slumber after drug use. They are unproductive and quickly lose their life savings, businesses or jobs. Their partners (except where they also are illicit drug users) and children are neglected and even physically abused. Some storytellers divorce and many end up being arrested and jailed for drug possession or drug-related crime. They bemoan the 'loss of face' that this brings [太没面子了] (Liang 2002, p. 240). The loss of face extends to their families and 'three generations of ancestors' [我丢了祖宗三代的脸] (Liang 2002, p. 217). They sum up their lives in drug addiction as 'unrestrained' [肆无忌惮 . . . 想做什么就做什么; 我就是控制不了自己] and degraded, like living in a 'quagmire' [泥潭] (Liang 2002, pp. 153, 155, 178–179, 244). They feel as if they are 'living at the lowest rung of society' [生活在社会的底层] (Liang 2002, p. 269).

After a long period of using illicit drugs or being in and out of government-run drug rehabilitation or re-education-through-labour facilities (see Chapter 2), storytellers are admitted to Daytop. In many stories, this occurs as a result of the dutiful efforts of the storyteller's mother, even where the relationship with the mother always had been very poor. Thereafter, one motivation in drug rehabilitation is repaying the mother's care and effort in organising treatment at Daytop. While life as a drug addict is unrestrained and degraded, Daytop brings control and 'personal integrity' [操守] (Liang 2002, p. 70). Personal 'errors' and rule 'violations' [犯错, 犯忌, 犯事] that are committed in Daytop are 'punished' [处罚] by means of group 'criticism' [批评, 评判], known as 'having one's head shaved' [被'剃头']; or an extended period of time-out in self-reflection, known as 'sitting out in the cold' ['坐冷板凳'] (Liang 2002, pp. 81–87, 99, 101, 155, 157).[3] Control is effected by the 'community' [社区] of which they are now a 'member' [成员] and which is led by the 'mighty' [伟大] leader, Director Yang [杨主任] (Liang 2002, pp. 101, 207). A person can 'walk away from the community' [走出社区] and can 'return to the community' [重返社区] (Liang 2002, pp. 82, 140, 246). Moreover, the community provides 'marginal people' [边缘人] with a 'cultural atmosphere' [文化气氛], 'a sense of belonging' [一种归属感], 'opportunities' [机会], and 'great strength, just like the Red Army on the Long March' [很大的力量, 就像红军长征] (Liang 2002, pp. 48–273).

The life stories in *Out from the Margins* conclude by affirming that 'persevering' [坚持] at Daytop has led to the formation of 'a completely new self' [人整个的焕然一新] (Liang 2002, pp. 100, 139, 224). Storytellers are 'reborn' [脱胎换骨] as 'moral human beings' [做人] (Liang 2002, pp. 111–241). They now can aspire to 'become a normal person' [我想变成一个正常人], in contrast to the 'abnormal person' [非正常人] who they had been, in most cases, since childhood (Liang 2002, pp. 76–260). Moreover, they can work to regain the 'social acknowledgement' [社会的认同] and 'respect' [被人尊敬; 人们的尊敬] that had been relinquished in drug addiction (Liang 2002, pp. 126, 140), when society 'spurned' [唾弃] them as 'trash' [垃圾], 'non-human' [非人] and 'heretics' [旁门左道] (Liang 2002, pp. 49, 54, 103, 223). On their 'return to society' [回到社会; 重返社会] (Liang 2002, pp. 186, 222, 245), they can 'live a normal life' [过正常的生活] and 'assimilate into the mainstream' [融入主流; 融进主流] with 'a regular job, a home of their own, and a wife and child' [有一份固定的工作, 有一个自己的家, 有妻子、孩子] (Liang 2002, pp. 223–224, 255, 273).

Analysis

The life stories in *Out from the Margins* recount Chinese people's experiences of opiate or opioid addiction and drug rehabilitation in the Daytop Drug Rehabilitation Village in mainland China. Most of the storytellers have been addicted to heroin, in keeping with illicit drug use patterns in mainland China, in particular, in Yunnan in the southwest border region (Biddulph 2013. See Chapter 1). Their life stories clearly bear out the institutional schema of the secular Daytop facility. However, they do so in a way that maintains cultural and political affinity with the mainland Chinese setting in which the life stories are told. This may stem from Daytop's foreign, albeit secular, origins, and its professional activity in a politically sensitive domain in mainland China (see Chapter 1). As a consequence, Daytop may purposely fashion an institutional narrative of drug addiction and rehabilitation that is culturally and politically palatable to the mainland Chinese authorities.

Storytellers compartmentalise their lives into two distinct and conflicting temporal periods, namely, the life from before and the life after joining the Daytop therapeutic community. The life from before is bad and the life of now is good. The badness of the life from before extends to before illicit drug use, with most storytellers' lives sullied from childhood. As a result, storytellers cannot point to a moral self from before drug addiction in order to counterbalance the immoral self during drug addiction, as observed in the mainland Chinese counterparts in Chapter 2. Likewise, a moral self from before drug addiction is not reengaged during drug rehabilitation. Instead, a completely new self is constructed, under the stewardship of the Daytop therapeutic community. Consequently, 'two distinct selves' [两个完全不同的我], inhabit the life stories in *Out from the Margins*: one 'moral' [做人的道德], namely, the new self; and the other 'despicable and shameless' [卑鄙无耻], namely, the self from before (Liang 2002, pp. 186, 205, 265).

The new self is not built upon an individual's life goals, needs or expectations. Rather, the new self is prescribed by the Daytop therapeutic community, where the storyteller lives during drug rehabilitation. This self is patterned on the 'normal person' [正常人] (Gao 2011) from 'mainstream society' [主流社会] (Liang 2002, pp. 168, 273) and, accordingly, conforms to gender norms in Chinese culture. The

54 *Institutional schema*

new man is 'manly' [有男子气] (Liang 2002, p. 103). He is righteous and readily employable and will marry and have a child. The new woman, on the other hand, abandons her successful former business pursuits; seeks to reconcile with her mother; is frugal in her day-to-day life; and resolves to be a responsible and caring mother and wife. Doing so cultivates the moral face [脸] that the storyteller has forsaken during drug addiction. This cultivation of face is a social phenomenon, which requires the storyteller to return to society (Hinze 2002; Wong 2000; Yang & Kleinman 2008).

The drug-addicted self from before, on the other hand, is embodied in the self-ascribed – or, more likely, institutionally assigned – identity, 'drug addict' [瘾君子; 隐君子]. This addict identity connotes 'ill repute' [劣迹斑斑] (Liang 2002, p. 267). It marks the bearer as 'truly offbeat and on the margins of society' [真正的'另类'、社会的边缘人] (Liang 2002, p. 260). It stands, therefore, in complete contradistinction to the new self, who is modelled on the 'normal person' [正常人] from 'mainstream society' [主流社会]. Drug addicts, by corollary, must be 'abnormal' [非正常人]. They are stigmatised in society by a process that marks them as 'discredit[ed]' and 'tainted' (Goffman, quoted in Link *et al.* 2004, p. 512. See also Kleinman *et al.* 2011; Lu, Fang & Wang 2008; Lu & Wang 2008). Link and Phelan (2001, p. 367) believe that this process of stigmatisation operates in the following way:

> In the first component, people distinguish and label human differences. In the second, dominant cultural beliefs link labeled persons to undesirable characteristics- to negative stereotypes. In the third, labeled persons are placed in distinct categories so as to accomplish some degree of separation of 'us' from 'them'. In the fourth, labeled persons experience status loss and discrimination that lead to unequal outcomes. Finally, stigmatization is entirely contingent on access to social, economic, and political power . . . Thus, we apply the term stigma when elements of labeling, stereotyping, separation, status loss, and discrimination co-occur in a power situation that allows the components of stigma to unfold.

Accordingly, the storytellers in *Out from the Margins* discursively validate the cultural stigma against drug addicts in mainland Chinese society by assuming labels [瘾君子; 隐君子] that connote disrepute, iniquity and the absence of humanity [劣迹斑斑; 垃圾; 非人]. Drug addicts are 'abnormal' [非正常人] and live outside of mainstream society [另类; 边缘人; 旁门左道]. They comprise an underclass that is unreliable and untrustworthy in the workplace and in interpersonal relationships. Only by creating a totally new self that is patterned on the 'normal person' [正常人] (Gao 2011), can they hope to overcome their social 'discrimination and isolation' [被歧视、被孤立] and return to society (Liang 2002, p. 224). This requires a relinquishing of freedom and a subordination of the self to the fellow members of the Daytop therapeutic community. The social marginality and disempowerment of drug addicts, in turn, is legitimised by contemporary Chinese cultural and political discourses, which cast drug addiction as antisocial and criminal behaviour (Luo *et al.* 2014. See also Chapters 1 & 2).

This stigmatised addict identity that is assumed by storytellers in *Out from the Margins* has only a tenuous link to illness. The life stories, for the most part, do not cast drug addicts as fundamentally ill or genetically programmed to become addicted to illicit drugs (Luo *et al.* 2014). The aetiology of their drug addiction may be psychopathological, stemming from character flaws or family dysfunction, but it is not innately pathophysiological. One storyteller does call drug addiction a 'grave disease' [沉疴] (Liang 2002, p. 267), while the expression 'symptom' (of an illness) [症状] is employed in three stories to describe the bodily manifestations of drug withdrawal (Liang 2002, pp. 151, 193, 237). Most storytellers, however, do not invoke the illness identity in drug addiction, most likely because this could biogenetically taint, not only themselves, but their family members, as is common in mental illness in Chinese culture (Ramsay 2008, 2013). Thus, the biomedical aetiological explanation for drug addiction may facilitate the forming of therapeutic communities in Western counterpart stories because, in the West, illness enables social connection and support (Muzak 2008. See Chapter 1). However, it does not appear to do so in the life stories in *Out from the Margins*, due to the deterrent effect of cultural stigma. The formation of the therapeutic community in the life stories in *Out from the Margins* more likely has institutional and cultural origins. The notion of the therapeutic community is a foundational principle of the Daytop Drug Rehabilitation Village. At the same time, there is a 'cultural prioritising' in mainland China 'of social relationships and defining self through connections with others' (Ramsay 2013, p. 31).

Storytellers commonly cast drug addiction in the life stories of *Out from the Margins* in the language of descent. Storytellers 'fall' [坠落, 跌进] into a 'very deep hole' [很深很深的洞] or 'abyss' [深渊], when addicted to illicit drugs (Liang 2002, pp. 61, 177, 245, 266). Daytop helps them to 'stand up' [站起来], through drug rehabilitation within the therapeutic community (Liang 2002, p. 143). In addition, spatial language distinguishes those inside the therapeutic community, that is, the 'members' [成员] who abide by the Daytop code, from those outside the therapeutic community, that is, the members who violate the Daytop code and then 'leave' [走出]. Similar language has been found to characterise counterpart stories in the West (see Chapter 1). Nevertheless, drug addiction and rehabilitation in the life stories in *Out from the Margins* are not heavily couched in the language of battle that characterises Western counterparts. Such language also characterises the mainland Chinese stories of drug addiction and recovery analysed in Chapter 2. The life stories in *Out from the Margins* may not personify illicit drugs as an enemy to be engaged in combat, because the storytellers wish to place the responsibility for drug addiction onto the illicit drug user and not the illicit drug.

56 *Institutional schema*

It is the illicit drug users who are to blame. They are sullied or flawed. Only with help and guidance from the Daytop therapeutic community can they create new moral selves with 'personal integrity' [操守] and return to society to live a normal life. Storytellers, therefore, are not liberated from the tyranny of illicit drugs, as they are in the Chapter 2 life stories. On the contrary, they must submit themselves to the control of the Daytop therapeutic community.

The commonalities across the life stories in *Out from the Margins* point to discursive shaping by the therapeutic community within which the stories have been told. This community, guided by the institution (Daytop), would have a 'preferred' story of drug addiction and rehabilitation, which would become apparent to community members as life stories are 'told and retold' during community activities (Ramsay 2013, p. 13). Members, therefore, may align their own stories with this prototypical community narrative. This would connect them to their fellow community members, while reinforcing 'the working logic of the treatment system' (Järvinen & Andersen 2009, p. 865. See Chapter 1). This treatment system is of North American origins. As a result, many narrative features of the life stories analysed in this chapter accord with those of Western counterparts, as identified in Chapter 1. Despite this, Chinese cultural and political discourses continue to shape these life stories. Normality and morality are gendered in accordance with Chinese cultural scripts. Face motivates drug rehabilitation and a return to society. Social belonging takes precedence over individual goals, needs or expectations. There is a reluctance to fully embrace the illness identity in drug addiction. Chinese cultural stigma is not questioned or challenged. Familiar political language describes the process of drug rehabilitation. As such, the life stories in *Out from the Margins* bear out the discursive schema of the institution, while maintaining Chinese cultural and political affinity.

Taiwanese life stories of drug addiction and rehabilitation

Dawn on the Black Seas: Rebirth Testimonies of Friends in Drug Rehabilitation [黑海中的晨曦: 戒毒朋友的重生見証] and *Young People, Treasure Your Youth!* [少年人, 寶貝你的年輕!] compile the life stories of nine Chinese people who reside in, or are still actively engaged with, the Operation Dawn [晨曦會] drug rehabilitation facilities in Taiwan. Operation Dawn is the largest non-penal[4] drug rehabilitation provider in Taiwan (Chou, Hung & Liao 2007). Other non-penal drug rehabilitation providers in Taiwan include The House of Grace and Agape House (Chou, Hung & Liao 2007). Operation Dawn, like The House of Grace and Agape House, is a Christian organisation (Chou, Hung & Liao 2007). It originated in Hong Kong in the 1960s and, in 1984, established a drug rehabilitation program in Taiwan, which at present, runs in twelve Operation Dawn facilities across Taiwan (Chou, Hung & Liao 2007). The free-of-charge program follows a Christian 'gospel rehabilitation' [福音戒毒] approach that 'does not rely on medication, nor self-will but only on the power of the gospel of Jesus Christ to achieve' drug rehabilitation (Operation Dawn 2013). Program activities aim to bring about 'individual, spiritual and physical' rehabilitative outcomes by means of 'realization', 'repentance' and 'transformation' (Operation Dawn 2013).

Both *Dawn on the Black Seas* and *Young People* are published by Operation Dawn's publishing arm, Dawn Press [晨曦出版社]. *Dawn on the Black Seas* was published in 2001 with Liu Min-he *et al.* [劉民和等 著] accredited as the volume's authors. The volume contains five first-person accounts of drug addiction and rehabilitation in Taiwan. All are life stories of Chinese men in their thirties. Four stories are self-written while one is transcribed by a second party. The stories range from eight to twenty-one pages in length. *Young People*, on the other hand, was published in 2003 with Shu Lian-wen *et al.* [束連文等 著] accredited as the volume's authors. It contains four first-person accounts of drug addiction and rehabilitation in Taiwan. Two are life stories of Chinese women and two are life stories of Chinese men. The former are self-written, while the latter are transcribed by a second party. The storytellers are aged in their twenties or thirties and their stories range from fifteen to twenty-one pages in length.

The Taiwanese life stories in *Dawn on the Black Seas* and *Young People* follow the narrative format of their mainland Chinese counterparts in *Out from the Margins*. The narrative moves from life as a child or teenager before illicit drug use, through illicit drug use and addiction, and concluding with life after a lengthy and successful period in drug rehabilitation. Unlike the mainland Chinese counterparts, opioids and amphetamines constitute the illicit drugs of abuse. The stories commence, as before, by recounting troubled childhood or teenage years, continuing into young adulthood. Some storytellers report feeling lonely and neglected in childhood [我卻連一個說話的對象也沒有; 享受不到親子之間的情誼, 一度還懷疑自己是父母親多餘的小孩; 享受不到親情的溫暖] (Liu *et al.* 2001, pp. 19, 86; Shu *et al.* 2003, p. 101). Others feel objectified by Chinese cultural values that cherish sons [父母有了我, 就代表跟祖宗有了個交代; 自己只是死去哥哥的替代品] and discount daughters [媽媽不喜歡女孩, 是肇因於 . . . 重男輕女] (Shu *et al.* 2003, pp. 101, 116, 134). Many storytellers are 'unruly' [狂野; 我暴跳如雷; 成天打架、鬧事] and 'rebellious' [叛逆; 被貼上問題學生的標籤] (Liu *et al.* 2001, pp. 69, 142; Shu *et al.* 2003, pp. 115, 135). One girl is overly timid and shy [膽小如鼠 . . . 我個性太軟] (Shu *et al.* 2003, pp. 154–155). In addition, beatings by parents for bad behaviour, not being scholarly or truanting are commonplace [打一下的嚴格方式處理; 對我拳打腳踢] (Shu *et al.* 2003, pp. 117, 137). All in all, the storytellers, like their mainland Chinese counterparts, are cast as sullied or having a 'distorted value system' [扭曲的價值觀] from childhood (Liu *et al.* 2001, p. 49). This leads them to 'deviate from the right way' [我都偏離了正路] and into illicit drug use and addiction (Liu *et al.* 2001, p. 86).

The right way in these life stories encompasses 'studying well, finding a job and showing filial respect to your parents' [好好的讀書、找一分工作、孝敬

58   *Institutional schema*

父母] (Shu *et al.* 2003, p. 100). The wrong path that most storytellers follow encompasses, for the men, joining an underworld gang [成為黑社會幫派中的一份子; 步入黑社會]; and, for the women, 'bringing unsavoury people home' [帶一些不三不四的人來家裡] or having a lesbian relationship (Liu *et al.* 2001, pp. 20, 87; Shu *et al.* 2003, p. 141). Such a lifestyle invariably is associated with 'vice' [惡習], including recreational drug use [「仙藥」] (Liu *et al.* 2001, p. 20; Shu *et al.* 2003, p. 163). The storytellers quickly succumb to addiction, where illicit drugs 'control' [轄制; 控制], 'bind' [捆綁], 'hook' [鉤住] or become 'one's own parents' [毒品纔是我的生身父母] (Liu *et al.* 2001, pp. 22, 88, 92, 112; Shu *et al.* 2003, pp. 107, 125, 131). Thereafter, they 'commit crime' [作奸犯科] and become 'crazed' and 'psychotic' [瘋子; 瘋了; 精神錯亂; 潑猴; 被害妄想症; 幻聽幻覺], or 'possessed' by devils and spirits [被邪靈附身; 被鬼附了; 中邪了; 著魔] (Liu *et al.* 2001, pp. 51, 113–114; Shu *et al.* 2003, pp. 108–168). In the depths of drug addiction, they encapsulate death[5] [打了第一針毒品時, 就已經死了; 行屍走肉] (Liu *et al.* 2001, pp. 45, 78, 86; Shu *et al.* 2003, p. 125). They encounter death [在死海中; 死路一條; 走上絕路] by attempting suicide [有了自殺的念頭; 自刎; 不如死去; 尋死; 自焚], or by watching associates die from drug overdoses [吸食過量 . . . 全身發黑而死; 吸過量死了], drug-related accidents [與卡車對面相撞, 登時腦漿迸流一地] and drug-related violence [活生生的燒死滅屍; 一群人持刀進來見人就砍] (Liu *et al.* 2001, pp. 22–115; Shu *et al.* 2003, pp. 109–170).

The storytellers seemingly are saved from an impending premature death by entering Operation Dawn, admission to which usually is organised by a caring family member. In Operation Dawn, they 'confess' [認罪] and 'repent' [悔悟; 悔改] the sin that has characterised their life to date (Liu *et al.* 2001, pp. 18–118). The 'newly created self' [新造的人] is forgiven and offered a 'new life' [新的生命; 新生] with faith in Jesus Christ (Liu *et al.* 2001, pp. 18–119; Shu *et al.* 2003, pp. 114, 151).[6] This faith sustains the new self through a relatively straightforward, but lengthy, drug rehabilitation program in Operation Dawn. On completion of the program, a 'healthy' [健健康康], 'moral human being' [做人] is able to re-join the family and pay back the unending love and support [苦口婆心; 沒有一天不想為我找一條出路] that had been given to the 'old self' [舊身] during drug addiction (Liu *et al.* 2001, pp. 18, 45, 92, 97; Shu *et al.* 2003, p. 169). Gratitude is expressed, even where the old self had been neglected, beaten, or even restrained using iron shackles [用鐵鍊把我鎖起來; 以手鍊、腳鍊把我鎖在房門內] by parents during childhood or during drug addiction (Liu *et al.* 2001, p. 44; Shu *et al.* 2003, p. 147). Thus, in the Taiwanese life stories of drug addiction and rehabilitation, the ultimate goal in recovery is not a return to society per se, but a return to and reconciliation with the family [能與家人和睦相處; 重新站立在他們面前; 與家人重拾親情] (Liu et al 2001, pp. 25, 98; Shu *et al.* 2003, p. 169). In so doing, a now moral self can atone for the 'unfilial behaviour' [不孝] and the loss of face [別人的指指點點; 拉下臉; 敗壞家風; 丟他們的臉] that the old self

Institutional schema 59

had brought upon the family during drug addiction (Liu *et al.* 2001, pp. 44, 99; Shu *et al.* 2003, pp. 147, 166, 168).

Analysis

The life stories in *Dawn on the Black Seas* and *Young People* recount Chinese people's experiences of opioid or amphetamines addiction and drug rehabilitation in the Operation Dawn drug rehabilitation facilities in Taiwan. The high incidence of heroin addiction, together with a marked incidence of amphetamines addiction, are in keeping with illicit drug use patterns across Taiwan as well as in metropolitan and coastal mainland China (Chou, Hung & Liao 2007. See Chapter 1). Similar to the life stories in *Out from the Margins*, the life stories in *Dawn on the Black Seas* and *Young People* clearly bear out the institutional schema of the Christian Operation Dawn organisation. This is accomplished in a way that maintains cultural and political affinity with the Taiwanese setting in which the life stories are told. This could stem from a purposeful attempt by the Christian Operation Dawn organisation to fashion an institutional narrative of drug addiction and rehabilitation that is locally palatable. Alternatively, it may stem from a broader indigenisation of Christianity in contemporary Taiwanese society. While the Communist mainland Chinese authorities maintain an intense distrust of organised religion, especially non-indigenous religion, Christianity in Taiwan has a long history that dates back to the arrival of Spanish (Catholic) and Dutch (Protestant) missionaries in the early seventeenth century (Kuo 2008; Lo 2011). Since this time, Christianity in Taiwan has been subject to the vicissitudes of Taiwanese governance, along with all facets of Taiwanese society (Kuo 2008; Lo 2011). Taiwan, successively, has been ruled by Spanish and Dutch colonists, the Qing dynasty, Japanese colonists, the mainland Chinese Nationalist Party, the Nationalist Party that fled the mainland following the Communist victory, a Nationalist Party dictatorship, and a current multiparty democracy. This, together with the existence of a rich and vibrant local Aboriginal culture in Taiwan, arguably manifest a tolerance [包容], at least at the political level, which accepts the Christian presence while facilitating its indigenisation. It is noteworthy that some of Taiwan's post-World War II leaders have been, at least notionally, Christian and may have used their Christianity to foster political support from the United States, in the face of a perceived threat from Communist mainland China (Kuo 2008).

The storytellers in *Dawn on the Black Seas* and *Young People*, like the storytellers in *Out from the Margins*, compartmentalise their lives into two distinct and conflicting temporal periods, namely, life from before and life after entering Operation Dawn. Life from before entering Operation Dawn is troubled and immoral. Childhood generally is sullied and unruly, and life as a drug addict is dangerous and 'debauched' [荒唐時光] (Shu *et al.* 2003, p. 170). Life after entering Operation Dawn, by contrast, is safe and decent. The storytellers find sanctuary and

60 *Institutional schema*

wellbeing in Operation Dawn. This is achieved by handing over their lives to Jesus Christ. Storytellers, therefore, assume two distinct identities in *Dawn on the Black Seas* and *Young People*: the 'moral human being' [做人] (Bakken 2000; Kleinman *et al.* 2011), who has newfound faith in Jesus Christ; and the 'big sinner' [大罪人], who dishonoured and defied her or his parents during childhood and turns to illicit drugs in adulthood [吸毒的我] (Liu *et al.* 2001, pp. 45, 118).

The sinners from before are not ostracised, isolated and alone [边缘人], in contrast to the mainland Chinese counterparts in *Out from the Margins*. Many retain connection with and support from their families and continue to reside in the family home. Others link up with, and get help from, members of the 'drug subculture' [煙毒文化], the lesbian community, or the 'sworn brotherhood' [結義] of the underworld (Liu *et al.* 2001, pp. 21, 48). They, therefore, retain a level of social connectedness and community membership that is absent in the mainland Chinese counterparts. Moreover, in line with Christian schema, the Taiwan storytellers still are human beings. They merely have gone astray. Jesus Christ saves them and forgives their past sins. These past sins often are gendered in line with Chinese cultural norms. Drug-addicted men join brotherhoods, but then behave 'unrighteously' [不義] (Liu *et al.* 2001, p. 99). Drug-addicted women find company in other women, but then engage in 'same-sex love' [同性相戀] (Shu *et al.* 2003, p. 160). They also can be 'insubordinate' [忤逆] to fathers and husbands; marry and then separate soon after [分道揚鑣]; become pregnant out of wedlock and then terminate the pregnancy [懷孕、墮胎]; use illicit drugs while pregnant [吸毒, 懷孕中如此]; or relinquish the care of their child to others [女兒, 交給媽媽] (Shu 2003 et al., pp. 141, 148, 160, 167). Operation Dawn teaches the sinners to be moral (drug-free) human beings [做人], who will return to their families, honour their parents [孝] and make productive contributions [禮], in order to atone for the support and care that their families had given them during drug addiction [忠]. As such, the new self is moral in both Christian and Confucian terms.

Storytellers do not assume an addict identity in *Dawn on the Black Seas* and *Young People*. More commonly, they take on an illness identity. They are 'infected with an illness' [染病], exhibit 'symptoms (of an illness)' [癥狀; 症狀], or suffer from mental illnesses such as 'paranoid disorder' [被害妄想症] and 'psychosis' [精神錯亂] (Liu *et al.* 2001, pp. 21, 23; Shu *et al.* 2003, pp. 146, 152, 168, 170). They also 'infect' other people with the illness of drug addiction [我身邊的十七位好朋友因我而染上吸毒] (Liu *et al.* 2001, p. 22). Storytellers, therefore, willingly take on the illness identity in drug addiction, despite the biogenetic taint that illness labels, in particular, those denoting mental illness, extend to their family members in Chinese culture (Ramsay 2008, 2013). Moreover, they actively spread their illness (drug addiction) to others. Taking on an illness identity, therefore, does not counter the moral censure that attends their sinful behaviour during drug addiction, as observed in the West (see Chapter 1). On the contrary, it amplifies it. The moral censure directed against the sinners from before also would be amplified by the use of the everyday language of madness [疯] and spirit possession to describe their drug addiction. Spirit possession taints a person's family in Chinese culture in a similar way to mental illness (Ramsay 2013; Yip 2007). There are two likely reasons for the storytellers' apparent willingness to use stigmatic language to describe their own drug addiction. First, many of the storytellers were addicted to amphetamines. The symptoms of amphetamines intoxication mimic psychotic illness (madness) and spirit possession. Second, being reborn [脱胎換骨] as a Christian would heal their illnesses and drive away the Devil and evil spirits. The new selves, accordingly, would be cleansed of the taints of the previous sinful selves. As a result, the 'felt stigma' that usually attends being mentally ill or possessed by spirits in Chinese culture would be wholly erased and the moral face of the family would be restored (Scambler 2004, p. 33).

Christian schema also may account for the widespread use of the language of death and the personification of illicit drugs in the life stories in *Dawn on the Black Seas* and *Young People*. Life as a drug addict in *Out from the Margins* was not life-threatening, but merely face-threatening. The mainland Chinese storytellers, therefore, can overcome their drug addiction through a community-based intervention that cultivates their moral face and returns them to society. The Taiwanese storytellers, by contrast, must be rescued from a looming, violent death that would lead to 'eternal damnation in Hell' [萬劫不復的無底坑] (Shu *et al.* 2003, p. 171). Jesus Christ is their saviour. He 'sets them free' [釋放] from illicit drugs, which are personified as the Devil [毒魔掌控; 與魔鬼短兵相接] (Liu *et al.* 2001, pp. 24, 99, 111). Illicit drugs, like the Devil, 'control' [轄制; 控制], 'bind' [捆綁], 'hook' [鉤住], 'possess' [附身; 附了; 中邪了; 著魔] and 'poison the mind' [心毒] (Liu *et al.* 2001, p. 50). One result of the use of such figurative language in *Dawn on the Black Seas* and *Young People* is that the responsibility for drug addiction discursively shifts back onto the illicit drugs, that is, the Devil, and away from the storyteller, who, just like most human beings, is a mere sinner (Tolton 2009).

The commonalities across the life stories in *Dawn on the Black Seas* and *Young People* point to discursive shaping by the Christian schema propagated by Operation Dawn. Storytellers align their life stories with this schema, even though only around 5% of the Taiwanese population is Christian (Kuo 2008; Lo 2011). As such, a storyteller's conversion to Christianity may have represented a considerable break from social and religious convention in Taiwan. In support of this, a number of the life stories allude to the outsider status of Christianity in Taiwan. Some people look on Christianity as 'no more than a tool borne of imperialist aggression' [基督教不過是帝國主義發展出來的侵略工具], which 'brainwashes' people [洗腦的], 'offends the ancestors' [信這種教是背祖忘宗], and is 'truly absurd and ridiculous' [實在荒謬可笑] (Liu *et al.* 2001, pp. 24, 47; Shu *et al.* 2003, p. 127). In light of such sentiment, or the aforementioned indigenisation of Christianity in Taiwan, the Operation Dawn life stories of drug addiction

62 *Institutional schema*

and rehabilitation maintain cultural and political affinity with the Taiwanese setting in which they are told. As a result, the storytellers' accounts are able to invoke Christian schema without offending Confucian morality and norms.

Hong Kong life stories of drug addiction and rehabilitation

The Hong Kong life stories of drug addiction and rehabilitation are drawn from four published sources: two are Chinese-language periodicals, *Drug Prohibition: The State of the Art* [禁毒: 最前線] and *Drum Beat*[7] [鼓聲]; and two are Chinese-language books, *We Love Zheng Sheng Kids*[8] [愛是這樣解毒] [*Lit. Love Sets Free From Drugs in this Way*] and *We are Good Zheng Sheng Kids* [我們是正生好孩子]. The two periodicals contain life stories of Chinese people who have undertaken drug rehabilitation in facilities administered by the secular non-government organisation, the Society for the Aid and Rehabilitation of Drug Abusers (SARDA) [香港戒毒會]. SARDA was established in Hong Kong in 1961 to provide free-of-charge, voluntary rehabilitative assistance and treatment to illicit drug users (SARDA 2011a). The organisation also carries out public drug preventative education and advises the Hong Kong regional government on illicit drug policy (SARDA 2011a). The two books, on the other hand, contain life stories of Chinese school-aged youth who have undertaken drug rehabilitation at the Christian Zheng Sheng College [基督教正生書院] (hereafter CZSC). CZSC is the first school-cum-drug-rehabilitation facility established in Asia and is located on a remote part of Lantau Island [大嶼山] in the Hong Kong Special Administrative Region (CZSC 2009, 2010). CSZC provides a school curricular and drug rehabilitative program based on Christian teachings for over 100 young people from across the region (CZSC 2009, 2010).

The periodical *Drug Prohibition* is collaboratively published by SARDA, the University of Hong Kong's School of Professional and Continuing Education (HKUSPACE) [香港大學專業進修學院], and the Community Health Organisation for Intervention, Care and Empowerment (CHOICE) [再思社區健康組織]. The periodical reports current academic knowledge on, therapeutic practice in, and government policy on illicit drug use, drug prevention strategy and drug rehabilitative treatment in Hong Kong. It also reports on the policing of narcotics and local trends in illicit drug use across the region. The periodical is irregularly published (at least one issue annually), with each issue containing one or two first-hand accounts of drug addiction and rehabilitation that have been written by local Chinese people. Issues 1 (2009) to 12 (2013) of *Drug Prohibition* contain twelve life stories of one to two pages in length. Chinese men wrote seven of the articles, while five are written by Chinese women. Their ages range from late teens to early forties. All issues of *Drug Prohibition* are published on the SARDA website: www.sarda.org.hk/.

The periodical *Drum Beat* is the internal bulletin of SARDA's Shek Kwu Chau Treatment and Rehabilitation Centre [香港戒毒會石鼓洲康復院]. The facility is located on the island of Cheung Chau [長洲] in the Hong Kong Special Administrative Region, where it provides a 'residential treatment and rehabilitation service for male drug abusers of all ages' that is based on a 'Therapeutic Community Model' (see pp. 50–62) (SARDA 2011b). The bulletin reports recent events at the facility and contains columns that are written by managerial and grass-roots staff. It is irregularly published (approximately one issue annually), with issues often containing one or more first-hand accounts of drug addiction and rehabilitation that have been written by Chinese clients. Issues 18 (2008), 19 (2009), 21 (2010) and 23 (2011) of *Drum Beat*, which are published on the SARDA website, contain six life stories of one to two pages in length. All are written by Chinese men whose ages, where identified, range from early twenties to late thirties. Taken together, *Drug Prohibition* and *Drum Beat* provide eighteen life stories of drug addiction and rehabilitation in the SARDA facilities. Men wrote thirteen of these stories and five are written by women. Their ages, for the most part, are evenly spread across late teens to early forties.

The two books *We are Good Zheng Sheng Kids* (2009) and *We Love Zheng Sheng Kids* (2010) are published by Breakthrough [突破出版社], a Christian publishing house that is based in Hong Kong. The accredited authors of both books are the students of CZSC [基督教正生書院同學]. The books portray daily life at CZSC by way of photographs and commentary from students. The books also contain eight first-hand accounts of drug addiction and rehabilitation that have been written by Chinese students. The stories are one to three pages in length, with six life stories written by male students and two life stories written by female students. The following synopsis and analysis of Hong Kong life stories of drug addiction and rehabilitation will compare and contrast these CZSC stories, created in a Christian facility, with the SARDA counterparts, created in secular facilities.

Life as a child is sullied or troubled in the Hong Kong life stories, like their mainland Chinese and Taiwanese counterparts. Some storytellers characterise themselves as simply 'bad' [壞人; 陋習] (CZSC 2010, p. 175; *Drum Beat 19*, p. 7). They may be 'bad tempered' [脾氣好差], 'stubborn and 'willful' [一向固執、任性; 我是一個非常任性和固執的人], 'vain' [虛榮感], 'indulgent' [放縱自己], 'undisciplined' [自己貪玩], 'irresponsible' [只識得「不負責任」; 好無責任感], or unconcerned about their families [唔識得關心下屋企人] (CZSC 2009, p. 47, 2010, p. 183; *Drug Prohibition 3*, p. 8, *4*, p. 7, *10*, p. 7; *Drum Beat 21*, p. 6, *23*, p. 8). Most storytellers, however, ultimately place the blame for their illicit drug use on peer-group pressure or family circumstance. Some are 'estranged from their families' [通常是獨自一個; 對屋企無歸屬感; 我和家人的關係一直都不太好], 'troubled' by their 'parents'' divorce [因為父母離婚, 我大受打擊; 我想起父母離婚的事情, 便將一顆毒品放進口裡], disturbed by 'tense family relations' [緊張的親戚關係中成長的我], or disadvantaged by 'family poverty' [我來自低下層的家庭] (CZSC 2010, pp. 163, 169; *Drug Prohibition 2*, p. 8, *4*, p. 7, *6*,

64 *Institutional schema*

p. 8, *11* p. 6; *Drum Beat 21* p. 6). Others are emotionally 'empty' [自在的空虛感], emotionally disturbed [當時自己感情出現問題, 心情不太好], 'friendless' [我自己就是沒有朋友的; 不懂得與人相處], or simply 'naïve' [天真] (CZSC 2009, p. 51, 2010, p. 163; *Drug Prohibition 2*, p. 8, *10*, p. 6, *11*, p. 6). Consequently, 'bad friends' [損友], 'bad classmates' [壞同學] or local street gangs ['邨童'; 小混混] introduce them to illicit drugs and they rapidly become addicted (CZSC 2010, p. 175; *Drug Prohibition 2*, p. 8, *3*, p. 8, *5*, p. 12, *6*, p. 8, *7*, p. 8). Heroin, ketamine and amphetamines are the most commonly used illicit drugs.

Storytellers tend to remain living in the family home while drug-addicted. They commit crime to support their habit, and sooner or later fall foul of the law and are directed to a drug rehabilitation facility. In the facility, whether secular or Christian, they 'learn' [學習] about themselves and their relationship with others [我慢慢學習要接受人們的批評及意見、要學習服從、要學習如何與人相處、要學習表達感受; 教導我正確的價值觀; 學到怎樣與人相處和待人接物] (CZSC 2009, p. 51; *Drug Prohibition 3*, p. 8, *6*, p. 9; *Drum Beat 23*, p. 6). They learn to be self-sufficient [學會自己照顧自己] through undertaking academic or vocational training (*Drum Beat 23*, p. 8). In addition, they are taught to let go of their pasts [學習忘記背後; 過去的已是過去]; set goals [為自己定下了人生目標; 訂下人生目標; 向目標進發]; and look forward to their futures [積極面對將來的人生; 未來其實就是掌握於我們的手中; 踏踏實實地走出我的未來; 我好好想清楚日後的日子; 為自己計劃將來; 步向理想的美好明天] (CZSC 2010, pp. 172, 183; *Drug Prohibition 1*, p. 7, *2*, p. 8, *3*, p. 8, *5*, p. 12, *9*, p. 10, *10*, pp. 7–8, *12*, p. 7; *Drum Beat 19*, p. 7). The primary outcomes of their rehabilitative 'education' and 'training' [教育; 教導; 訓練; 操練] include newfound senses of 'self-worth', 'self-fulfilment' and 'self-confidence' [進修, 增值及充實自己; 提升自己的水平和價值; 我自己可以重拾自信] (CZSC 2009, p. 47; *Drug Prohibition 2*, p. 8, *3*, p. 8, *7*, p. 9, *10*, pp. 7–8, *11*, p. 7; *Drum Beat 18*, p. 3).

Following drug rehabilitation, be it in the secular SARDA or the Christian CZSC facility, storytellers expect to return to their families or to establish independent lives. Some feel a need to reconcile with family members [重新建立了互信關懷的家庭關係; 不再令家人擔心; 與家人和諧相處; 背起一家人的責任; 大大修復了我與家人的關係; 我和家人的關係開始有改善] (*Drug Prohibition 2*, p. 8, *5*, p. 12, *6*, p. 8, *7*, p. 9, *11*, p. 7; *Drum Beat 23*, p. 8). They want to repay their families for standing by them during the vagaries of drug addiction [家人給予無盡的支持; 給我最大的支持是家人], when families often suffered the most [當時都無理屋企人點睇; 自己更加傷盡了家人的心; 最遺憾的是令家人傷心和失望; 首當其衝的就是我的家人] (CZSC 2010, p. 172; *Drug Prohibition 5*, p. 12, *7*, p. 8, *9*, p. 10, *10*, p. 7, *12*, p. 7). Like the Taiwanese counterpart stories, previous unfilial behaviour [我也不能盡孝道; 自己好不孝] seemingly can be offset by a newfound filial piety (*Drug Prohibition 12*, p. 7; *Drum Beat 23*, p. 7). An equal number of storytellers, nevertheless, do not plan to return to their families. They feel empowered by their newfound senses of self-worth, self-fulfilment and self-confidence. Individualist sensibilities appear to prevail over collectivist sensibilities in these life stories, with storytellers looking to establish independently productive lives. Thus, in contrast to the Taiwanese and mainland Chinese counterpart stories, returning to the family or returning to society as a good citizen is not prioritised in many of the Hong Kong life stories of drug addiction and rehabilitation.

Analysis

The Hong Kong life stories recount Chinese people's experiences of heroin, ketamine and amphetamines addiction and drug rehabilitation in the secular SARDA and the Christian CZSC drug rehabilitation facilities. The storytellers have been addicted to a wide range of illicit drugs, encompassing opioids, dissociative agents and stimulants, in keeping with illicit drug use patterns in Hong Kong (see Chapter 1). Their life stories clearly bear out the institutional schema of the secular SARDA and the Christian CZSC facilities. These schema appear to be grounded in contemporary social welfare practice in Hong Kong, regardless of the level of government affiliation of the drug rehabilitation facility or whether the facility is secular or Christian. As a result, the Hong Kong life stories of drug addiction and rehabilitation appear to maintain political affinity, but only partial cultural affinity, in distinction to their mainland Chinese and Taiwanese counterparts.

The Hong Kong life stories of drug addiction and rehabilitation are characterised by a future-looking temporality. Whether drug rehabilitation took place in a secular (SARDA) or Christian (CZSC) facility, the stories emphasise a life that is not yet experienced but is deemed to hold promise, due to the education received during drug rehabilitation. Identities are constructed in line with this future-looking temporality. The self from before [以前的我; 從前的我; 以前吸毒嘅我; 以前既我; 從前的我; 以前嘅自己] lacks direction, goals and a future [未有任何方向或目標; 沒有將來; 毫無目標的生; 冇將來; 我沒有想過自己的未來會怎樣; 完全無方向、無目標; 無想過什麼目標; 我從來不會為自己定下任何目標; 迷失方向] (CZSC 2009, p. 51; *Drug Prohibition 2*, p. 8, *3*, p. 8, *4*, p. 7, *5*, p. 12, *6*, p. 8, *7*, p. 9, *10*, p. 7, *12*, p. 7; *Drum Beat 21*, p. 6, *23*, p. 6). The new self, on the other hand, possesses the skills, knowledge and insight to move forward in a drug-free life that holds 'fulfilling' and 'worthwhile' personal and vocational opportunities [增值及充實自己; 提升自己的水平和價值; 獲得滿足感及自我價值; 充實感] (*Drug Prohibition 9*, p. 10, *10*, pp. 7–8; *Drum Beat 21*, p. 6).

A greater subjective continuity between the self from before and the new self distinguishes the Hong Kong life stories from their mainland Chinese and Taiwanese counterparts. This continuity is realised by way of a true, good inner-self, who possesses a certain level of 'conscience, dignity and human connection' [良心、尊嚴、人性溝通] (*Drug Prohibition 4*, p. 7). This true self is temporarily

66 *Institutional schema*

'lost' in drug addiction [我自己都迷失了; 迷失了自己] to a 'phony' drug-addicted 'self' [虛假的自我] (CZSC 2010, p. 175; *Drug Prohibition 3*, p. 8). The true self, however, is rediscovered and fully engaged when storytellers become 'students' [學員] in a drug rehabilitation facility and 'learn' [學習] how to 'say no to drugs' [齊齊向毒品說不] (*Drug Prohibition 2*, p. 8, *4*, p. 7, *5*, p. 12, *7*, p. 8, *10*, p. 8). Being 'drug-free' [操守] semantically equates to storytellers regaining their true inner 'personal integrity' [操守], and this allows them to progress toward living either independent lives or family-oriented lives as 'moral human beings' [做人] (CZSC 2009, p. 51; *Drug Prohibition 1*, p. 7, *3*, p. 8, *4*, p. 7, *6*, p. 9, *7*, p. 9, *9*, p. 10, *10*, p. 7; *Drum Beat 18*, p. 3, *19*, p. 7).

The student identity is taken on in drug rehabilitation, regardless of the storyteller's age or whether or not the rehabilitation facility functions as a properly constituted school (Gardner & Poole 2009). Such an identity normalises the person in drug rehabilitation. The person is neither ill and in need of biomedical treatment, nor a sinner requiring penance. The person is a student, an identity that all people assume at some stage in their lives. Moreover, taking on this everyday identity likely counters, to some extent, the stigmatised identity – 'drug addict' [道友] – that Hong Kong society commonly ascribes to illicit drug users (*Drug Prohibition 4*, p. 7; Laidler 2003). This addict identity marks illicit drug users as social outcasts [被社會排斥; 被社會遺棄的; 生活在社會邊緣] who can never change [「銅油醒始終是裝銅油], because they are enmeshed in a 'culture from beneath the overpass' [「天桥底文化」] (CZSC 2009, p. 47; *Drug Prohibition 10*, p. 8; *Drum Beat 18*, p. 3, *19*, p. 7). In Hong Kong, highly 'negative labels' are routinely 'attached to' this addict identity [加上負面標籤], stereotyping illicit drug users as 'unwanted dregs' [不受歡迎的地底泥], 'young good-for-nothings' [爛仔] and 'scum, degenerates, non-human, losers, . . . "jailbirds" and a waste of life' [人渣、敗類、無人性、瀾泥、. . . 監「躉」、唔死都冇用 . . . 以前嘅人就係用呢D字眼嚟稱呼我] (CZSC 2009, pp. 47, 51; *Drug Prohibition 2*, p. 8, *4*, p. 7). This negative labelling, typecasting and marginalisation of illicit drug users in Hong Kong society, coupled with the location of drug rehabilitation facilities in often quite remote parts of the Special Administrative Region, realise Link and Phelan's (2001) definition of social stigma discussed earlier in the chapter.

Stigmatising language is accompanied by a negative personification of illicit drugs in the Hong Kong life stories. Illicit drugs are personified as 'he' [「他」] and an 'easily invited, yet not easily seen off, 'bad friend'' [這個易請難送的「壞朋友」], who can 'control' [受毒品支配; 被毒品控制], 'enslave' [盲目地做毒品的奴隸], 'hold captive' [被毒品囚禁], 'wrest away' [自己七年青春、金錢、連身體的健康都被它奪去了] and be 'officially farewelled' [正式跟毒品道別] (*Drug Prohibition 3*, p. 8, *4*, p. 7, *6*, p. 8, *10*, p. 6, *11*, pp. 6–7, *12*, p. 7). Such personification discursively shifts the blame for drug addiction away from the storyteller and onto the illicit drug (Tolton 2009). As noted earlier in this section, storytellers also tend to direct the blame for drug addiction away from themselves

Institutional schema   67

and onto bad friends and their family circumstance. Thus, a true, good inner-self temporarily is led astray by external forces in the Hong Kong life stories. Thereafter, education restores this self.

Somewhat unexpectedly, there are few clear differences between the SARDA and the CZSC life stories of drug addiction and rehabilitation, even though the former is a secular organisation and the latter is a Christian organisation. Storytellers universally are cast, not as intrinsically bad, but merely in need of education to reengage their true, good inner-selves. As a consequence, drug rehabilitation equates to education. During drug rehabilitation, storytellers take on the identity of a student, regardless of their age, gender, or whether they are attending the CZSC school or a SARDA treatment and rehabilitation centre. The education that they receive equips them for futures that may or may not be closely entwined with their families. The stigma toward illicit drug users in Hong Kong society, which a number of the life stories allude to, may explain this observed similarity between the SARDA and the CZSC stories. Storytellers may resist the stigmatic notion that they are essentially bad and find refuge in the normative identity, student. Chinese cultural stigma may explain why storytellers do not embrace an illness identity, as is common in the West (see Chapters 1 & 2 and earlier in this chapter). However, social stigma also was encountered in the mainland Chinese life stories, where it is accepted and the storytellers return to the same society that had stigmatised them for using illicit drugs. The Hong Kong life stories, on the other hand, generally counter and, at times, openly challenge social stigma.

An explanation for these differing discursive responses to social stigma in the mainland Chinese and Hong Kong life stories may be found in the discursive schema of the institution. This also may explain the similarity between the secular SARDA and the Christian CZSC life stories. Social welfare services, often provided by charitable organisations such as Tung Wah [東華], have a long and largely unbroken history in Hong Kong, in contrast to mainland China and Taiwan, whose histories are marked by political instability, revolutions, foreign occupations and war (Jones 1990; Kleinman *et al.* 2011; Lo 2011; Munn 2000). This has provided a relatively coherent and proactive approach to social welfare in Hong Kong that, particularly since the late 1960s, espouses liberal notions of client-centredness and client-empowerment (Jones 1990; Lo 2011). This likely informs the social welfare practices in the SARDA and the CZSC drug rehabilitation facilities and, as a consequence, discursively shapes the Hong Kong life stories of drug addiction and rehabilitation, when compared to their mainland Chinese and Taiwanese counterparts, in ways that destigmatise drug addiction and empower the individual.

Conclusion

The analysis of the mainland Chinese, Taiwanese and Hong Kong life stories of drug addiction and rehabilitation has shown the differential interplay of cultural,

68 *Institutional schema*

political and institutional discourses in shaping temporality, subjectivity and language use. Cultural discourse appears to shape an emphasis on social belonging, filial piety and attention to face in the mainland Chinese and Taiwanese life stories. It also appears to construct normality and morality in these stories, in line with normative gender scripts in Chinese culture. Cultural discourse further provides the negative labels that dehumanise, marginalise and disempower illicit drug users in a stereotypical way in the mainland Chinese and Hong Kong life stories. These labels remain unchallenged in the mainland Chinese life stories, with storytellers aiming to return to the same society that has stigmatised them. The labels, however, are countered or contested in the Hong Kong life stories, where storytellers cast themselves as intrinsically good people and assume a student identity during their drug rehabilitation. Negative labels of this type are mostly absent from the Taiwanese life stories, where storytellers cast themselves as sinners, as all people are in Christian schema.

Political discourse may direct the mainland Chinese storytellers' return to society, rather than to their families, as the Taiwanese storytellers and some Hong Kong storytellers do. Good citizens in socialist mainland China demonstrate their political merit by productively contributing to society (see Chapter 2). Political considerations also may silence the candid reporting of the death and violence that surrounds heroin use and trafficking in southwestern mainland China. The Taiwanese life stories do not underplay the death and violence that surrounds illicit drug use and trafficking in Taiwan. Political and cultural considerations, nevertheless, may direct the Taiwanese storytellers to return to their families after drug rehabilitation in Operation Dawn, rather than devote their lives, as born-again Christians, to more individualistic Christian evangelical and missionary pursuits.

Institutional discourse appears to shape the mainland Chinese, Taiwanese and Hong Kong life stories of drug addiction and rehabilitation, with storytellers, in many instances, aligning their life stories with institutionally 'preferred' schema (Ramsay 2013, p. 13). Doing so provides storytellers with a sense of belonging, while discursively validating their institutional drug rehabilitation program. These programs are wholly secular in mainland China; largely Christian in Taiwan's non-penal sector (Chou, Hung & Liao 2007; Taiwan Ministry of Justice 2010); and both secular and Christian in Hong Kong in order to cater to 'drug abusers from varying background[s]' with 'different needs' (Narcotics Division 2009). The mainland Chinese storytellers, accordingly, are transformed into completely new drug-free and normal selves, as a result of their membership of the Daytop therapeutic community. The Taiwanese storytellers, on the other hand, are saved from an impending, violent death and subsequent eternal damnation in Hell, by being born again as sinless, drug-free selves while in Operation Dawn. Meanwhile, the Hong Kong storytellers retain their essential inner-goodness and become empowered, in non-gender-specific ways, by newfound senses of

Institutional schema 69

self-worth, self-fulfilment and self-confidence, as a result of being everyday students of the CZSC school or a SARDA treatment and rehabilitation centre. Both Christian CSZC and secular SARDA appear to embrace the discursive schema of social welfare services in Hong Kong, which espouses liberal notions of client-centredness and client-empowerment (Jones 1990; Lo 2011).

Nevertheless, institutional discourse shapes the mainland Chinese and Taiwanese life stories of drug addiction and rehabilitation in ways that align with prevailing cultural and political discourses. For Daytop, this likely stems from pragmatic considerations, in light of its foreign origins and the political sensitivities that surround illicit drug use in mainland China. For Operation Dawn, this likely stems from an apparent indigenisation of Christianity in Taiwan, together with its prominent standing and influence in Taiwanese politics. Institutional discourse, on the other hand, shapes the Hong Kong life stories of drug addiction and rehabilitation in ways that appreciably resist cultural discourse. This can be attributed to a long-standing activist social welfare agenda in Hong Kong. As a result, the Hong Kong life stories of drug addiction and rehabilitation appear to be more discursively empowering than their mainland Chinese and Taiwanese counterparts. The life stories analysed in Chapter 2 and this chapter recount an insider's perspective of drug addiction, rehabilitation and recovery in mainland China, Taiwan and Hong Kong. Chapter 4 shifts attention to the outsider's perspective by analysing filmic stories of drug addiction, rehabilitation and recovery in mainland China, Taiwan and Hong Kong.

Notes

1 The expression 'storyteller' denotes the person who has been addicted to illicit drugs and then undertaken a drug rehabilitation program. The account of this experience may be a first-person written account or a first-person oral account that has been transcribed by a second party.
2 During the Cultural Revolution, educated youth [知识青年, 简称: '知青'] were sent from the urban areas down to the countryside [下乡] to learn from the peasants about rural life.
3 The similarity with activities of the Cultural Revolution is noted by one storyteller [我的感觉是在搞'文化大革命'] (Liang 2002, p. 43).
4 Government-run drug rehabilitation services in Taiwan, for the most part, are prison-based (Chou, Hung & Liao 2007).
5 Baumler (2007, p. 204) states that death was an inescapable outcome of opium addiction in 'public and private anti-opium propaganda' from Republican era China. Baumler (2007, p. 203) claims that such discourse originated from the Christian 'temperance movement' in China.
6 Baumler (2007) states that the notion of a 'new life' for drug addicts in recovery characterised institutional stories of opium addiction in late-Qing and early Republican era China. Baumler (2007, p. 49) believes that '[f]or the missionaries, this tied in well with the narrative of [Christian] conversion, for Chinese nationalists it tied in well with the narrative of national awakening.'
7 The published English-language title of the periodical.
8 The published English-language title of the book.

70 *Institutional schema*

References

Bakken, B. 2000. *The exemplary society: human improvement, social control, and the dangers of modernity in China.* Oxford: Oxford University Press.

Baumler, A. 2007. *The Chinese and opium under the Republic: worse than floods and wild beasts.* New York, NY: SUNY Press.

Biddulph, S. 2013. Compulsory drug rehabilitation in China. In F. Rahman and N. Crofts (eds) *Drug law reform in East and Southeast Asia* (pp. 233–244). Lanham, MD: Lexington.

Chou, T. C., Hung, Y. J. and Liao, F. C. 2007. A study on factors affecting the abstention of drug abuse in private rehabilitation institutes in Taiwan – Operation Dawn Taiwan as an example. *Flinders Journal of Law Reform*, 10 (3), 737–758.

CZSC students [基督教正生書院同學]. 2009. *We are good Zheng Sheng kids* [我們是正生好孩子]. Hong Kong: Breakthrough [突破出版社].

CZSC students [基督教正生書院同學]. 2010. *We love Zheng Sheng kids* [愛是這樣解毒]. Hong Kong: Breakthrough [突破出版社].

Daytop. 2012a. *About us.* Retrieved from www.daytop.org/about.html#wha 17 August 2013.

Daytop. 2012b. *Our history.* Retrieved from www.daytop.org/history.html 17 August 2013.

Drug Prohibition: The State of the Art [禁毒: 最前線]. 2009–2013. Issues 1–12.

Drum Beat [鼓聲]. 2008–2011. Issues 18, 19, 21, 23.

Elliott, J. 2005. *Using narrative in social research: qualitative and quantitative approaches.* Thousand Oaks, CA: Sage.

Gao, H. 2011. *Women and heroin addiction in China's changing society.* New York, NY: Routledge.

Gardner, P. J. and Poole, J. M. 2009. One story at a time: narrative therapy, older adults, and addictions. *Journal of Applied Gerontology*, 28 (5), 600–620.

Hinze, C. 2002. *Re-thinking 'face': pursuing an emic-etic understanding of Chinese mian and lian and English face.* Unpublished doctoral dissertation. St Lucia, QLD: The University of Queensland.

Järvinen, M. and Andersen, D. 2009. Creating problematic identities: the making of the chronic addict. *Substance Use and Misuse*, 44, 865–885.

Jones, C. 1990. *Promoting prosperity: the Hong Kong way of social policy.* Hong Kong: Chinese University Press.

Kleinman, A., Yan, Y., Jun, J., Lee, S., Zhang, E., Pan, T., Wu, F. and Guo, J. 2011. *Deep China: the moral life of the person: what anthropology and psychiatry tell us about China today.* Berkeley: University of California Press.

Kuo, C. T. 2008. *Religion and democracy in Taiwan.* Albany, NY: SUNY Press.

Laidler, K. J. 2003. Globalization and the illicit drugs trade in Hong Kong. In C. Sumner (ed.) *The Blackwell companion to criminology.* Blackwell Reference Online. Retrieved from www.blackwellreference.com/subscriber/tocnode.html?id=g9780631220923_chunk_g978063122092322 18 November 2014.

Liang, P. [梁苹]. 2002. *Out from the margins* [走出边缘]. Kunming: Yunnan People's Publishing House [云南人民出版社].

Link, B. and Phelan, J. 2001. Conceptualizing stigma. *Annual Review of Sociology*, 27, 363–385.

Link, B., Yang, L., Phelan, J. and Collins, P. 2004. Measuring mental illness stigma. *Schizophrenia Bulletin*, 30 (3), 511–541.

Liu, M. H., *et al.* [劉民和等著]. 2001. *Dawn on the black seas: rebirth testimonies of friends in drug rehabilitation* [黑海中的晨曦: 戒毒朋友的重生見証]. Taipei: Dawn Press [晨曦出版社].

Lo, L. K. 2011. Taiwan, Hong Kong, Macao. In P. C. Phan (ed.) *Christianities in Asia* (pp. 173–183). Maldan, MA: Wiley-Blackwell.

Lu, L., Fang, Y. and Wang, X. 2008. Drug abuse in China: past, present and future. *Cellular and Molecular Neurobiology*, 28, 479–490.

Lu, L. and Wang, X. 2008. Drug addiction in China. *Annals of the New York Academy of Sciences*, 1141, 304–317.

Luo, T., Wang, J., Li, Y., Wang, X., Tan, L., Deng, Q., Thakoor, J. P. D. and Hao, W. 2014. Stigmatization of people with drug dependence in China: a community-based study in Hunan province. *Drug and Alcohol Dependence*, 134, 285–289.

Munn, C. 2000. The Hong Kong opium revenue, 1845–1885. In T. Brook and B. T. Wakabayashi (eds) *Opium regimes: China, Britain, and Japan, 1839–1952* (pp. 105–126). Berkeley: University of California Press.

Muzak, J. 2008. "Addiction got me what I needed": depression and drug addiction in Elizabeth Wurtzel's memoirs. In H. Clark (ed.) *Depression and narrative: telling the dark* (pp. 97–109). Albany, NY: SUNY Press.

Narcotics Division, Security Bureau, the Government of the Hong Kong Special Administrative Region. 2009. *Voluntary in-patient treatment/residential drug rehabilitation programmes*. Retrieved from www.nd.gov.hk/en/6–1–2.htm 14 October 2013.

Operation Dawn. 2013. *Our program*. Retrieved from www.opdawn.org/program/ 4 September 2013.

Ramsay, G. 2008. *Shaping minds: a discourse analysis of Chinese-language community mental health literature*. Amsterdam: John Benjamins.

Ramsay, G. 2013. *Mental illness, dementia and family in China*. London: Routledge.

SARDA. 2011a. *History and aims*. Retrieved from www.sarda.org.hk/en/Objective.html 17 September 2013.

SARDA. 2011b. *Shek Kwu Chau Treatment and Rehabilitation Centre*. Retrieved from www.sarda.org.hk/en/SKCTRCH.html 17 September 2013.

Scambler, G. 2004. Re-framing stigma: felt and enacted stigma and challenges to the sociology of chronic and disabling conditions. *Social Theory and Health*, 2, 29–46.

Shu, L. W., *et al.* [束連文等著]. 2003. *Young people, treasure your youth!* [少年人, 寶貝你的年輕!]. Taipei: Dawn Press [晨曦出版社].

Taiwan Ministry of Justice [法務部]. 2010. *Quitting drugs: stop, look, listen* [戒毒停看聽]. Retrieved from http://refrain.moj.gov.tw/lp.asp?ctNode=401&ctUnit=121&baseDSD=7&mp=1&ps 15 October 2013.

Tolton, L. 2009. *Legitimation of violence against women in Colombia: a feminist critical discourse analytic study*. Unpublished doctoral dissertation. St Lucia, QLD: The University of Queensland.

Tong, W. [佟薇]. 2013, June 26. Difficulties encountered as the people's force moves forward in drug rehabilitation [戒毒民间力量艰难前行]. *Kunming Daily* [昆明日报]. Retrieved from http://daily.clzg.cn/html/2013–06/26/content_359163.htm 27 August 2013.

Wong, D. 2000. Stress factors and mental health of carers with relatives suffering from schizophrenia in Hong Kong: implications for culturally sensitive practices. *British Journal of Social Work*, 30, 365–382.

Yang, L. H. and Kleinman, A. 2008. 'Face' and the embodiment of stigma in China: the cases of schizophrenia and AIDS. *Social Science and Medicine*, 67, 398–408.

Yip, K. S. 2007. *Mental health service in the People's Republic of China: current status and future developments*. New York, NY: Nova Science Publishers.

Yunnan People's Publishing House. 2010. Retrieved from http://ynpress.yunshow.com/ 17 August 2013.

4 Marginalisation and palliation

Filmic stories of drug addiction, rehabilitation and recovery

This chapter examines how cultural, political and institutional discourses shape filmic stories of drug addiction, rehabilitation and recovery that are recounted in six contemporary film and television productions: two from mainland China, two from Taiwan and two from Hong Kong. The filmic stories recount the experience of drug addiction, rehabilitation and recovery of Chinese men, women and young adults. Like the life stories in Chapter 3, they originate from three neighbouring Chinese communities that have differing political systems and histories. In contrast to the life stories in Chapters 2 and 3, they are fictional or quasi-documentary accounts that, to a large extent, present a filmmaker's or television maker's 'outsider' perspective on drug addiction, rehabilitation and recovery (Ramsay 2013). The chapter's analysis of the filmic stories proceeds by, first, summarising the story of a drug addict that is portrayed in a film or television production; and, second, examining how cultural, political and institutional discourses shape temporality, subjectivity and language use in this story. The chapter compares and contrasts the analytic findings for the mainland Chinese, Taiwanese and Hong Kong filmic stories. It also compares and contrasts these findings with those for the life stories that are analysed in Chapters 2 and 3.

The cultural meta-narrative of drug addiction

This chapter's analysis of filmic stories usefully complements the analyses of life stories that have been undertaken in Chapters 2 and 3. This is because the filmmaker's or television maker's perspective on drug addiction, rehabilitation and recovery will more readily draw on 'the prevailing meta-narrative that circulates in a cultural community . . . aspects of which may remain hidden from view in life stories told by those inside the experience' (Ramsay 2013, p. 61). This meta-narrative equates to the dominant story of drug addiction that characterises culturally Chinese communities such as mainland China, Taiwan and Hong Kong.

The ensuing analysis will identify the character and resonance of this cultural meta-narrative across the six film and television productions from mainland

74 *Marginalisation and palliation*

China, Taiwan and Hong Kong. In this way, the analysis will ascertain whether the political systems and histories of geographical communities can have a bearing on the manner in which filmic stories engage the prevailing cultural meta-narrative. In addition, the analysis will consider whether these filmic stories discursively malign and marginalise the Chinese drug addicts in ways similar to the life stories in Chapters 2 and 3. It also will consider whether the filmic stories, alternatively, discursively palliate the Chinese drug addicts and, so, absolve them of the moral transgressions that they commit during drug addiction. In either case, the analysis will point out how these stories utilise the key narrative processes of temporality, subjectivity and language use, in order to achieve a greater marginalisation or palliation of the Chinese drug addict.

Mainland Chinese filmic stories

Two mainland Chinese films that tell the stories of Chinese people with drug addiction are analysed in this section. The 2001 film *Quitting*[1] [昨天] [*Lit*. Yesterday] is directed by Zhang Yang [张扬], a well-known contemporary mainland Chinese film director. *Quitting* tells the story of Jia Hongsheng's [贾宏声] drug addiction, rehabilitation and recovery in Beijing in the 1990s. Jia, a young man in his late twenties, had been a well-known mainland Chinese actor during the late 1980s and early 1990s, but had slipped into obscurity as a result of his drug addiction. The film employs a quasi-documentary style, with Jia, his family and other cast members playing their own characters in the film. Sadly, in real life, Jia committed suicide in 2010. He was in his forties. The other film, *The War of Two*[2] [两个人的战争], is a 2005 remake of a 1997 television serial drama, *Red Recipe* [红处方] [*Lit*. Red Prescription]. The television serial drama, in turn, was based on a novel of the same title by mainland Chinese literary writer Bi Shumin [毕淑敏]. Both the 2005 film and the 1997 television serial drama were produced by Tianjin Television [天津电视台] and were directed by Dong Zhiqiang [董志强], a less-well-known but prolific mainland Chinese film and television director. *The War of Two* tells the story of Pei Pei's [佩佩] drug addiction, rehabilitation and recovery in Tianjin, a mainland Chinese city, during the 1990s. Pei Pei, a young woman in her late teens, is unemployed and cared for at home by her widowed mother. The film focuses in particular on their 'mother-daughter relationship', a hallmark of many films of the period (Vanderstaay 2011, p. 69).

Quitting

The film begins with a *vox populi* about Jia Hongsheng. Members of the public share their mixed opinions of Jia as an actor, some noting his drug addiction. Jia's story then begins with the arrival of his parents from their home in the northeast of China. They have retired early to come to Beijing to care for their son, due to his 'troubles and difficulties' [这么大的麻烦和困难]. This is their duty as his parents [作为父母应该过来照顾他]. Jia is indifferent upon meeting his parents and simply turns his back on them and returns to his bedroom, closing the door. He initially ignores them upon rising the following day, then mocks them as 'peasants' for using laundry soap for bathing [这是农民用的] and admonishes his mother for entering his room without his permission [谁让你进来]. He rudely orders her to 'get out!' [出去!], even though she merely was cleaning the unkempt room while Jia was bathing.

Jia's parents initially voice their dissatisfaction with his current indolence and poor financial circumstances [拿什么养活自己]. Jia dismisses their criticisms and, in turn, criticises his father for his use of northeastern dialect. The father speaks to Jia privately, expressing that Jia's life is no longer 'normal' [正常] and that he is not the person he was before [你和过去不一样了]. The father accuses Jia of still using illicit drugs [你还在吸毒啊!] and slaps him. Troubled by Jia's behaviour toward them, the parents seek medical advice. They are told to indulge Jia's every wish, which they try to do with some success. They buy him a bicycle, which he finds ugly. However, after some adjustments, he starts taking the bicycle out on regular rides. The parents diligently follow him, in fear that he is going out to buy illicit drugs.

Jia's story briefly turns back to his initiation into illicit drug use. At the time, in the early 1990s, he had acted in many productions and had burnt out mentally [脑子都拍空了]. Jia begins using illicit drugs with co-workers during rehearsals for a stage play in which he had a major role. His 'reaction' to illicit drugs is 'especially intense; unlike anyone else's' [反映就特别强烈, 和所有人都不一样]. At the time, Jia reports that his co-workers had mocked his acting. He had wanted to prove that he could 'become an actor admired by all' [一定要成为让所有人都佩服的演员]. He also wanted to show that he was 'fashionable' [时髦]. Using illicit drugs was one way to achieve these aims. Jia's mother and a co-worker concur that the essential character flaw that had led to Jia's drug addiction was his 'vanity' [虚荣]. This vanity, in turn, is linked to his disdain for his parents' peasant backgrounds.

Returning to the time of the family co-residing in Beijing, Jia's relationship with his parents ostensibly has improved. The medical advice to indulge his every wish seems to have paid off. Jia's father regularly accompanies him on a daily walk, dressed, on Jia's insistence, in tight jeans. The father, however, remains 'somewhat afraid' of Jia [心里总是有点儿怕他] and unhesitatingly agrees to a request from Jia to buy beer. The father and son sit under a freeway and drink the beer together, once again, on Jia's insistence. The father drinks, even though he has had issues with alcohol in the past. While sitting under the freeway, Jia recites the lyrics of a favourite Beatles song and his father agrees to buy Jia a Beatles music cassette. Over time, Jia becomes more communicative with both of his parents and in a tender moment, one day under the freeway, he acknowledges

76   *Marginalisation and palliation*

his father as his 'Dad' [你是我爹]. This developing connection between Jia and his parents, however, is ruptured one morning when he demands that they give him money to buy noodles at the local street stall. He had been out all night long and they suspect him of having used illicit drugs. They claim that they have no money. He does not believe them [你怎么老没钱呀, 你!] and angrily threatens to smash their television set if they do not give in to his demand. They capitulate. Later on, during his daily walk and rest under the freeway, Jia suddenly begins cursing passersby. He 'thinks that they all are idiots' [我感觉他们都是白痴]. He, on the other hand, is the son of Beatles' legend, John Lennon.

At this juncture, Jia's filmic story reflects back on his past friendship with an art designer, who also was a talented rock musician. The friend moves in with Jia and paints a mural of John Lennon on the wall of his bedroom. The two spend their days listening to rock music and using illicit drugs. Eventually, however, they grow apart and, when the friend finds a girlfriend, the friendship comes to an end. This causes Jia to completely cut himself off from people. He feels unhappy with other people and with himself [好像就是想和自己掷气]. Contributing to this feeling is Jia's dissatisfaction with acting. He resolves to never perform again and destroys his video cassettes and television set. He then bangs his head repeatedly on the wall of his apartment. Later on, he approaches a musician friend to start a rock music band. Jia views acting as 'too pretentious' [演戏太虚伪呀], while rock music is 'real' [是真的]. The friend agrees and teaches Jia to play the guitar. He, however, finds it awkward to communicate with Jia and grows fearful of him [越来越害怕]. He leaves Jia after only two weeks, leaving Jia feeling 'disillusioned with everyone' [我对所有的人都失望了]. Jia spends time alone, gazing aimlessly out of his apartment window. One day, he observes a cloud take the form of a dragon. The dragon has his eyes. Jia now is destitute. He steals cabbages from his neighbour for food. His younger sister, who has moved in with him, pays his utility bills and stocks his refrigerator.

Returning to the time of the family co-residing in Beijing, Jia turns down an offer of an acting role. His parents are taken aback by this. Jia, however, derides acting as 'deceitful' [骗人]. His parents are insulted by this, as they have been actors for all of their lives. Jia hurtfully snaps, 'you have deceived people for all of your life, you just don't know it' [自己骗了一辈子人不知道自己干什么的]. Jia's parents believe that they have always behaved as 'clean moral human beings' [清清白白做人]. Yet, Jia callously accuses them of deceiving themselves in thinking that they had come to Beijing to help out their son. Adding insult to injury, later that night, Jia questions his parents over his heritage. He is convinced that he is John Lennon's son. His delusions and hallucinations soon worsen. In the daytime, he can see the dragon outside of his apartment window once again, while, at night, he argues loudly with himself and smashes things violently. The parents seek medical advice and the doctors diagnose drug-induced psychosis, in Jia's absence. Jia's parents are warned that he may harm someone, if he is not watched carefully. The parents return home and search Jia's room, where they find illicit drugs. They confront Jia on his return home. Jia is unrepentant and angry that they have gone through his belongings. He finds it hypocritical that his father would be concerned about his illicit drug use, when the father 'has been a drunk' for his 'entire life' [你这一辈子是酒鬼, 你管不了我].

On Jia's twenty-ninth birthday, he insists that his father drink beer with him. After many beers, Jia refutes that his father is his real father. He proclaims that John Lennon is his father. He states that a peasant could never be his father. Jia then proceeds to aggressively question whether his parents' generation has meaningful and happy lives. The father is confused by his son's tirade. Jia subsequently declares that he 'will make' him 'understand' [今天我让你明白]. With this, he repeatedly and violently slaps his father's face. The entire family now lives in fear of Jia [恐惧, 每时每刻都潜伏在我们身边]. He loses his mother's support when he denies that she is his mother. His sister insists that he be admitted to a hospital. Jia, meanwhile, is paranoid that 'everyone around' him 'is trying to harm' him [我感觉所有的人都想害]. He entertains thoughts of death. Police officers, however, soon arrive to detain Jia. They had been summoned by the local neighbourhood committee [居委会] and Jia's mother. The police treat him kindly and escort him to a hospital. In the hospital, Jia repeats his delusional thoughts to medical staff. He is placed in a ward with a number of men with mental illness. He takes on their appearance, dressing in the hospital pyjamas that they wear. He also eats with them and communes with them in the activities yard. Jia's parents visit him regularly and bring him food. He, however, becomes unhappy about being in the hospital and curses his parents for allowing him to be admitted. Moreover, he angrily refuses to take his medication, following which he is retrained on his bed and compelled to take the medication.

One night in the hospital, Jia is revisited by the dragon. The dragon questions Jia about his identity [它问我: 你是谁?]. Jia replies with his name and his former vocations and dreams. The dragon corrects Jia, declaring that 'you are nothing; you are just a person' [你什么都不是, 你就是一个人]. The dragon adds that Jia is in the hospital as 'punishment' [惩罚] for his past 'evil' [恶]. Only here can he be 'cleansed' [清理出去]. The following day Jia is interviewed by mental health specialists. They decide that he must remain in the facility. Three months later, Jia appears to have adjusted to life in the hospital. By chance, he runs into his former drug buddy, who has been admitted to a neighbouring facility. Jia tells his friend that he 'finds it alright' [我觉得还行] in the facility, and that he wishes to stay here until he can swear off illicit drugs and alcohol. The friend informs him that the friend's former girlfriend, in fact, had died while using illicit drugs. After a year's stay in hospital, Jia leaves, apparently recovered. He is attentive and civil to his family. He no longer is angered by his parents' use of laundry soap for personal use, and he readily accepts his mother reminding him to take his medication. On the night of Jia's return from hospital, the family celebrates his

78 *Marginalisation and palliation*

thirtieth birthday, which his parents had forgotten, but for which he has gone out and bought food. The father offers to go to the store to buy beer to celebrate the occasion, but Jia turns him down: he 'has quit' [我戒了]. The film concludes with Jia's family going about their regular, everyday activities.

Analysis

Drug addiction in *Quitting* is presented as morally transgressive behaviour that equates to mental illness. Like mental illness, it only can be effectively treated by way of acute medical intervention. The transgressive nature of drug addiction is foregrounded in *Quitting* by the film's temporal focus on Jia's life during drug addiction and, in particular, the impact of his drug addiction on his family. There are no depictions of Jia's life from before drug addiction, for example his childhood together with his family in northeast China. Depiction of this period of his life may have counterbalanced the immoral behaviour that characterises his life during drug addiction. His life in recovery from drug addiction takes a distinct turn for the better, upon returning home to live an everyday life with his family after a protracted stay in a psychiatric-hospital-cum-drug-rehabilitation-facility. However, he now carries an illness identity that would taint him and his family for the rest of their lives in Chinese culture (Ramsay 2008, 2013). As a consequence, Jia is constructed as an immoral human being, whose drug addiction has needlessly troubled, burdened and defiled his family. This contrasts with his elderly parents' and his younger sister's moral human conduct [做人]. His parents fulfil their culturally prescribed responsibilities and care for their child when he is in need, even though they must sacrifice their acting careers by retiring early. They fully comply with medical advice as they care for their mentally ill son, even though this comes at great cost to their own self-respect and their financial wellbeing. They only abandon the care of their son in the home when violence intervenes. Abandoning care in such a circumstance does not necessarily violate their cultural obligations in caregiving for a family member (Ramsay 2013).

Jia, on the other hand, is a cold, callous, selfish and unfilial young man when drug-addicted. He disrespects his parents by ignoring them, chastising them, threatening them, taking advantage of their generosity, and mocking their peasant backgrounds and their dialect-inflected manner of speech. These behaviours grossly violate Chinese cultural norms and values, even in contemporary mainland Chinese society where filiality is taking on new meanings (Cheung & Kwan 2009). For a moment, *Quitting* proffers a more sympathetic portrayal of Jia, when he begins to communicate with his parents and to call his father 'Dad'. Any emergent sympathetic feelings, however, are shattered by Jia's extreme moral transgression in viciously beating his elderly father, in a deluded attempt to make him understand the meaning of 'life' [人为什么要活着] and 'happiness' [什么叫快乐]. These are notions that Jia believes his parents' generation does not understand [你们这一代人从来都没有活明白过]. The fundamental cause of Jia's illicit drug use, namely his innate vanity, also limits any sympathy that may have been generated by the apparent pressures of his acting career. This vanity not only manifests in an intense desire to be liked and admired by peers and the general public, but also in a rejection of, and ongoing contempt for, his family's peasant roots.

The drug addict in *Quitting* is not only morally transgressive, but also marked by subjective fragility. Jia lives a largely solitary existence before his family moves into his apartment. He repeatedly fails to maintain connections with others. His friendships are short-lived and he has no romantic interests. People quickly distance themselves from Jia, because they fear him. Fear is a constant motif throughout *Quitting*. Both family and friends fear Jia. Jia, in turn, fears the dragon that haunts him during his drug addiction. The dragon calls attention to his insignificance and his subjective fragility during drug addiction. He 'is nothing; just a person' [你什么都不是, 你就是一个人]. He could not maintain an identity as an actor or rock musician, or maintain active membership of the acting and rock music communities. He does not competently play the role of son to his elderly parents or the role of older brother to his younger sister. He does not take on, nor is he assigned, the label of drug addict in his story. Moreover, he is not overtly connected to an illicit-drug-using community. The only identity and community connection that Jia successfully maintains in *Quitting* is that of patient in the psychiatric hospital, where he is treated for drug addiction and comorbid psychosis. His embracing of this identity paves the way for his recovery from drug addiction and his return to his family, where he now behaves in a culturally normative manner.

Linguistically and figuratively, drug addiction in *Quitting* is biomedicalised as mental illness (madness). Health professionals play a prominent role in Jia's story, with a consistently beneficial impact. Medical advice improves the relationship between Jia and his family, after the parents move into his apartment. Health professionals also correctly diagnose his comorbid psychosis and warn of the violence that could eventuate if he is not kept under constant scrutiny. Finally, Jia's recovery from drug addiction only occurs after his involuntary admission to a psychiatric hospital. Jia is not 'normal' [正常]. This is a state of being commonly ascribed to people with a mental illness in Chinese culture (Ramsay 2013). In addition, Jia is feared. Fear constitutes a common reaction to people with a mental illness in Chinese culture and significantly contributes to the intense cultural stigma that is directed against them by Chinese society (Kleinman *et al.* 2011; Ramsay 2013). This fear stems from a deemed heightened potential for people with a mental illness to commit violent acts. Such an association between mental illness and random violence, in particular, is propagated by the mainland Chinese press (Kleinman *et al.* 2011). As a consequence, it is unsurprising that, in *Quitting*, the progressively worsening psychotic episodes that mark Jia's drug addiction culminate in a disturbing act of violence against his unsuspecting father.

80 *Marginalisation and palliation*

In sum, Jia's story of drug addiction, rehabilitation and recovery, as depicted in *Quitting*, aligns with a dominant meta-narrative in Chinese culture that presents drug addiction as morally transgressive and something to be feared. Kleinman *et al.* (2011, p. 255) observe that illicit drug use in mainland China is not just an expression of 'personal lifestyle or individual morality', but a distinct 'betrayal of the family'. In his film, Zhang Yang foregrounds this familial dimension to moral transgression in drug addiction, in line with the cultural meta-narrative. He does not foreground broader social transgressions, such as criminality and violating gender norms, which are prominent in the mainland Chinese life stories that are analysed in Chapters 2 and 3. As such, Jia's transgressions against (and betrayal of) his family when drug-addicted, which culminate in a callous act of family violence, enhance the emotional import of the vagaries of drug addiction as portrayed in *Quitting*. Drug addiction also leaves his family permanently tainted with the shame of mental illness, a fate worse than death in Chinese culture (Ramsay 2008, 2013).

While cultural discourse appears to shape this filmic story in these ways, political (and possibly institutional) discourse may shape the benevolent portrayals of the arresting police officers and the staff of the psychiatric hospital. The latter come across as caring and understanding professionals, even though, at one point, they forcibly bind Jia to his bed in order to procure his behavioural and pharmacotherapeutic compliance. Political discourse also may direct that Jia does not successfully quit illicit drugs through his own efforts or those of his family. Rather, well-intentioned intervention by the state and its affiliated institutions – the neighbourhood committee, the police and the psychiatric hospital – leads Jia away from the vagaries of drug addiction and onto the path of recovery.

The War of Two

The film begins with Pei Pei's mother frantically searching for her daughter on the city streets. Pei Pei has run away from a drug rehabilitation facility. She phones her boyfriend, Gao Peng [高朋], a high-class art and heroin dealer, and meets him at a club. As the pair plays billiards, she impudently belittles him for being servile to his female drug-dealing partner [你用不着这么崇拜她, 没劲. 我原来以为你挺像回事儿的, 可是现在你也让我失望]. Pei Pei considers her to be nothing but a common drug dealer [她有什么了不起的, 不就是一个毒贩吗?]. Gao Peng responds that the pair should not see each other anymore. He feels that this will be to both of their benefit. Pei Pei replies that he is the first person who she wanted to see after escaping from the drug rehabilitation facility, yet now he just makes her feel sick [没想到一见面, 你让我这么恶心]. She storms off, declaring that it is easy to find a man in this world [天下的男人, 有的是!].

Outside the club, Pei Pei reunites with her boyfriend. She intends to go home with him, but her mother arrives at the club. She asks her mother why she has wasted her time looking for her, when she should just consider her daughter to be dead [妈, 你说你到处找我干吗? 这么多余吗? 你就当我死了多清静]. She, nevertheless, elects to return home with her. Back at home, Pei Pei ignores her mother when she speaks to her. When her mother goes out to buy some groceries, she immediately uses some heroin that she has hidden in her clothes. The mother returns to find Pei Pei obviously affected by illicit drugs. Pei Pei condescendingly avows that 'heroin is the most wonderful thing in the world' [世上最美好的东西就是海洛因啊]. She adds that she 'can never give it up' [戒, 我是戒不了了] and that there is nothing that her mother can do to stop her from using heroin [你又不能把我怎么样?]. The mother patiently replies that she has bought some fish for their dinner and some new sleeping attire for Pei Pei to wear at night. She then cooks dinner, telling Pei Pei that she could never abandon her [佩佩, 妈妈怎么会不管你呢?]. As she works in the kitchen, she suggests that they should visit another drug rehabilitation facility the following day. Pei Pei, however, angrily rejects the idea. She claims that she would rather commit suicide than quit using illicit drugs [你要真的让我去戒毒, 我就真的死给你看: 跳楼啊、摸电门啊、吃安眠药、上吊啊。 活、死了, 我没什么]. She curses her mother for giving birth to her, making her suffer in life, and then denying her the simplest of pleasures in life that heroin brings [干吗要生我, 这不存心让我痛苦吗?! . . . 刚刚想离开家痛快地飘几天, 你倒好, 满世界找我, 到处张扬]. She also admonishes her mother for exposing her heroin addiction to the world and causing them both to lose face [你不嫌丢人, 我还嫌丢人呢]. She states that 'it is now clear' to her 'that the grandeur of ecstasy is greater than the grandeur of this world, and the love of heroin is greater than a father's or mother's love' [我算是看透了, 这个世界, 天大地大, 不如摇头丸大, 爹亲娘亲不如海洛因亲]. She then takes some money from her mother's drawer and goes out, proclaiming, as she leaves, that she 'already is a woman' [已经是个女人了].

Pei Pei meets Gao Peng and his drug-dealing partner at a dance club. Inside the club, she recalls that this is where she had first used illicit drugs. At that time, Gao Peng's drug-dealing partner had supplied heroin to her for free. The drug-dealing partner asks Pei Pei about her future plans. Pei Pei replies that the drug dealer need not worry about her future; that she can make her own way in life [你用不着操心这个, 我自己的路, 我自己会走]. She informs the pair that she intends to become a drug dealer, just like them, only better. She then insults Gao Peng's drug-dealing partner and leaves after reassuring the pair that she will not report them to the police. Pei Pei's mother is waiting for her in the foyer of the dance club. She apologises to Pei Pei for having made her angry and offers her some of her favourite chewing gum. Pei Pei says that she does not like that flavour. She angrily asks her mother 'what the hell are you up to?!' [你到底想干什么?!] and storms outside. The pair returns home together in a taxi, where the mother professes how lonely she had felt when Pei Pei was in the drug rehabilitation facility. The mother shows Pei Pei a photograph of her deceased father and laments that

82   *Marginalisation and palliation*

things would have been different now, if he were still alive [要是你爸爸还活着, 我们家就不会这样, 你也不会这样]. Pei Pei's father was a People's Liberation Army soldier, who had sacrificed his life to save the lives of two comrades during an exercise in Tibet. Pei Pei disrespectfully throws the photograph of her father face-down onto her bed. Her mother angrily insists that Pei Pei turn the photograph over and look at her father [你看着你爸爸]. She then slaps Pei Pei, despairing as to how 'inhuman' her heroin-addicted daughter has become [难道海洛因就把你变得怎么没有人心吗?!]. She tells Pei Pei that she cannot care for her anymore and that she can 'use drugs until' she 'dies' [你吸死算了, 我再也不会管你了]. After the mother has left the room, Pei Pei turns over the photograph of her father and pensively gazes at it.

Two days later, Pei Pei has decided to quit illicit drugs and rehabilitate at home. She flushes her remaining supply of heroin down the toilet. Her mother comforts her while she suffers the inevitable drug withdrawal symptoms. Sometime later, Pei Pei is in recovery from drug addiction. She is kind and considerate to her mother, who now leaves her alone at home, albeit locked in. Gao Peng, however, manages to contact Pei Pei and send her some heroin. She accepts the heroin, hesitates, flushes some down the toilet, but hides one satchel behind the photograph of her martyred father. She then tries to get out of the apartment, but her mother has locked her in. Later on, she uses the heroin that she had hidden behind the photograph. Her mother eventually returns home, excited that Pei Pei's recent drug test had come up negative. Pei Pei asks her permission to go out that night to a music recital. The mother, however, is reluctant. She fears that Pei Pei will fall back into illicit drug use, not realising that she already has relapsed. Pei Pei threatens that she will start using heroin again, if she never can be allowed to go out [那我如果一辈子待在家里的话, 我戒了毒又有什么用呀. 我还不如接着吸呢]. As a result, the mother gives in to her daughter's request.

That night, Pei Pei meets her boyfriend and procures more heroin. He convinces her to surreptitiously addict her mother to heroin, so that the mother will leave her alone. When Pei Pei returns home, her mother is furious. She knows that Pei Pei did not go to the music recital. Pei Pei boasts that she, in fact, had casual sex in a hotel room. She asserts that quitting illicit drugs does not require her 'to give up everything' [我戒毒, 干吗把什么都戒了?]. The mother collapses on hearing this news. Pei Pei takes advantage of the opportunity to offer her mother a glass of water that she has laced with heroin. After her mother drinks the water, Pei Pei expressionlessly tells her to 'get some rest and all will be fine' [好好睡一觉就没事了]. Some days later, both mother and daughter are addicted to heroin. The mother, who is unaware that she, too, is addicted, finds out that Pei Pei has failed her most recent drug test. Pei Pei is wholly unconcerned, declaring that 'heroin could not be heroin if people could give it up' [海洛因要是能戒, 那还叫海洛因吗?]. She reveals that she surreptitiously has addicted her mother to heroin, teasingly displaying a satchel of heroin in her hand. She assures her mother that

Marginalisation and palliation 83

'the feeling that heroin gives will be forever etched in your memory' [海洛因的感觉就会让你刻骨铭心]. The mother is distraught. She brands her daughter a 'killer' [毒手], whose 'most basic humanity' has been taken away by heroin [海洛因能使你丧失最起码的人心]. She reports Pei Pei to the police, who come to arrest her. The mother laments, 'Mama cannot take care of you anymore, so let the government take care of you' [妈妈已经管不了你, 让政府来管教你吧]. Pei Pei curses her mother as 'shameless' [你才是恬不知耻] and escapes from the apartment before the police arrive.

Pei Pei goes to live with Gao Peng. Some days later, she tells him that she is going to visit her mother for her birthday. She imagines that her mother 'now must be craving' heroin and 'awaiting rescue' by her daughter [她现在也熬得差不多了, 正等着我回去救她呢]. Pei Pei's mother, however, is not pleased to see her. Pei Pei offers her some fruit juice laced with heroin, which the mother initially rejects but then drinks. Afterward, the mother goes into the kitchen and laces a birthday cake, which Pei Pei has bought for her, with poison. At the last minute, however, she warns off Pei Pei from eating the cake. Pei Pei disregards her mother's warnings and madly eats the cake, even though she now suspects that it contains poison that may kill her. She muses, 'Heroin is really fabulous. It can make you, such a kind mother, become so vicious' [海洛因真是了不起, 能让你这么善良的妈妈也改变得这么狠毒]. Within moments, Pei Pei collapses. She is hospitalised and placed in a drug rehabilitation facility. Her mother confesses to the attending doctor that she has lost all hope that Pei Pei could ever be a 'normal person' [正常人] (Gao 2011), and that 'she is heading for destruction and degradation' [她走向毁灭, 走向堕落]. Pei Pei, in the meantime, initially rejects the detoxification treatment that is prescribed to her by the doctor. She coldly accuses her mother, who brings her the medicine, of wanting to further poison her. A kind woman nurse, however, counsels Pei Pei to fully reflect on her behaviour [你好想想]. Thereafter, she elects to rehabilitate and return home with her mother.

Back at home, Pei Pei is kind and attentive to her mother and agrees to study to become a nurse. Once again, Gao Peng contacts her ten days later. He claims that he loves her and proposes marriage. He also confesses to being a drug addict and to lacing the groceries, which Pei Pei's mother had just bought at the market, with heroin. As a result, Pei Pei meets him at a café where she begs him to give up heroin. He repeats his marriage proposal and takes her to his villa, where he claims to have a reserve of expensive alcohol. They drink the alcohol and, while Gao Peng is asleep, Pei Pei binds him to the bed and covers him in packages of heroin. He awakes, startled. He tells her that he had laced the chewing gum, which he had given her at the café, with heroin. She replies that she had known this all along and, so, had switched the chewing gum. She then violently stuffs the packet of heroin-laced chewing gum into her boyfriend's mouth. He chokes, spits it out, and angrily calls her 'a stinking slut' [你干吗, 臭婊子?]. Pei Pei proceeds to smash several of the bottles of alcohol on the bedroom floor and to pour

84 *Marginalisation and palliation*

alcohol over the tethered boyfriend. She emotionlessly tells him that 'it's too late' [太晚了]. She then ignites some matches and sets fire to the room. Pei Pei and Gao Peng are burnt to death in the ensuing inferno.[3]

Analysis

Drug addiction in *The War of Two* is presented as morally transgressive behaviour that inevitably leads to death. The transgressive nature of drug addiction is foregrounded in *The War of Two* by the film's temporal focus on Pei Pei's life during drug addiction and, in particular, the impact of her drug addiction on her widowed mother. There are no depictions of Pei Pei's life from before drug addiction, for example her childhood with her parents in Tibet. Her life in recovery from drug addiction furthermore is short-lived and marked by a violent murder-suicide. Scant attention, therefore, is given in the film to episodes in Pei Pei's life that could counterbalance the immoral behaviour that characterises her life during drug addiction. Pei Pei's immoral behaviour in drug addiction greatly impacts her family. This underscores the transgressive nature of her drug addiction in Chinese culture, as in *Quitting* (Kleinman *et al.* 2011). She is unkind, deceitful, selfish, manipulative and condescending to her widowed mother, who makes every effort and sacrifice to care for her troubled daughter. She deliberately addicts her mother to heroin, which drives her to poison her drug-addicted daughter, just so she can be put into a hospital and treated for her heroin addiction. Pei Pei also shamelessly disrespects the memory of her martyred father, by hiding a satchel of heroin behind the treasured photograph of him in his military uniform.

Pei Pei's moral transgressions during drug addiction are further accentuated by her corrupted performance of normative womanhood in Chinese culture. She takes on the identity of a modern, self-sufficient mainland Chinese woman (Guo 2010; Mann 2011). However, she seeks out financial gain in the lucrative local heroin trade. She also conflates self-confidence and self-conviction with brashness and arrogance, and misconstrues feminine autonomy as sexual promiscuity. This deeply offends her conservative mother. In her role as a filial daughter, she chooses to live with her mother, but only when there is nowhere else to live. She also willingly addicts her mother to heroin, because it is a pleasure that very few people can afford [我这样也是在孝顺你吗? 有些人想吸海洛因, 还吸不到]. This corrupted performance of normative womanhood in Chinese culture stands in contrast to the virtuous performance by the kind woman nurse who looks after Pei Pei in the government-run drug rehabilitation facility and motivates her to reflect on her heroin use and embrace recovery.

Pei Pei's corrupted performance of normative womanhood in Chinese culture, coupled with her moral transgressions during drug addiction, seemingly condemn her to death in *The War of Two*. Her climactic murder-suicide is equally unfeminine, on two accounts. First, her act resembles the 'honourable death' of *wu* [武]

Marginalisation and palliation   85

('martial') men in Chinese chivalry tales of old (Maggs 2012, pp. 65, 68). This is because she is able to atone for her previous moral failings, by eliminating from society an evil menace [高朋做的孽太多了] who 'deserved to be punished' [他应该受到惩罚]. Second, the justness of her deadly act is symbolically evoked by covering Gao Peng with packets of heroin, before setting fire to him and his stash of illicit drugs. The mainland Chinese government ritualistically incinerates confiscated illicit drugs in public, as part of anti-drug campaigns and as a prelude to the execution of convicted drug criminals (Levin 2015; Liang & Lu 2013; Lu, Miethe & Liang 2009; Trevaskes 2007, 2013; Zhou 1999, 2000a, 2000b). This contemporary 'political ritual' harks back to the destruction of foreign opium by legendary anti-opium crusader, Lin Zexu [林则徐], in southern China in 1839, in the lead up to the Opium Wars (Baumler 2007, p. 9). Lin Zexu's heroic act and the ensuing wars are decidedly masculine phenomena.

Language use in *The War of Two* discursively conforms to these masculinised notions of (just) death and violence. *War* invokes the political language of the mainland Chinese government's 'people's war against drugs' [人民禁毒战争] (Liang & Lu 2013, p. 315. See Chapter 2). *War* also connotes death and killing. Both Pei Pei and her mother equate heroin addiction to death and killing. Pei Pei proclaims that death by suicide is preferable to giving up heroin. In the end, she suicides (and murders). The masculinised death and violence that characterises this filmic story of a mainland Chinese woman drug addict is absent from the counterpart story of a mainland Chinese male drug addict in *Quitting*. Jia is able to atone for his previous moral failings, by simply returning to participate in and contribute to everyday family life. That said, he remains marked by mental illness, which is a fate worse than death in Chinese culture (Ramsay 2008, 2013). Jia also is not denigrated by way of gendered language in *Quitting*. Pei Pei, on the other hand, is labelled a 'stinking slut' [臭婊子]. Such language encodes her transgression of normative womanhood in Chinese culture. It also discursively aligns with mainland Chinese mass media depictions of women drug addicts 'as the most shameless human beings on the earth' (Zhou 1999, p. 119). Common to the two mainland Chinese filmic stories are the descriptions of drug addicts as abnormal. Such language discursively connects them to people with a mental illness, thereby marking them as violent and to be feared (Kleinman *et al.* 2011). Jia's attack on his father is disturbing, but Pei Pei kills. This may be because she has no moral man to support her and guide her in her recovery from drug addiction, unlike Wang, the mainland Chinese woman drug addict in *Struggle Spirit* (see Chapter 2). The moral man in Pei Pei's life, namely, her martyred father, is dead.

In sum, Pei Pei's story of drug addiction, rehabilitation and recovery, as depicted in *The War of Two*, aligns with a dominant meta-narrative in Chinese culture that presents drug addiction as morally transgressive and something to be feared. The familial dimension to transgression in drug addiction is foregrounded in the

86 *Marginalisation and palliation*

mainland Chinese filmic story, in line with the cultural meta-narrative (Kleinman *et al.* 2011). Betrayal of the family also featured in *Quitting*. The woman drug addict's moral and cultural disembodiment (Kleinman *et al.* 2011; Traphagan 2000), however, is more complete. Ostensibly traditional behaviours as a daughter and a woman in Chinese culture are corrupted: Pei Pei considers it filial to addict her mother to heroin; and her suicide, as a disgraced woman, is carried out in a masculine and callously violent manner. It appears that the woman drug addict's corrupted performance of normative gender in Chinese culture, coupled with her moral transgressions during drug addiction, seal her mortal and violent fate in *The War of Two*, especially in the absence of a moral man to support her and guide her in her recovery from drug addiction (Cai 2005). A considerably more sanguine fate awaited her morally transgressive, yet, arguably, masculine, male counterpart in *Quitting*.

While cultural discourse appears to shape this filmic story in these ways, political (and possibly institutional) discourse may shape the benevolent portrayal of the government-run drug rehabilitation facility, where Pei Pei rehabilitates and recovers from her heroin addiction. The staff of this facility is kind, honourable and dedicated. A similar portrayal characterises the mainland Chinese film, *Quitting*. Political discourse also may shape the use of the language of war and the allusions to contemporary and past national drug campaigns in the film.

Taiwanese filmic stories

Two Taiwanese films that tell the stories of Chinese people with drug addiction are analysed in this section. The 2007 film *Help Me Eros*[4] [幫幫我愛神] is directed by Lee Kang-sheng [李康生], a well-known contemporary Taiwanese actor and, more recently, film director. *Help Me Eros* tells the story of Ah Jie's [阿杰] drug addiction in present-day Kaohsiung [高雄], a large city in southern Taiwan. Ah Jie, a young man in his late twenties, has lost his job and now devotes all his time and energy to his substantial marijuana habit. The film is marked by dark humour and magic realist elements that tie in with the film's depiction of drug-induced fantasy and illusion. The 2011 film *Jump Ashin!*[5] [翻滾吧! 阿信], on the other hand, is directed by Lin Yu-hsien [林育賢], a less well-known contemporary Taiwanese film director. *Jump Ashin!* is based on a true story and tells the life story of Ashin [阿信], an accomplished Taiwanese gymnast who won a national gold medal in the 1990s. A subplot of the film tells the story of drug addiction and recovery for Ashin's best friend, Pickle [菜脯], a likeable street hoodlum. The friendship between rural-dwelling Ashin and Pickle becomes particularly close when they are in their late teens. The two young men spend a great deal of time together when Ashin is forced to stop gymnastics, because his mother, a widow who runs a fruit stall, can no longer afford to fund his gymnastics' endeavours.

Marginalisation and palliation 87

Help Me Eros

Ah Jie's story begins with him in a drug-induced stupor in the lounge room of his apartment. He smokes a marijuana joint as his television shows a cooking program, where a fish is prepared for consumption while it is still alive. As the host of the television show comments that the fish appears 'to be saying: help me!' [牠在講救救我!], Ah Jie attempts to phone his helpline counsellor. He is unsuccessful in reaching her. Ah Jie next appears in the small greenhouse that is secured in a closet of his apartment, where he grows copious amounts of marijuana. He hyperventilates for quite a lengthy period, blowing carbon dioxide into the greenhouse for his marijuana plants' respiration. The next day, Ah Jie sleeps at his former workplace: he was a stockbroker. On the way home, he buys cigarettes at a tobacco and betel nut kiosk that is located below his apartment building. The kiosk is staffed by scantily dressed young women [檳榔西施], who sometimes offer sexual favours to their customers. Ah Jie pays with an out-of-circulation coin, while conning a free betel nut from the young saleswoman.

Ah Jie returns to his apartment, which has a repossession notice on the door [封條]. He goes inside and tends to his greenhouse. He recites religious verse about life and death and hyperventilates in the greenhouse, in order to supply carbon dioxide to his marijuana plants. He then phones his helpline counsellor to inform her that he, now, is jobless and unemployable. As they talk, a kettle squeals unattended on the gas cooker in his kitchen. He is boiling water for his staple diet, instant noodles. He tells the counsellor of his devotion to marijuana, 'It is my life. Without it I would die' [它是我的生命啊, 沒有它我會死掉]. He pleads for help from the counsellor: 'You must help me, please, I'm going to die!' [妳一定要幫幫我, 拜託, 快死了!]. She directs him to open up the windows of his apartment and relax somewhere comfortable. This settles him down. In order to get some cash, Ah Jie goes out to pawn furniture and belongings at the local pawnbroker shop. On the way to the shop, he runs into the young tobacco and betel nut kiosk saleswoman, who wants him to reimburse her for the out-of-circulation money that he previously had given her. He tells her that he has not brought his wallet with him, but then pawns his designer wallet for cash at the pawnbroker shop. On his return home, he calls the helpline counsellor again and asks her for her MSN email address, so that he can reach her more easily. She appears reluctant, so he gives her his MSN email address: HELPME178@hotmail.com.

Back on the street, Ah Jie again runs into the young kiosk saleswoman and helps her with her motor scooter. They go for a ride together on her scooter and he takes her to a car-yard, where he steals his repossessed car. They joyride in the car. He tells her that he 'can hardly go on living anymore' [我快活不下去了], much to her amusement. They drive to a car park where he introduces the young saleswoman to marijuana. She is a novice to illicit drugs. They smoke a marijuana joint 'shotgun' fashion, a highly sexualised way of smoking whereby one

88   *Marginalisation and palliation*

person blows exhaled smoke into the partner's mouth. Stoned, they return home to his apartment where they have very vigorous and acrobatic sex. Resting in bed after sex, Ah Jie receives an MSN instant message from his helpline counsellor. The MSN chat screen shows that his nickname is 'Marijuana-is-God' [大麻是神]. While the young kiosk saleswoman lies naked beside him, Ah Jie and his counsellor profess feelings for each other. He tells the counsellor, 'In the whole world, only you care about me dearly' [全世界只有你最關心我]. He then asks the counsellor who is the 'fatty' [胖子] in the photograph in her MSN instant message window. Her photograph shows two women: one slender and one very overweight. Ah Jie thinks that the counsellor is the slender woman, when, in fact, she is the overweight woman. The counsellor pretends to be the slender woman, as Ah Jie mistakenly believes her to be. As the two continue to chat on MSN, the young kiosk saleswoman awakes and has oral sex with Ah Jie.

The following day, while the young kiosk saleswoman moves into his apartment, Ah Jie tracks down the slender girl in the MSN photograph, who he believes to be his helpline counsellor, and stalks her as she moves about the city. That night, Ah Jie smokes marijuana with the young kiosk saleswoman and two of her co-workers. He smokes 'shotgun' fashion with all three young women, then takes the two visiting co-workers into his greenhouse and smokes more marijuana with them, before taking them onto the roof of his apartment building and having group sex with them. The next day he, once again, stalks the slender woman, who he believes to be his helpline counsellor. He follows her to the counselling office, where he discovers that the overweight woman, in fact, is his counsellor. He quickly leaves the office, when his counsellor is not looking, using the emergency exit. Back home, his electricity and water supply have been cut off due to non-payment of the utility bills. He asks the young kiosk saleswoman to bring him some water, which she believes is for drinking purposes. Ah Jie gets extremely angry with her, because he had wanted a large quantity of water to water his marijuana plants. He fears that, 'without water, they will die' [它門不加水會死]. He rudely orders the young saleswoman to go out and buy him water for the plants. She is livid and retaliates by destroying a number of his beloved plants. Ah Jie, in turn, throws her belongings out of his window and onto the pavement below, in front of the tobacco and betel nut kiosk.

The young kiosk saleswoman leaves town, leaving Ah Jie alone again to spend his days tending to his marijuana plants. He tries to make contact with the young saleswoman, but without any success. Without her financial support, he returns to pawning his possessions for cash. He wastes the money, however, on lottery tickets. The tickets are all losing tickets. In despair, he contacts the helpline counsellor, who immediately sets off for his apartment. She retains strong feelings for Ah Jie – even though he had abandoned her in her office when he had realised she was unattractive – probably because she had recently discovered that her husband was secretly cross-dressing with a male friend with whom he had been spending a great deal of time of late. Ah Jie bathes naked in a public fountain and then returns home, where he attempts suicide by gassing himself in his kitchen. The gas bottle runs dry, however, so the attempt is unsuccessful. He awakes quite intoxicated by the gas and stumbles through his apartment, climbing up to his windows. He opens the windows, takes some breaths, and starts reciting religious verse that contemplates the multiple lives that are formed from the death of one grain of seed [一粒麥子不落在地裡死了, 仍舊是一粒. 若是死了, 就結出許多籽粒來]. He then jumps or falls from the windows, presumably to his death, although, curiously, no body lies on the pavement below his apartment, just showers of lottery tickets. The helpline counsellor arrives at Ah Jie's unlocked apartment, but she is too late to save him.

Analysis

Drug addiction in *Help Me Eros* is presented as morally transgressive behaviour that inevitably leads to death. The transgressive nature of drug addiction is foregrounded in *Help Me Eros* by the film's temporal focus on Ah Jie's life during drug addiction and the absence of attention to his life from before and after drug addiction. As a result, the transgressive acts that he commits during drug addiction cannot be counterbalanced by virtuous displays from before or after drug addiction. He remains hopelessly addicted to marijuana throughout his filmic story. Marijuana is his sole concern in life. It is his 'god' [大麻是神]. It causes him to lose his job and to cheat, deceive, use and steal from others in order to get by financially. It causes him to go naked in public and to allure young women into illicit drug use and wanton fornication. It also makes him aggressive, to a young woman who is helping him to get by, when his supply of illicit drugs comes under threat.

Ah Jie is not masculine, despite his vigorous sexual prowess. He procures sex by duping the young, scantily dressed tobacco and betel nut saleswomen, who offer sexual favours to other men on the street below his apartment. Yet, he is unable sustain a relationship with these women and, instead, stalks a slim, bright and attractive helpline counsellor, who is a work colleague of his own helpline counsellor. His illicit-drug-induced conceit, spurred on by his own counsellor's deception, deludes him into believing that the slim, bright and attractive helpline counsellor is attracted to him. Ah Jie further contravenes normative manhood in Chinese culture by not having a job and not supporting his parents or a wife and child (see Chapter 2). He appears to have no family at all. He also has no male friends and, therefore, cannot perform acts of male-bonding (see Chapter 2). On the contrary, he solely relies on women to advise him in his day-to-day life and to financially support him when he is penniless. Once that he feels that he has lost the support of these women, he attempts suicide in what normally would be considered a non-masculine way in Chinese culture (Kleinman *et al.* 2011; Maggs 2012; Pearson & Liu 2002; Pearson *et al.* 2002; Wu 2009).

90 *Marginalisation and palliation*

Ah Jie's flawed masculinity is accentuated in *Help Me Eros* by repeated linguistic and figurative allusions to his doleful vulnerability and fixation with death. He is helpless, depending on illicit drugs, sex and the debasement of women in order to create meaning in his life. His helplessness is signified in the title of the film: *Help Me Eros*; through the dying cries of the fish on the television cooking program: 'help me!' [救救我!]; through Ah Jie's frantic telephone call to his helpline counsellor: 'You must help me, please, I'm going to die!' [妳一定要幫幫我, 拜託, 快死了!]; and in his MSN email address: 'HELPME178@hotmail.com'. Moreover, his helplessness interlaces with a fear of death that shrouds his day-to-day existence. The fish is dying, he is dying, and his beloved marijuana plants are dying. In the end, he recites religious verse about life and death and then, presumably, dies. With this, Ah Jie's ever-present fear of an impending death, seemingly, is vindicated.

In sum, Ah Jie's story of drug addiction, as depicted in *Help Me Eros*, aligns with a dominant meta-narrative in Chinese culture that presents drug addiction as morally transgressive and something to be feared. Ah Jie's transgressions in *Help Me Eros* are not committed against his family, as they are in the mainland Chinese films, *Quitting* and *The War of Two*. This is because Ah Jie does not appear to have a family. Instead, Ah Jie contravenes cultural conventions, the law and sexual mores, by cheating, deceiving, stealing and salaciously corrupting young women in a non-masculine way. His transgressions are not counterbalanced by displays of moral behaviour from before, during or after drug addiction. Rather, they are accentuated by his contravention of normative masculinity in Chinese culture. As a consequence, little sympathy is generated for the drug addict in *Help Me Eros*, leading up to, and upon, his apparent death. He secures no moral capital throughout his filmic story, even in his apparent death. This death bears out a cultural meta-narrative that links drug addiction to fears of death and violence. As a consequence, the fear espoused by the meta-narrative, as well as by Ah Jie throughout the film, is vindicated by the film's ending.

Jump Ashin!

Pickle's story begins with Ashin and him on motor scooters delivering goods. They share a cigarette, as they wait for a train to pass at a level crossing. After the train passes, they knowingly hold up traffic. This causes the driver of the car behind them to impatiently beep his horn. Pickle is sharing a sexual fantasy with Ashin. Pickle curses the young male car driver and challenges him to a fight. Ashin, however, steps in and smashes in the front windscreen of the car. Later on Pickle, Ashin and two other young street punks meet a gang of young Chinese men for a street fight. Pickle's streetwise-ness and Ashin's gymnastics' talent make the pair formidable opponents in the ensuing melee. Ashin ends up saving Pickle's hide, following which the pair impulsively kiss, much to the consternation of all present, including the two young friends.

Marginalisation and palliation 91

A seemingly subliminal homosexual attraction between the two young friends is further insinuated when Ashin tells the young female attendant of the billiard hall, where the pair hangs out, that he [我啦] is Pickle's favourite type of girl. Pickle, nonetheless, appears sexually interested in the young female attendant. He starts a brawl with patrons at the billiard hall and then retreats to chat up the attendant. Ashin appears unimpressed by this and continues brawling. The pair triumphs in the fight when Pickle returns to the fray. That night, while the pair eats at a street stall, Pickle smashes two beer bottles that they have been drinking from, in order to test their usefulness in a street brawl. The next night, while eating at the same street stall, local gangsters harass the hardworking stall vendor. Pickle smashes a beer bottle in order to draw the attention of the gangsters away from the stall vendor. The gangsters yield to the threats of the pair. The following day, the gangsters seek out the pair at Ashin's mother's fruit stall and ask them to join their gang. The gangsters consider the pair 'to be quite courageous' [你們兩個膽識不錯]. The pair, however, brashly refuses the offer. Pickle insults the face of the gang leader, whose name is Papaya, by offering him two 'sweet' [甜的喔] papayas from the fruit stall for free.

One night, Pickle runs into Papaya at a local nightclub. Papaya offers him a vial of amphetamine [安]. Papaya says that 'it's popular to smoke this nowadays' [現在流行抽這個啦]. He tosses a vial to Pickle and challenges him to try it [你怕喔]. Pickle initially wants to return the amphetamine to Papaya, but he already has walked away. Later on, Pickle is slightly aggressive toward Ashin at work. This is out of character for the young larrikin. Ashin angrily orders him to move some goods. Pickle sulkily does so and then abruptly speeds off on his motor scooter ahead of Ashin, despite Ashin's calls for him to wait. Ashin pursues Pickle, who is driving fast and recklessly, until he crashes on a country laneway. Ashin rushes to him, concerned that he may have injured himself. Pickle appears wholly unperturbed and states that he, in fact, feels 'awesome' [爽啦]. Ashin comments that Pickle 'has been acting weird recently' [你最近怪怪的]. Pickle responds that he has not slept for a week and suggests that the pair 'go out that night to get some action' [晚上陪我去把馬子]. They end up running into Papaya at the local nightclub. Pickle sets up Ashin for a dance challenge with Papaya, which Ashin wins, much to Papaya's chagrin. Pickle proudly declares that 'this is my brother!' [這我兄弟啦], and then sneaks off to smoke amphetamine. However, there is none left. He immediately becomes extremely agitated. He seeks out Papaya and politely asks him for more drugs. Papaya teases Pickle by showing him vials of amphetamine and then tossing them around to his gang members. Papaya refuses to sell the drugs to Pickle and then beats him. Pickle, now on his knees, respectfully apologises to Papaya for having embarrassed him in public at the nightclub [木瓜老大, 對不起啦]. Papaya and his gang members only beat him more. Following the beating, while Pickle lies bloodied on the pavement, Papaya gives him the amphetamine on the condition that he brings Ashin to him.

92 *Marginalisation and palliation*

In line with Papaya's demand, Pickle invites Ashin for a snack at a night stall. On arrival, Ashin finds that the stall is closed and Pickle is nowhere to be seen. Pickle hides, crying behind the night stall, as Ashin is ambushed and severely beaten by Papaya's gang. Pickle, however, suddenly emerges and appears to kill Papaya,[6] just as he was about to hit Ashin with a baseball bat. The pair runs away in fear to Taipei. Pickle soon grows gaunt, weak and unwell from drug withdrawal. Ashin cares for him in their small apartment. He brings him food and looks for a job for both of them. Pickle's only concern, however, is to obtain money to buy amphetamine. He begs Ashin for money, avowing that they are 'brothers' [我們不是兄弟嗎]. When Ashin angrily refuses, Pickle tries to placate him by eating the food that Ashin had brought him. Ashin has thrown the food on the floor in his rage, but Pickle scrambles over and eats it anyway. He eats with his hands in an unseemly way and then vomits up the food, but continues on eating regardless. He repeatedly asserts, as he eats, 'we are brothers' [我們是兄弟勒]. He vows that he will give up amphetamine and does not use illicit drugs again in the film.

The pair finds work as waiters in a nightclub that is frequented by underworld patrons. The patrons treat the pair poorly. Pickle offends one unscrupulous patron, a gang leader, who retaliates by attacking him. Ashin intervenes, but Pickle wildly threatens the gang leader with a knife. Pickle survives the altercation, due to the intervention of the nightclub owner, a godfather. Thereafter, Pickle and Ashin serve as the godfather's henchmen, violently beating rival gang members and trashing their premises. One day, the godfather offers the pair a million Taiwanese dollars[7] to do a hit on a rival gang leader. It is the unscrupulous gangster with whom Pickle had had the altercation earlier on. Pickle eagerly accepts the task. Later that night, he tells Ashin that he likes life in Taipei. Ashin, on the other hand, wants to return home. He does not like 'working as someone else's minion' [作別人小弟]. Pickle says that he fears imprisonment or a reprisal death, if they return home. He reminds Ashin that it was he who committed the murder [人是我殺的]. Anyway, he expects 'to be a gangland boss soon and, after that, it will be' his 'turn to protect' Ashin 'whenever anything happens' [我告訴你, 我馬上就會做老大了, 以後發生什麼事情, 換我罩你]. That night, Pickle leaves a letter for Ashin, in which he confesses his betrayal of Ashin on the night of the apparent murder. He declares that he 'is just a loser' [我真的很沒用] and 'unworthy to be' Ashin's 'brother' [我不配當你的兄弟]. He tells Ashin to return home and resume his gymnastics' career. He asks Ashin to take the hit money that was supplied by the godfather and give it to his father. He also asks Ashin to tell his father that 'he can't beat' him 'anymore' and 'to take good care of himself' [說以後他再也打不到我了, 要好好照顧自己]. Pickle attempts the brazen hit on the rival gang leader, but, as expected, he is unsuccessful. In retaliation, the gang members severely beat him, take him outside and execute him on the street. Before he is shot, he mutters with an ironic smile, 'Now, I can go back to Yilan', his hometown [這樣我就可以回宜蘭了]. The last word he calls out is 'Ashin!'

Marginalisation and palliation   93

Analysis

Drug addiction in *Jump Ashin!* is presented as morally transgressive behaviour that inevitably leads to death. It causes the affable, proud and loyal young larrikin, Pickle, to become surly, servile and treacherous, to the point that he is willing to betray his beloved long-term male companion, Ashin. Pickle's transgressions, however, are counterbalanced in *Jump Ashin!* by the temporal attention given to his life from before and after drug addiction. This is in contrast to the preceding three films analysed in this chapter. His life from before and after drug addiction is righteous [义], loyal [忠] and filial [孝], in a way that conforms with normative masculinity in Chinese culture, specifically, *wu* [武] ('martial') masculinity (Cai 2005; Louie 2002; Lu 2012). His life from before also points to a reason for his drug addiction: his father beat him and his mother left home, when he was a child.

Before drug addiction, Pickle is an honourable young larrikin, whose mischievous antics rarely cross the boundaries of normative behaviour for a young man from the Taiwanese countryside. He intimidates strangers, but only impatient men. He drinks alcohol at a late night street stall, but protects the stall's vendor when he is threatened by local gangsters. He brawls with young hoodlums in public, but only to back up his best friend, Ashin. Ashin is a talented local gymnast and the hero of the film. Pickle also refuses to join a local street gang that traffics in illicit drugs, and tries to turn down a free sample of amphetamines that the leader of the local street gang offers him one night. After drug addiction, he perpetrates gangland violence, but in partnership with Ashin and only in accordance with their godfather's directives.

Pickle's masculine righteousness only is surpassed by his hetero-normative bond with the man he loves. He calls Ashin his 'brother' [兄弟]. The pair spends most of their daily lives together, side-by-side, until Pickle is killed. They back each other up during street fights, each man's fighting prowess complementing the other's. They share food, cigarettes and alcohol, as well as a single-roomed dwelling when living in Taipei. Ashin takes care of Pickle when he is suffering from drug withdrawal, and Pickle promises to take care of Ashin when he becomes a gangland boss. Neither man has a girlfriend or engages in sexual activity with a woman. Although both men are sexually interested in women, they kiss, albeit on impulse; and they equate their relationship, hetero-normatively, to that of boyfriend-girlfriend. Tellingly, the last word that is uttered by Pickle before he dies alone on a Taipei street is 'Ashin'.

Pickle's masculine righteousness, hetero-normative fraternity and filial piety coalesce at the conclusion of his filmic story, when he magnanimously gives up his own life for Ashin and his father. His death releases Ashin from his fraternal obligations to Pickle and absolves him of any culpability in Papaya's apparent murder [人是我殺的]. Thereupon, Ashin is able to resume his gymnastics' career. His death also secures the financial wellbeing of his ageing and

94   *Marginalisation and palliation*

unaccompanied father, even though he had beaten him as a child. In this way, Pickle's death, while suicidal in essence, emulates the 'honourable death' of *wu* men in the Chinese chivalry tales of old (Maggs 2012, pp. 65, 68). This stands in contrast to Ah Jie's self-indulgent and feminised death in the Taiwanese film, *Help Me Eros*.

In sum, Pickle's story of drug addiction and recovery, as depicted in *Jump Ashin!* aligns with a dominant meta-narrative in Chinese culture that presents drug addiction as morally transgressive and something to be feared. Even the most loyal of men can be corrupted by, and ultimately die as a result of, drug addiction. The transgressions that a man commits when he is drug-addicted, nevertheless, may be absolved by behaving in accordance with normative manhood when not drug-addicted. Death still ensues, but an honourable death.

Hong Kong filmic stories

Two Hong Kong television serial dramas that tell the stories of Chinese people with drug addiction are analysed in this section. The two productions form part of a special television series, *Drug Battle*[8] [毒海浮生] (*Lit.* Floating upon the Drug Seas), which is produced by the Television Department of Radio Television Hong Kong [香港電台電視部], in conjunction with the P.A.T.H.S. to Adulthood [共創成長路] project. Radio Television Hong Kong [香港電台] is a government-funded public broadcaster in Hong Kong. It is widely regarded to uphold editorial independence. The P.A.T.H.S. to Adulthood project is funded by The Hong Kong Jockey Club Charities Trust [香港賽馬會慈善信託基金] and seeks to promote healthy living and the personal and moral development of young people in Hong Kong (P.A.T.H.S. to Adulthood 2012). The project is steered by a research team and the social welfare and education departments of the Hong Kong regional government (P.A.T.H.S. to Adulthood 2012).

The quasi-documentary television serial dramas depict the common causes of, and issues surrounding, drug addiction in the Hong Kong Special Administrative Region. Each episode of the serial dramas, which lasts approximately twenty-five minutes, tells a progressive tale of a young person's drug addiction (approximately twenty minutes), followed by a short public drug education message that is presented by a local cartoon artist or a local health professional (approximately five minutes). One of the serial dramas, *He Is Not Lonely* [他不寂寞], was broadcast over three nights during late 2012 and early 2013. It recounts the story of drug addiction, rehabilitation and recovery for two male Chinese youth, Ah Hou [阿豪] and Ah Him [阿謙]. The pair had lived in the same urban housing tenement when they were very young. The other serial drama, *Happily Sharing, Seventeen Years of Age* [開心 share 十七歲], was broadcast over three nights during January 2013. It recounts the story of drug addiction, rehabilitation and recovery for two female Chinese youth, seventeen-year-old Lemon Tea

[檸茶] and twenty-year-old Ah San [阿臣]. The pair resides in the same urban neighbourhood in Hong Kong.

He Is Not Lonely

The television serial drama begins with Ah Hou and Ah Him as young boys, playing together in the large apartment block where their families live. Ah Hou lives with his elderly grandmother. His parents, who are divorced, live elsewhere with their new partners. Ah Him, on the other hand, lives with his affluent, hardworking parents, who employ a nanny to care for him. That night at dinner, Ah Hou's grandmother tells him that his mother 'apparently won't have time to come and visit' him 'this week' [這個星期你媽好像沒空來探望你]. Meanwhile, Ah Him eats dinner with his nanny, lamenting that his parents 'regularly don't get home until real late' [他們經常很晚才回家]. Sometime later, Ah Him's family moves away from the tenement. Both boys seem unhappy about the move.

Eight years on, Ah Hou, now a teenager, returns home one night to the tenement. He is late for dinner. He expresses concern to his grandmother that she bundles newspapers for such a meagre income. She replies that she has to do it in order to meet their daily living expenses [不撿的話, 怎夠維持生活]. She then asks if Ah Hou had asked his parents about buying a new cell phone. He replies that he had not asked them, because it just would be a waste of time [說了也沒有用]. The next day at school, Ah Hou leaves the toilet block and notices items of clothing falling from above. Much to Ah Hou's and his classmates' amusement, a classmate, who is high on methamphetamine (colloquially known as 'ice') [吸食「冰」], has stripped off his school uniform and is parading naked around the school precinct. Ah Hou and his classmates are hurriedly ushered away by teachers. After school, Ah Hou goes window shopping with his girlfriend. She is unhappy because Ah Hou has no money to buy her things. He promises her that he will buy her gifts with money that he is saving for her birthday [不要緊, 下月你生日, 我儲錢買給你]. Later on, Ah Hou hangs out at the local park with some friends, who are in a street gang. They chat about girls. One friend boasts that their gang leader had shared some ketamine (colloquially known as 'K') with the group of friends [老大那天真豪爽, 請大家索K], which Ah Hou, naturally, had missed out on. Another friend observes that Ah Hou would never take illicit drugs, even if he were forced to [他這個人餵到嘴邊也不懂吃!]. Ah Hou humbly replies, 'How can I play up without any money?' [沒有錢, 怎玩得起?].

As a gang member heads off to deliver illicit drugs to a local customer (in fact, it is Ah Him), Ah Hou notices an approaching police patrol. He tips off the drug dealers and they are able to escape. Ah Hou is rewarded for tipping off the drug dealers. He now can sell illicit drugs on the street. He eagerly buys a quantity of spoons and small plastic satchels, which he uses to divvy up the drugs in his bedroom. Ah Hou is successful and makes quite a lot of money from drug dealing,

96   *Marginalisation and palliation*

but he wants more. One of the gang members suggests that Ah Hou could gain more customers by giving out free samples, and that he could spread the ketamine further by cutting it with additive, which he does. With the money that he has earned, Ah Hou takes his girlfriend out shopping for expensive gifts at the mall. Here, he sees his mother with her new husband and child. Ah Hou quickly exits the mall, trying to avoid her. She, however, sees him and pursues him out onto the street. She tells him how busy she has been, offers to send him money and then leaves. Ah Hou is depressed by this encounter with his mother. He returns home to find that his father is just leaving the apartment. The father says that he cannot stay to eat dinner with him and his grandmother. This further depresses Ah Hou. He, nevertheless, is kind and considerate to his grandmother at dinner, sharing food with her.

The next day Ah Hou has a barbeque with his drug-dealing friends. One of the friends has been caught with illicit drugs and sentenced to juvenile detention. Ah Hou still is depressed by the lack of attention that he had received from his parents the previous day. His friends suggest that he try ketamine [有煩惱便索K], which he does. He soon is addicted. He uses ketamine at school, even in the classroom during lessons. On New Year's Eve, Ah Hou parties with his drug-dealing friends. He uses large quantities of ketamine and ecstasy, and then stumbles aimlessly around the streets in a drug stupor. He is noticed by the police, who search him and find illicit drugs. As a result, he is arrested. On sentencing, Ah Hou is sent to Zheng Sheng College [正生書院] for long-term drug rehabilitation (see Chapter 3). His grandmother is heartbroken. At the facility he nevertheless, 'can continue to study and, most importantly, establish a proper life value system' [他可以在那裡繼續求學, 最重要是建立正確的人生價值觀]. Day-to-day life in Zheng Sheng College is difficult for Ah Hou. He is struck by the number of young 'fellow students' [同學] who are on 'regular, follow-up' treatment for comorbid mental illness [十多歲便要定期到腦科、精神科覆診]. While bathing with male staff and students in the communal bathroom, however, Ah Hou finds motivation and strength in the fraternal bonds and fellowship of the Zheng Sheng College staff and students [這裡的生活真的很難熬, 但眼見同工、老師和我們一同起居飲食, 何苦呢?].

Ah Hou's mother and father visit him at Zheng Sheng College. They bring him food and ask him about his daily routine in the facility. He asks after his grandmother and then asks about how his parents had met; this is the topic of an essay that he must write for school work. The parents tell a story of the young father falling asleep while at the movies on a date with the mother, because he was tired from overworking. Ah Hou responds with a story of grandmother falling asleep while at the movies with him, for similar reasons. Later on, Ah Hou plays basketball with his fellow students. He falls heavily and they help him up. A male staff member treats his wounded knee. As he does so, the staff member tells Ah Hou that he has kept an elaborate tattoo on his head as a reminder that, as a youth, he

Marginalisation and palliation 97

'also had gone astray', just like the students in Zheng Sheng College [把它留下來是給自己一個儆醒, 我年輕時也曾像你們誤入歧途]. The staff member adds that, were it not for Zheng Sheng College, he 'would have been locked up in Stanley Prison or Pik Uk Prison, or living an inhuman existence on the outside' [因犯事而關在赤柱或壁屋監獄, 或在外面過著非人生活]. Ah Hou's story concludes with a visit from his parents and his grandmother. The family is reunited and Ah Hou is content.

The film shifts to Ah Him, showing him as a teenager, eight years after moving away from Ah Hou's tenement. Ah Him is at school, alone, watching other boys playing basketball on the school courts. Some schoolgirls, who also are watching the boys play basketball, spot Ah Him, who now wears glasses, and make fun of him. They call him 'four eyes' [四眼哥哥]. After school, Ah Him's mother phones him to make sure that he is on his way to the evening tuition school. She tells him that she and his father will be home very late that night. Ah Him goes into an electronic goods store, where he runs into the schoolgirls who had made fun of him earlier. They continue to tease him, calling him a 'weirdo' [怪模怪樣的]. He moves on to a convenience store, where he eats a microwave dinner, alone. Ah Him returns home to an empty apartment. The fridge is covered in post-it messages from his mother. He ignores them and plays computer games, alone in his bedroom.

That weekend, Ah Him's parents are home and quarrel over money. They already have had to let Ah Him's nanny go. Ah Him shows little interest in the situation and goes out to the computer game parlour to get away from his parents. At the game parlour, Ah Him buys and immediately uses ketamine. He hallucinates as he plays a shooting game, imagining that the victims who he shoots are the schoolgirls who had teased him. The next morning, Ah Him's father hassles him for oversleeping. Ah Him rises, gets some cash from his mother and immediately goes out again. While travelling on a public bus, he watches a young man and his girlfriend get on board. Ah Him looks longingly at the pair enjoying each other's company while sitting together on the bus. Later on, Ah Him is back at home, alone, lying on the sofa in a drug stupor. His mother returns home. She mistakenly believes that he is tired.

Ah Him now uses ketamine heavily at home, when alone. He does so, alone, on New Year's Eve. One day when his mother is home, he becomes unwell due to drug withdrawal. His mother, thinking that he is ill, fusses over him, wanting him to see a doctor. This makes Ah Him extremely aggravated and he rushes out to buy some ketamine. His mother pursues him until he falls over on the pavement, in great pain. He has sprained his ankle. His mother, who now is aware of Ah Him's drug addiction, lies to his father by claiming that the injury had occurred when Ah Him was playing basketball with classmates. After the father goes out, she implores Ah Him to quit using illicit drugs [你千萬不要再吸毒]. Ah Him, in turn, implores his mother to not tell his father, fearing that 'he will beat' him

98 *Marginalisation and palliation*

'to death' [你千萬不要告訴他, 否則他會打死我]. He then surreptitiously orders more ketamine and has it delivered to his front door. Ah Him's mother is distraught and tells his father that he has been using illicit drugs. The father is furious and severely beats Ah Him in his bedroom before manhandling him into the bathroom, where he forces Ah Him's head into a basin under a running water faucet. Ah Him cries. At the conclusion of Ah Him's story, he is visibly mentally ill. He witlessly hallucinates, alone in the bathroom of his apartment, banging his fists and wildly clawing at his face. His face distorts into a grotesque image. He cries out loudly as he violently smashes items in the bathroom.

Analysis

Drug addiction in *He Is Not Lonely* is presented as morally transgressive behaviour that inevitably leads to incarceration or madness. It causes Ah Hou and Ah Him to deceive others, commit crime and go mad. These transgressions, nevertheless, are mitigated by the root cause of their drug addiction, namely, a lack of attention from their parents during childhood. Ah Hou's parents are divorced and live separately with their respective new partners. He is raised by his grandmother and rarely sees his parents. Ah Him's parents are rarely at home, due to their busy careers. As a young boy, he is cared for by a nanny and, in adolescence, he is allowed to wander the streets without adult supervision. The temporal focus in *He Is Not Lonely* on the life as a child from before drug addiction, therefore, displaces the blame for the later drug addiction in adolescence onto the parents (Tolton 2009). They should have cared for their sons more attentively, rather than delegate their care to a grandmother or a nanny. Moreover, parental blame is accentuated in the filmic stories by the parents' divergent reactions to finding out that their sons are drug addicts. Ah Hou's parents reunite and spend more time with their son. This heralds his apparent recovery from drug addiction. Ah Him's parents, on the other hand, self-deny or physically abuse their son. This exacerbates his drug addiction and drives him to madness.

Both of the drug addicts in *He Is Not Lonely* are schoolboys, who are from imperfect home environments. Ah Hou consistently behaves in accordance with normative masculinity in Chinese culture, while Ah Him does not. Ah Hou exhibits hetero-normative fraternity through his relationships at school with other schoolboys; his association with the local street gang; and his communal life with the male staff and students of the drug rehabilitation facility. He is athletic (*wu* masculinity) and displays business acumen through his success and innovation as a street drug dealer (*wen* masculinity) (Louie 2002, 2015). He also behaves righteously [义] through his concern and consideration by publicly acknowledging his grandmother's toil and ensuing fatigue; honouring his promise to his girlfriend to buy her expensive gifts; initially not using illicit drugs, despite his friends selling and using illicit drugs themselves; and thwarting the arrest of his friends, at some risk to himself. Ah Him, on the contrary, has no male (or female) friends. He is alone when at school, on the street, on the bus, at home, and during festive occasions. Girls mock his behaviour and appearance. He uses illicit drugs when alone in the stairwell of a building or when alone at home. Ah Hou, on the other hand, only used illicit drugs when he was with friends or around other people at school. Ah Him is not good at sports and merely watches from the sidelines. He has no source of income, bar the money that he acquires from his mother by deception. Unlike Ah Hou, he does not crave the attention of his father. He is cold and indifferent toward his parents, and sometimes aggressive and violent toward them and others. He takes great pleasure in imagining himself shooting the schoolgirls who had mocked him at school and at the mall, and he is physically aggressive to his mother when she presses him about going to see a doctor about his apparent ill health. Moreover, he ultimately harms himself when psychotic at the conclusion of his filmic story.

Ah Hou's consistent performance of normative masculinity in Chinese culture, in particular, the hetero-normative fraternity that marks his life at Zheng Sheng College – as well as his reunion with his parents while in the drug rehabilitation facility – seem to pave the way for his apparent recovery from drug addiction. In contrast, the emasculated Ah Him, who is pressured and beaten, rather than supported, by his parents, descends into madness. Contravening normative gender in Chinese culture, therefore, appears to condemn Ah Him to a fate worse than death in Chinese culture, namely, mental illness (Ramsay 2008, 2013). However, he is not alone in suffering this fate at the hands of drug addiction. Ah Hou's high school classmate goes mad after using methamphetamine. A number of Ah Hou's fellow students at Zheng Sheng College are on long-term medical treatment for mental illness. An association between illicit drug use and mental illness also characterises the mainland Chinese films analysed in this chapter.

In sum, Ah Hou's and Ah Him's drug addictions, as depicted in *He Is Not Lonely*, align with a dominant meta-narrative in Chinese culture that presents drug addiction as morally transgressive and something to be feared. The transgressions committed during drug addiction will lead to madness, a fate worse than death in Chinese culture, or incarceration. Ah Him and a number of Ah Hou's drug-addicted acquaintances go mad. Ah Hou, his street-gang friend, and his staff mentor and fellow students at Zheng Sheng College are incarcerated for drug-related crime. The transgressions committed during drug addiction, however, are mitigated by parental neglect from a young age,[9] and by behaving in accordance with normative masculinity in Chinese culture. Cultural discourse pertaining to familial responsibility and gender norms, therefore, appear to be selectively drawn on in the television serial drama to palliate or marginalise the young drug addict.

While cultural discourse appears to shape the filmic stories of Ah Hou and Ah Him in these ways, the discursive schema of social work services in Hong Kong (see Chapter 3) may account for the shifting of the blame for drug addiction

100   *Marginalisation and palliation*

away from the drug addict and onto their parents. Institutional discourse also may shape the casting of people in drug rehabilitation as students, the equating of drug rehabilitation to education, and the suggestion that recovery from drug addiction requires a structured institutional intervention. Institutional discourse appears to shape the Hong Kong life stories of drug addiction and rehabilitation that are analysed in Chapter 3 in a similar way.

Happily Sharing, Seventeen Years of Age

The television serial drama begins with Lemon Tea at her after-school job, serving at a convenience store. After work, she returns home and finds a note from her mother saying that she had to rush back to her job at a casino in Macao and, so, could not see her. The mother said that she had left some money for her on the table and that she should phone her if the money is not enough. Lemon Tea takes the money and goes out. The next morning she visits her boyfriend's apartment and prepares him some breakfast. On hearing a noise in an adjacent room, she calls out: 'Honey' [老公]. However, it is his father. The boyfriend has gone out already. He eventually returns home, takes the food that Lemon Tea had prepared for him, and asks her for some money to buy a new cell phone. Lemon Tea obligingly gives him the money that her mother had left for her. He thanks her, calling her 'Honey' [老婆], and then rushes off out of the apartment without her.

Later at school, Lemon Tea is in a toilet block with schoolmates. She shares ketamine with them. They cheerfully propose a toast [乾杯] and then prepare to inhale the illicit drugs. They thank Lemon Tea for sharing the drugs. She replies that 'good things certainly must be shared around' [好東西當然要一起分享]. A suspicious teacher comes into the toilet block and finds illicit-drug-using paraphernalia in a cubicle. As a result, Lemon Tea is suspended from school. She is quite blasé about the suspension. Her mother is busy working in Macao and, in Lemon Tea's mind, even if she were to die, her mother probably would not be able to find the time to organise her funeral [我死了, 她也沒有空替我收屍]. Lemon Tea also dismisses the 'loss of face' [丟臉] that is brought upon her older sister, due to her suspension from school. She takes care of Lemon Tea in the mother's absence. Lemon Tea, however, 'doesn't take any notice of her' and has 'absolutely no relationship with her' [我懶得理會她. 我跟她完全沒有關係]. She resolves to work more hours at her job at the convenience store and to spend more time with her boyfriend, even though 'he just doesn't take any notice' of her [他才懶得理會我].

Later that evening, Lemon Tea goes to visit her boyfriend at his apartment. He, however, rushes out soon after she arrives. She heads off to a karaoke bar, where she has organised to buy illicit drugs. At the karaoke bar, Lemon Tea is sexually fondled by a drunken male acquaintance. She protests that she has a boyfriend, but the young man continues to fondle her, stating that 'at the moment' he 'wants

Marginalisation and palliation 101

to drink lemon tea' [我現在要喝檸檬茶]. She goes outside and phones her boyfriend, but he just asks her to take his computer to the store and get it repaired. He adds that he will get home very late that night, so there would be no point in calling him thereafter. Lemon Tea is upset by the phone call and returns to the bar, where she treats those present to ketamine. Her boyfriend, however, happens to be in a private room of the same bar. An acquaintance enters the room and comments on the 'tawdry' [失禮] behaviour of a young woman, who she saw openly using ketamine at the bar. The boyfriend takes a look and sees that it is Lemon Tea. Back at his apartment, the boyfriend aggressively confronts Lemon Tea about her using ketamine. He beats her, calling her a 'damned K sister' [你這死K妹]. He rages that she has caused him to 'lose face' [真讓我丟臉]. Lemon Tea pushes him away. He stomps off in a huff, declaring that he does not want to see her. This makes Lemon Tea cry.

The following day Lemon Tea resolves to give up ketamine [我以後不索K]. Back at work at the convenience store, she chastises a Chinese customer who had called the store's well-mannered young delivery man a 'young Blackie' [黑個仔]. He is South Asian. The customer is enraged and calls Lemon Tea a 'stinking bitch' [臭三八] and leaves. The young delivery man tells Lemon Tea not to be upset, since this often happens to him [其實很多人叫我黑個仔, 你不必理會他]. He then asks her out, but she turns him down. After work, she visits her boyfriend at his apartment and finds an opened condom wrapper in his bedroom. He dismisses it and offers her some marijuana. She immediately vomits, recalling the smell of marijuana in her mother's room when she was a young girl. She also recalls, at the time, her older sister calling her a 'good for nothing' [不中用] and flushing her head in the toilet [吃糞便好了]. The sister blames Lemon Tea for their parents' drug addiction [他們吸毒也是因為你] and for why their father had abandoned the family [你出生後, 爸爸便離開我們]. When she recovers from her nausea, she asks her boyfriend why he had admonished her for using ketamine when, in fact, he smokes marijuana. He replies that 'using K is uncool; only fools use K' [索K不夠酷, 傻瓜才去索K]. Lemon Tea begs him to give up marijuana, since she 'had already given up K for' him [我已為你戒掉K仔了]. He says that he will think about it and comments that she looks fat. She blames it on having given up using ketamine [人家說戒K會長胖的].

Lemon Tea decides to try methamphetamine, because her friend tells her that it can help people to lose weight. One day, she meets the friend in a public toilet and declares that she has lost some weight. She adds that she 'really feels that using ice is much better than using K' [我真的覺得僕冰比索K好]. She returns to her boyfriend's apartment, where he is furious that she is using methamphetamine. He calls her a 'hopeless damned K sister' [死K妹, 你沒救了] and a 'pathetic stinking bitch' [你面目可憐 . . . 臭三八]. He orders her to leave, but she refuses. She reminds him that she supports him financially and that he uses illicit drugs as well. He replies that methamphetamine users are 'abnormal' [僕冰的人是失常的], and

102   *Marginalisation and palliation*

then manhandles her out of the apartment. She wanders around the streets, forlorn, until she stumbles across a young woman drug addict, who has overdosed in the local park (in fact, it is Ah San). She immediately phones the emergency services. Thereafter, she resolves to quit using methamphetamine.

That morning, Lemon Tea goes to work at the convenience store, only to be told by the store's manager that she has been sacked on suspicion of illicit drug use. The manager had been finding empty illicit drug satchels on the floor of the store. She angrily denies that the satchels belong to her, storms outside and goes to brood in the local park. The South Asian delivery man happened to observe all of this and follows her to the park. She warns him off becoming her friend, since she uses illicit drugs, her boyfriend has left her, and her family has no time for her. She even 'doesn't like to look at' herself [我也不想見到自己]. The kind delivery man consoles her, telling her that 'in fact, many people look down on' him as well [其實很多人看不起我]. She proceeds to tell the delivery man about coming across the young woman in the park, who had overdosed on illicit drugs, and that she had not waited around for the ambulance to arrive, because she had methamphetamine on her. She laments that she, 'like her, certainly will die' [我和她一樣, 必死無疑]. The kind delivery man replies that the young woman who had overdosed was lucky that Lemon Tea had stumbled upon her, otherwise she may have died. He then invites Lemon Tea to have breakfast with him. Soon after, her former boyfriend texts her, telling her that he wants to get back together with her and that he needs some money. Lemon Tea initially hesitates and then accepts the invitation for breakfast with the kind delivery man.

Ah San, who resides in the same neighbourhood as Lemon Tea, is first seen returning home to her apartment with some breakfast for her seventeen-year-old girlfriend. The pair is in a lesbian relationship. Her partner is asleep, so Ah San sits at a table, divvying up ketamine into small plastic satchels for street dealing. The partner awakes, hugs Ah San and suggests that the pair use some of the ketamine [你陪我索點K]. Ah San is unwilling, saying that the ketamine is for business purposes and not for their recreational use [開工不能索]. She tells her partner to eat some chocolate instead. The partner complains that chocolate will only make her 'fat and then no one will want to marry' her [發胖了, 誰娶我?]. Ah San promises that she will marry her [我娶吧]. Her partner then snatches several satchels of ketamine to 'happily share' with a friend who she is meeting later [待會兒約了朋友, 要開心分享嘛]. That evening, Ah San deals illicit drugs on the local street. Afterward, she drinks alcohol and uses ketamine at home with her partner.

One day, Ah San's drug boss visits her apartment, which doubles as an illicit drug depot for his gang. He does not want her partner to live there, because he feels that 'she eventually will bring trouble' for Ah San [總有一天她會連累你]. As the drug boss is leaving, the partner returns and asks Ah San to buy her a watch that she has seen in a store. It costs over 80,000 Hong Kong Dollars.[10] Ah San informs her that the drug boss has asked her to move out of the apartment. Her partner is reluctant to leave, but capitulates when Ah San tells her that she may lose her job and their ready source of cash and ketamine, if she does not heed her boss's directive. The pair then use ketamine to cheer up. Sometime later, the partner visits Ah San in her apartment. Ah San confides that her partner 'now is the only family' that she has following the death of her father [自從我爸去世後, 我只有一個人, 你現在是我唯一的親人]. She then prepares some ketamine for the pair to use, but her nose starts to bleed. At that moment, the drug boss enters the apartment unannounced and is angry to find her partner there. Because of this, and evidence that Ah San has been cutting and reselling his stores of ketamine, he sacks Ah San and advises her to quit using illicit drugs.

Ah San soon lands a job as a hairdresser. She is very talented at her new job. Her partner, on the other hand, becomes an escort girl [做援交]. Ah San is furious when she discovers that her partner has taken up such a vocation and that she allows her male clients to fondle her. The partner argues that she only is doing it for the money. Ah San replies that they should simply reduce their expenses by giving up ketamine. The partner angrily reminds Ah San that it was she who had 'lost a job' as a street dealer, due to using too much ketamine [索K掉了工作的是你, 可不是我]. She then storms off. Ah San, forlorn, overdoses on ketamine, alone at the local park. By chance, she is rescued from a certain death by Lemon Tea. Ah San is released from a facility six months later, having successfully overcome her drug addiction [死過翻生, 我已經戒毒]. She walks down the road, alone but 'clear-headed' [清醒].

Analysis

Drug addiction in *Happily Sharing* is presented as morally transgressive behaviour that leads to death or incarceration, unless the young woman drug addict is rescued by a moral man. Lemon Tea uses and shares illicit drugs with friends and, as a result, gets suspended from school. This shames her family, in particular, the older sister who raised her. She eventually loses her boyfriend and her job, due to her illicit drug use. A moral man, nevertheless, supports her and guides her into recovery from her drug addiction. Ah San, meanwhile, sells illicit drugs that she has stolen from her gangland boss. She becomes unwell and loses her job and, eventually, her girlfriend, due to her illicit drug use. As a result, she attempts suicide. She recovers from her drug addiction after long-term internment in a government-run drug rehabilitation facility.

Temporality and normative sexuality in Chinese culture appear to palliate Lemon Tea's moral transgressions during drug addiction, while accentuating Ah San's. The temporal focus on Lemon Tea's life from before drug addiction, as a neglected and abused child, displaces the blame for her drug addiction onto her family (Tolton 2009). Her father and mother used illicit drugs when she was a

104 *Marginalisation and palliation*

young girl. Her father left home when she was very young and her mother generally is absent, since she works and resides in Macao. The older sister who raised Lemon Tea had mistreated and abused her when she was a young child. She now is estranged from the sister and has little contact with her mother. Thus, similar to *He Is Not Lonely, Happily Sharing* implies that the drug addict's parents should have cared for her more attentively, rather than delegating her care to her resentful older sister, who blames her for the parents' transgressions.

By contrast, there is scant temporal attention to Ah San's life from before drug addiction in her filmic story. She appears to have had an untroubled childhood, apart from the recent death of her father. She, alone, carries the blame for her transgressions during drug addiction. Moreover, these transgressions are more serious than Lemon Tea's. Ah San peddles illicit drugs on the streets of Hong Kong. Lemon Tea has a legitimate job in a neighbourhood convenience store. Ah San steals illicit drugs from her gangland boss and sells them on to customers of her own. Lemon Tea is a hard-working and trustworthy employee, apart from using illicit drugs. As a result, heterosexual Lemon Tea holds a comparatively higher moral standing than homosexual Ah San in *Happily Sharing*. Her higher moral standing, together with her heterosexuality, allows her to attract the attention of a moral man, who rescues her from drug addiction. Ah San, on the other hand, cannot attract the attention of such a man, due to her lower moral standing and her homosexuality. She attempts suicide, by chance is rescued by Lemon Tea and, over a long period of time, recovers from her drug addiction alone in a government-run drug rehabilitation facility. Homosexuality remains transgressive behaviour in a conservative Chinese culture that continues to place great importance on patrilineal continuity (Kleinman *et al.* 2011). Homosexuality, therefore, is readily linked discursively to drug addiction in the Hong Kong television serial drama, as in Western literary writings from bygone times (Melley 2002; Viano 2002).

While Lemon Tea carries less moral censure than Ah San, she, nevertheless, remains the object of stigmatised language that signifies the marginal status of drug addicts in Hong Kong (see Chapter 3), in particular, female drug addicts (Addenbrooke 2011; Hersey 2005; Hirschman 1995; Infantino 1999; Muzak 2008; Zhou 1999. See also Chapters 1 & 2). Time and again, she is disparaged as 'abnormal' [失常], 'tawdry' [失禮], 'stupid' [傻瓜], 'worthless' [不中用], 'hopeless' [沒救了] and 'pathetic' [可憐]; or branded a 'damned K sister' [死K妹] and a 'stinking bitch' [臭三八]. Even the moral man who supports her and guides her in her recovery from drug addiction attracts a racial slur [黑個仔]. Derogatory language that is directed at gender and race does not feature in *He Is Not Lonely*.

In sum, Lemon Tea's and Ah San's drug addictions, as depicted in *Happily Sharing*, align with a dominant meta-narrative in Chinese culture that presents drug addiction as morally transgressive and something to be feared. The transgressions that are committed during drug addiction may lead to (near) death or long-term

Marginalisation and palliation 105

incarceration, unless the young female drug addict is able to find a moral man to support her and guide her in her recovery from drug addiction. This bears a discursive resemblance to the life story of the mainland Chinese woman drug addict, Wang, in *Struggle Spirit* (see Chapter 2). Clearly, only heterosexual women (Lemon Tea and Wang) can attract the attention of a moral man. They also hold a comparatively higher moral standing than their lesbian counterparts in *Happily Sharing* and *Struggle Spirit*, who are destined to attempt suicide or endure long-term incarceration. Any transgressions that heterosexual Lemon Tea commits during drug addiction are mitigated by parental neglect and sibling abuse at a young age, and by having a culturally normative sexual identity. Cultural discourse pertaining to familial responsibility and sexual norms, therefore, are selectively drawn on in *Happily Sharing* to palliate or marginalise the young female drug addict.

While cultural discourse appears to shape the filmic stories of Lemon Tea and Ah San in these ways, the discursive schema of social work services in Hong Kong (see Chapter 3) may account for the shifting of the blame for drug addiction away from the drug addict and onto her parents and her older sister, at least where the drug addict is heterosexual. Institutional discourse appears to shape the Hong Kong life stories of drug addiction and rehabilitation that are analysed in Chapter 3 in a similar way.

Conclusion

The chapter has examined how cultural, political and institutional discourses shape temporality, subjectivity and language use in mainland Chinese, Taiwanese and Hong Kong filmic stories of drug addiction, rehabilitation and recovery. Drug addiction is presented as morally transgressive and fearful behaviour in these filmic stories that originate from three Chinese communities with disparate political systems and histories. Such a portrayal of drug addiction is in line with the dominant meta-narrative in Chinese culture. The mainland Chinese and Taiwanese films, *Quitting*, *The War of Two* and *Help Me Eros*, foreground moral transgression in drug addiction by giving scant attention to the lives of the drug addicts from before or after drug addiction. Accounts of the lives of the drug addicts during these periods in the Taiwanese and Hong Kong productions, *Jump Ashin!*, *He Is Not Lonely* and *Happily Sharing*, counterbalance the negative behaviour that characterises their lives during drug addiction. In *Jump Ashin!*, Pickle's righteous masculinity from before and after drug addiction atones for his betrayal of the man he loves, when drug-addicted. Likewise, parental neglect and sibling abuse of young heterosexual drug addicts in *He Is Not Lonely* and *Happily Sharing* help to explain their duplicity and wrongdoing during drug addiction.

Moral transgression in drug addiction is further accentuated in the two mainland Chinese films by their depictions of the drug addicts' bad behaviour toward their families. Jia and Pei Pei are unkind, cold, callous, disrespectful, deceitful,

106   *Marginalisation and palliation*

selfish, manipulative, condescending and threatening towards their parents. They go so far as to physically harm their parents: Jia beats his father, while Pei Pei addicts her mother to heroin. This constitutes extremely unfilial behaviour in Chinese culture. It also epitomises the 'betrayal of the family' that is a hallmark of drug addiction in mainland China (Kleinman *et al.* 2011, p. 255). The moral transgressions that are committed by the drug addicts in the Taiwanese and Hong Kong productions, on the other hand, tend to be directed against acquaintances, friends, partners and broader society, but not their families.

Conforming to normative masculinity in Chinese culture atones for the moral transgressions that are committed by the male drug addict. In the Taiwanese film, *Jump Ashin!*, the culturally masculine Pickle redeems himself at the conclusion of his filmic story, by overcoming his drug addiction and sacrificing his life in the same way that *wu* heroes do in the Chinese chivalry tales of old (Maggs 2012). In the Hong Kong television serial drama, *He Is Not Lonely*, the culturally masculine Ah Hou overcomes his drug addiction and reconnects with his estranged parents at the conclusion of his filmic story, by availing himself of the hetero-normative fraternity that is fostered at Zheng Sheng College. By contrast, violating normative masculinity in Chinese culture serves to further marginalise the male drug addict and condemn him to a dishonourable death or a fate worse than death. In the Taiwanese film, *Help Me Eros*, the culturally emasculated Ah Jie attempts suicide in a normatively feminine way at the conclusion of his filmic story and, while unsuccessful, apparently dies anyway. In the Hong Kong television serial drama, *He Is Not Lonely*, the culturally emasculated Ah Him succumbs to irredeemable madness at the conclusion of his filmic story.

Female drug addicts, meanwhile, are sexualised in their filmic stories. In the mainland Chinese film, *The War of Two*, Pei Pei is openly and arrogantly sexually promiscuous during drug addiction. In the Hong Kong television serial drama, *Happily Sharing*, Lemon Tea is groped by a male acquaintance at a nightclub, while Ah San's girlfriend becomes an escort girl. Moreover, language use in the filmic stories confirms the discursive position of female drug addicts in Chinese culture 'as the most shameless human beings on the earth' (Zhou 1999, p. 119). They are branded, in gendered terms, as a stinking slut, stinking bitch and damned K sister. Male drug addicts are not. Gender disempowerment also manifests in the need for the female drug addict to enlist the support and guidance of a moral man in order to recover from her drug addiction. Lemon Tea succeeds, because of the kind delivery man. Pei Pei fails, because her martyred father is dead. Ah San cannot but fail, because she is a lesbian. Cultural discourse shapes Wang's life story in *Struggle Spirit*, which is analysed in Chapter 2, in a similar way.

Woman not only are sexualised and degraded in the filmic stories, they also never serve as moral guides. In the mainland Chinese film, *Quitting*, Jia's mother and sister dearly love their drug-addicted son and brother, but they abandon his care when he becomes violent due to comorbid psychosis. In the mainland

Marginalisation and palliation   107

Chinese film, *The War of Two*, Pei Pei's mother is devoted to her drug-addicted daughter, but abandons her care and attempts to poison her, albeit with good intentions. In the Taiwanese film, *Help Me Eros*, Ah Jie's woman helpline counsellor is kind and conscientious, but she deceives Ah Jie about her appearance, is gluttonous with food, and in one scene of the film, masturbates in a bathtub full of eels that her cross-dressing husband intends to cook for her dinner. Meanwhile, in the Taiwanese film, *Jump Ashin!*, and the Hong Kong television serial dramas, the mothers of the drug addicts are absent or neglect their child.

While the filmic stories selectively draw on cultural discourse to further marginalise or palliate the drug addict in these ways, political discourse may shape the prominence of punishment [惩罚] in the mainland Chinese filmic stories. Drug addicts, and not their families, are to blame for their drug addiction, and, accordingly, must be punished for their 'evil' [恶; 孽]. This discursively aligns with the strict enforcement of the laws that criminalise illicit drug use in mainland China (Biddulph & Xie 2011; Liang & Lu 2013; Lu, Miethe & Liang 2009; Lu & Wang 2008; Trevaskes 2013; Yang *et al.* 2014; Zhou 1999, 2000a. See Chapter 1). Jia and Pei Pei are arrested or pursued by the police. Pei Pei kills herself and her drug-trafficking boyfriend in a way that invokes a familiar criminal-justice ritual in mainland China, namely, the burning of illicit drug pyres (Levin 2015; Liang & Lu 2013; Trevaskes 2013). Political discourse also may direct that the mainland Chinese drug addicts mix in bourgeois social circles. Neither drug addict associates with members of the former model political classes of worker, peasant and soldier [工农兵]. Jia is a successful film and television actor, and mocks his moral parents' peasant backgrounds. Pei Pei socialises in her boyfriend's contemporary-art-dealing circles, and disrespects her moral father's martyrdom as a People's Liberation Army soldier in Tibet. By contrast, the Taiwanese drug addicts are young, single (former) working men, while the Hong Kong drug addicts are young school-age people, apart from the lesbian. This is in keeping with the institutional reality of drug addiction in Taiwan and Hong Kong (see Chapters 1 & 3).

Political and institutional discourses may shape the positive portrayal of drug rehabilitation facilities in the mainland Chinese and Hong Kong productions. They are medical facilities in the mainland Chinese filmic stories and primarily corrective educational facilities in the Hong Kong filmic stories. The latter, accordingly, cast people in drug rehabilitation as students. This is in keeping with the discursive schema of social welfare services in Hong Kong. Institutional discourse shapes the Hong Kong life stories of drug addiction and rehabilitation in Chapter 3 in a similar way.

Chapters 2 to 4 have identified how salient cultural, political and institutional discourses are engaged or contested in contemporary Chinese life stories and filmic stories of drug addiction, rehabilitation and recovery. Chapter 5, which concludes the book, will summarise the analytic findings from these chapters. This summary will draw attention to the interrelationships and interconnections

108 *Marginalisation and palliation*

between the key narrative processes that contribute to sense-making in these stories: the temporal and causal ordering of life events, the claiming and refashioning of identities, and language use. It also will draw attention to those narrative features that are common to many of the Chinese stories of drug addiction, regardless of their geographical origin or the status of their storyteller as an insider or outsider. Awareness of these features and the discourses that shape them would be of value to people whose professional and personal responsibilities bring them into contact with Chinese people who are addicted to illicit drugs. This awareness could assist them to make sense of the stories that drug addicts tell them, and to appreciate the societal and structural pressures on former or recovering drug addicts to conform to certain stereotypes and life trajectories. At the same time, the summary will draw attention to the narrative differences that characterise stories that are told in differing geographical locations. These differences remind people whose professional and personal responsibilities bring them into contact with Chinese people who are addicted to illicit drugs that mainland Chinese, Taiwanese and Hong Kong people can tell similar, but not identical, stories about drug addiction. Finally, the chapter will discuss the key issues pertaining to morality, gender, exemplarity, institutional schema, disempowerment and stigma, which arise through the analysis of the life stories and filmic stories in Chapters 2–4. These issues resonate beyond the immediate experience of drug addiction that is recounted in the Chinese stories.

Notes

1 The published English-language title of the film.
2 The published English-language title of the film.
3 In the television serial drama counterpart, Pei Pei escapes the fire and suffers an unknown fate. Pei Pei, however, is a secondary character in *Red Recipe*. The primary woman drug addict in *Red Recipe*, a high-class contemporary art dealer, ultimately goes mad and attempts to murder the kind, honourable and dedicated woman director of the government-run drug rehabilitation facility. Madness constitutes a fate worse than death in Chinese culture (Ramsay 2008, 2013).
4 The published English-language title of the film.
5 The published English-language title of the film.
6 Later on in the film, it is revealed that Papaya, in fact, did not die.
7 This amounts to around $40,000 USD.
8 The published English-language title of the production.
9 Gao (2011) observes that parental neglect that leads to drug addiction in adulthood may encompass emotional and physical abuse, but rarely extends to sexual abuse in mainland China.
10 Over $10,000 USD.

References

Addenbrooke, M. 2011. *Survivors of addiction: narratives of recovery*. New York, NY: Routledge.

Baumler, A. 2007. *The Chinese and opium under the Republic: worse than floods and wild beasts.* New York, NY: SUNY Press.

Biddulph, S. and Xie, C. 2011. Regulating drug dependency in China: the 2008 PRC Drug Prohibition Law. *British Journal of Criminology*, 51, 978–996.

Cai, R. 2005. Gender imaginations in *Crouching Tiger, Hidden Dragon* and the *Wuxia* world. *Positions: East Asia Cultures Critique*, 13 (2), 441–471.

Cheung, C. K. and Kwan, A. Y. H. 2009. The erosion of filial piety by modernisation in Chinese cities. *Ageing and Society*, 29, 179–198.

Gao, H. 2011. *Women and heroin addiction in China's changing society.* New York, NY: Routledge.

Guo, Y. 2010. China's celebrity mothers: female virtues, patriotism and social harmony. In L. Edwards and E. Jeffreys (eds) *Celebrity in China* (pp. 45–66). Hong Kong: Hong Kong University Press.

Happily sharing, seventeen years of age [開心 share 十七歲]. 2013. Hong Kong: Television Department of Radio Television Hong Kong [香港電台電視部]/ P.A.T.H.S. to Adulthood [共創成長路].

He is not lonely [他不寂寞]. 2012/2013. Hong Kong: Television Department of Radio Television Hong Kong [香港電台電視部]/ P.A.T.H.S. to Adulthood [共創成長路].

Help me Eros [幫幫我愛神]. 2007. Taipei: Link International [聯成國際事業].

Hersey, C. 2005. Script(ing) treatment: representations of recovery from addiction in Hollywood film. *Contemporary Drug Problems*, 32, 467–493.

Hirschman, E. C. 1995. The cinematic depiction of drug addiction: a semiotic account. *Semiotica*, 104 (1/2), 119–164.

Infantino, S. C. 1999. Female addiction and sacrifice: literary tradition or user's manual? In J. Lilienfeld and J. Oxford (eds) *The languages of addiction* (pp. 91–102). New York, NY: St. Martin's Press.

Jump Ashin! [翻滾吧! 阿信]. 2011. Taipei: Deltamac [得利影視].

Kleinman, A., Yan, Y., Jun, J., Lee, S., Zhang, E., Pan, T., Wu, F. and Guo, J. 2011. *Deep China: the moral life of the person: what anthropology and psychiatry tell us about China today.* Berkeley: University of California Press.

Levin, D. 2015, January 24. Despite a crackdown, use of illegal drugs in China continues unabated. *The New York Times*. Retrieved from www.nytimes.com/2015/01/25/world/despite-a-crackdown-use-of-illegal-drugs-in-china-continues-unabated.html 24 February 2015.

Liang, B. and Lu, H. 2013. Discourses of drug problems and drug control in China: reports in the *People's Daily*, 1946–2009. *China Information*, 27 (3), 301–326.

Louie, K. 2002. *Theorising Chinese masculinity: society and gender in China.* Cambridge, UK: Cambridge University Press.

Louie, K. 2015. *Chinese masculinities in a globalizing world.* New York, NY: Routledge.

Lu, H., Miethe, T. D. and Liang, B. 2009. *China's drug practices and policies: regulating controlled substances in a global context.* Farnham, UK: Ashgate.

Lu, L. and Wang, X. 2008. Drug addiction in China. *Annals of the New York Academy of Sciences*, 1141, 304–317.

Lu, Y. 2012. *Heroic masculinity and male homosociality in Three Kingdoms and Le Morte Darthur.* Unpublished doctoral dissertation. St Lucia, QLD: The University of Queensland.

Maggs, E. 2012. *A cultural analysis of suicide in the Chinese classical novels Romance of the Three Kingdoms and Dream of Red Mansion.* Unpublished BA Honours dissertation. St Lucia, QLD: The University of Queensland.

110 *Marginalisation and palliation*

Mann, S. 2011. *Gender and sexuality in modern Chinese history*. New York, NY: Cambridge University Press.

Melley, T. 2002. A terminal case: William Burroughs and the logic of addiction. In J. F. Brodie and M. Redfield (eds) *High anxieties: cultural studies in addiction* (pp. 38–60). Berkeley: University of California Press.

Muzak, J. 2008. "Addiction got me what I needed": depression and drug addiction in Elizabeth Wurtzel's memoirs. In H. Clark (ed.) *Depression and narrative: telling the dark* (pp. 97–109). Albany, NY: SUNY Press.

P.A.T.H.S. to Adulthood. 2012. *Project aims*. Retrieved from www.paths.hk/app/webroot/en-US/info/info.php 12 February 2014.

Pearson, V. and Liu, M. 2002. Ling's death: an ethnography of a Chinese woman's suicide. *Suicide and Life – Threatening Behaviour*, 32 (4), 347–358.

Pearson, V., Phillips, M. R., He, F. and Ji, H. 2002. Attempted suicide among young rural women in the People's Republic of China: possibilities for prevention. *Suicide and Life – Threatening Behaviour*, 32 (4), 359–369.

Quitting [昨天]. 2001. Xian: Xian Film Studio [西安电影制片厂].

Ramsay, G. 2008. *Shaping minds: a discourse analysis of Chinese-language community mental health literature*. Amsterdam: John Benjamins.

Ramsay, G. 2013. *Mental illness, dementia and family in China*. London: Routledge.

The war of two [两个人的战争]. 2005. Tianjin: Tianjin Television [天津电视台].

Tolton, L. 2009. *Legitimation of violence against women in Colombia: a feminist critical discourse analytic study*. Unpublished doctoral dissertation. St Lucia, QLD: The University of Queensland.

Traphagan, J. W. 2000. *Taming oblivion: aging bodies and the fear of senility in Japan*. New York, NY: State University of New York Press.

Trevaskes, S. 2007. *Courts and criminal justice in contemporary China*. Lanham, MD: Lexington.

Trevaskes, S. 2013. Drug policy in China. In F. Rahman and N. Crofts (eds) *Drug law reform in East and Southeast Asia* (pp. 221–232). Lanham, MD: Lexington.

Vanderstaay, L. M. C. 2011. *A textual analysis of female consciousness in twenty-first century Chinese women directors' films*. Unpublished doctoral dissertation. St Lucia, QLD: The University of Queensland.

Viano, M. 2002. An intoxicated screen: reflections on film and drugs. In J. F. Brodie and M. Redfield (eds) *High anxieties: cultural studies in addiction* (pp. 134–158). Berkeley: University of California Press.

Wu, F. 2009. *Suicide and justice: a Chinese perspective*. New York, NY: Routledge.

Yang, M., Zhou, L., Hao, W. and Xiao, S. Y. 2014. Drug policy in China: progress and challenges. *The Lancet*, 383 (9916), 509.

Zhou, Y. 1999. *Anti-drug crusades in twentieth-century China: nationalism, history, and state building*. Lanham, MD: Rowman and Littlefield.

Zhou, Y. 2000a. *China's anti-drug campaign in the reform era*. Singapore: World Scientific and Singapore University Press.

Zhou, Y. 2000b. Nationalism, identity, and state-building: the antidrug crusade in the People's Republic, 1949–1952. In T. Brook and B. T. Wakabayashi (eds) *Opium regimes: China, Britain, and Japan, 1839–1952* (pp. 380–404). Berkeley: University of California Press.

5 Conclusion

Chinese Stories of Drug Addiction: Beyond the Opium Dens has identified how salient discourses can shape life stories and filmic stories of drug addiction from mainland China, Taiwan and Hong Kong. The book confirms that these stories, which are told by people who are inside the experience of drug addiction as well as outside of it, are not merely singular, individualised accounts of drug addiction. In many instances, key narrative features, such as the temporal and causal ordering of life events, the claiming and refashioning of identities, and language use, bear out prevailing cultural, political and institutional conceptions and understandings of drug addiction, rehabilitation and recovery. As a result, the stories 'perform' drug addiction as much as they 'inform' about drug addiction (Davies 1997a. See Chapter 1). The book concludes that, in order to make greater sense of the Chinese stories of drug addiction, it is important to appreciate the wider notions of morality, gender, familial responsibility, civic duty, stigma and rehabilitative therapeutic reasoning that are in play in a geographical community.

An exemplar of immorality

Harding (1986, p. 79) describes drug addiction 'as an exemplar of abnormality'. The Chinese stories of drug addiction construct it as an exemplar of immorality (Lu, Miethe & Liang 2009). Drug addicts in the stories invariably contravene cherished cultural norms and values that define proper and honourable conduct within the Chinese family and society. The mainland Chinese drug addicts typically betray their families (Kleinman *et al.* 2011). Drug-addicted mothers abandon their children, rather than give up illicit drugs. Drug-addicted children inflict unconscionable physical harm on their parents. The Taiwanese and Hong Kong drug addicts, on the other hand, typically transgress against society. They join miscreant subcultures and commit crime. They wantonly deceive their friends and acquaintances. Meanwhile, women drug addicts from all three geographical regions – and the emasculated male drug addict – usually are sexually suspect or promiscuous.

112 Conclusion

This immorality that is culturally ascribed to Chinese drug addicts causes them to lose face [脸] (Kleinman *et al.* 2011). They, potentially, also harm the face of their immediate family members. Children, in particular, can be permanently tarnished by the criminal transgressions of their drug-addicted parents [父母作奸犯科, 子女必须低人一等]. Of deeper gravity for the drug addicts themselves is their 'social creation' as 'nonpersons' (Kleinman *et al.* 2011, p. 258). This stems from their failure to live up to culturally prescribed responsibilities and expectations, by not being filial, productive, respectable, decent, civil and loyal to members of their family and society (Kleinman *et al.* 2011). As a consequence, they forgo their 'rights' as human beings and members of society (Kleinman *et al.* 2011, p. 243). This readily enables their removal from society by way of arbitrary incarceration or, until recent times in mainland China and Taiwan, state execution.

Incarceration and death are common motifs across the Chinese stories of drug addiction. All of the mainland Chinese drug addicts and most of the Hong Kong drug addicts are forcibly detained for a period of time at some point in their stories. The Taiwanese drug addicts, meanwhile, constantly face death or madness, a fate worse than death in Chinese culture (Ramsay 2008, 2013). Death also features in the mainland Chinese stories, and, on occasion, in the Hong Kong stories. Madness, however, only features in the mainland Chinese and Hong Kong *filmic* stories. The intense stigma against mental illness in Chinese culture may explain the absence of accounts of madness in the mainland Chinese and Hong Kong *life* stories. This cultural stigma taints both the sufferer and his or her family members (Ramsay 2008, 2013). People, therefore, would be reluctant to invoke mental illness in their life stories (Ramsay 2013).

The status of drug addicts as non-persons in Chinese culture clearly manifests in the language used to describe them in the mainland Chinese and Hong Kong stories of drug addiction. Drug addicts in these stories are assigned an identity that is signified by Chinese expressions [瘾君子; 隐君子; 吸毒者; 道友] that connote 'disrepute and iniquity' [劣迹斑斑]. In addition, the drug addicts are commonly labelled as 'non-persons' [非人; 無人性]. As such, they readily can be socially discarded as 'unwanted dregs' [不受歡迎的地底泥], 'scum' [人渣], 'degenerates' [敗類], 'losers' [瀾泥] and 'a waste of life' [唔死都冇用]. Although such stigmatic language is absent from the Taiwanese stories, the Taiwanese drug addict in *Help Me Eros* is portrayed in like terms and dies ignobly at the conclusion of his filmic story. Women drug addicts, in particular, attract venal, stigmatic labels in the Chinese stories of drug addiction. They frequently are branded using gendered and, often, sexualised expressions, such as 'heroin sister' [白粉妹], 'damned K sister' [死K妹], 'stinking slut' [臭婊子] and 'stinking bitch' [臭三八]. Such language discursively aligns with their depictions in the Chinese mass media, Zhou (1999, p. 119) reports, 'as the most shameless human beings on the earth'. Their Chinese cultural shamelessness is accentuated, Dikötter, Laamann and Zhou (2004, p. 113) observe, by their 'giving birth to "addicted" infants'.

Conclusion 113

Normative gender in Chinese culture, therefore, gains discursive significance in the life stories and filmic stories of drug addiction. The gendered and sexualised slurs that the Chinese woman drug addict frequently attracts goes hand in hand with her portrayal in the stories as sexually promiscuous (Pei Pei, the Operation Dawn women, Lemon Tea and Ah San's girlfriend) or of dubious sexuality by Chinese cultural norms (Wang's fellow inmate, the Operation Dawn women and Ah San). By contrast, the male drug addict does not attract such slurs. Those men who are portrayed to be sexually promiscuous (Ah Jie) or of dubious sexuality by Chinese cultural norms (Ah Him) are emasculated and die ignobly, or go mad, at the conclusion of their stories. The masculine man, on the other hand, is able to redeem himself in the stories. His moral transgressions that are committed during drug addiction can be atoned for by displays of *wen* [文] (literary) or *wu* [武] (martial) masculinity before or after drug addiction. This can lead him into a seemingly successful and enduring recovery from drug addiction (Wen, the Daytop men and Ah Hou), where he is able to 'return to society' [回归社会; 重返社会] or to his family as a 'moral man' [男子汉]. Alternatively, he may die after his recovery from drug addiction, but in an honourable, righteous and normatively masculine way (Pickle).

The mainland Chinese life stories that are analysed in Chapter 2 utilise this gendered morality in drug addiction by creating political exemplars. Bakken (2000, p. 1) notes the importance of these political 'exemplars' [榜样] in a mainland Chinese state where the 'morality and . . . physical, mental, and behavioural qualities' of its citizens have 'become important for the sake of state power and the nation' (see also Brady 2002, 2008, 2009, 2012). In the life stories, only men are exemplary in drug addiction. Wen is a meritorious citizen before and after drug addiction. He is a successful individual entrepreneur, who lives a modest, unpretentious life [小康水平] despite his business acumen. He is a loyal and devoted family man, who has unswerving respect for the Chinese state and the authorities. He is masculine and proactively contributes to society. Although Wen transgresses when drug-addicted, he maintains a semblance of morality by continuing to look after his family and, for the most part, continuing to work and earn money. He never resorts to crime as most drug addicts do, including his wife. Moreover, he respects the authorities at all times and is motivated by his esteem for the venerated male leaders of China, Sun Yat-sen and Mao Zedong, to take the initiative to quit drugs. He steadfastly persists in his self-rehabilitative endeavour and successfully becomes drug-free in recovery, even though he and his son are abandoned by his drug-addicted wife. The semblance of morality that Wen maintains during drug-addiction is plausible because it is consistent with his conduct from before and after drug addiction. It also is plausible due to his everydayness and his largely seamless performance of Chinese masculinity before, during and after drug addiction.

The woman drug addict, by contrast, cannot be exemplary. Wang is a successful businesswoman before and after drug addiction. She, however, divorces her

114   *Conclusion*

husband when she becomes bored with him, and lives an independent life separated from her natal family and daughter when she recovers from drug addiction. During and after drug addiction she is indulgent, assertive, rebellious and disrespectful toward the authorities. She considers herself to be extraordinary throughout her life story and willingly associates with lesbians. Wang claims a semblance of morality during drug addiction, by refusing to commit crime or engage in licentious acts in order to fund her drug addiction, and by selflessly helping out her fellow inmates in the re-education-through-labour facility. The plausibility of this claim to morality, however, is diminished in her story due to her habitually unfeminine behaviour, her subjective fragility and inconsistency, and her repeated assertions of exceptionality and extraordinariness. As a result, exemplarity in Wang's story is afforded to Deputy Director Guo, the male governor [所长] of the re-education-through-labour facility where she is an inmate for several years. He is a high-ranking model socialist cadre. Moreover, Wang considers him to be wise, just, upright, righteous, rational and masculine. She looks to him for support and guidance in her recovery from drug addiction, and attributes all her success in overcoming drug addiction to him.

The morality of the everyday body in recovery

Gibson, Acquah and Robinson (2004, p. 608) describe recovery from drug addiction as a process which espouses the 'morality of the everyday body'. The Chinese stories of drug addiction, likewise, discursively champion a return in recovery to a 'normal' [正常] everyday existence in society or with one's family. An important measure of the recovering drug addicts' everydayness in these stories is a gendering of their bodies in line with Chinese cultural norms. As a consequence, their reclaiming of morality by being drug-free in recovery – commonly denoted by a Chinese expression [操守] that literally means to possess 'personal integrity' – becomes discursively bound to the performance of normative gender in Chinese culture.

In recovery from drug addiction, men aspire to work hard, be productive and support their families. Women, meanwhile, aspire to be competent wives, mothers or daughters. An exception is found in some of the Hong Kong life stories, where people in recovery seek to live independent and autonomous lives. The process by which drug addicts set about achieving their everyday morality in recovery also is gendered in the Chinese stories. Masculine men can recover primarily on their own initiative (Wen), with the help of a close male friend (Pickle), or with the support of a drug rehabilitation facility that fosters heteronormative bonding or has a patriarch in charge (Ah Hou and the Daytop, Operation Dawn and CZSC men). Heterosexual women, meanwhile, can recover with the help and guidance of a moral man (Wang and Lemon Tea), or with the support of a patriarchal drug rehabilitation facility (the Daytop, Operation Dawn and CZSC women). Where there is no moral man or patriarchal institution to support and guide these women into recovery, they are doomed to suffer Pei Pei's and Ah San's tragic fates of death or near fatal overdose. In line with this masculinisation of the process of recovery in the Chinese stories of drug addiction, women never hold the position of moral guide. Wen's recovery from drug addiction is facilitated by the Xinjiang Aunty, but he makes the critical decision to quit illicit drugs of his own accord and, on his return home to Xian, singlehandedly remains drug-free by wholly and steadfastly reengaging his meritorious and masculine self from before drug addiction. Moreover, the Xinjiang Aunty, while motherly in line with gender norms in Chinese culture, also is a strict and disciplined People's Liberation Army veteran.

Gender also appears to impact on the durability of recovery from drug addiction in the Chinese life stories and filmic stories. Men recover with greater certainty, while women recover with greater fragility. The phenomenon is most evident in the mainland Chinese stories. Pei Pei catastrophically relapses from her brief recovery from drug addiction and commits murder-suicide. Wang eventually achieves a long-term recovery from drug addiction, but her emergent non-addict identity in recovery is forever haunted by her drug-addicted self from before. Wen, by contrast, is able to successfully unfasten his drug-addicted self from his recaptured moral self in recovery. Even Jia, who is mentally ill as a result of his drug addiction, appears to leave behind his drug-addicted self from before, as he lives an everyday life with his family at the conclusion of his filmic story.[1] This greater durability of a man's recovery from drug addiction may stem from his greater ability, in the stories, to maintain a semblance of normative masculinity during drug addiction. He, subsequently, can draw on and readily nurture these traces of masculinity, as he develops his emergent moral and masculine non-addict identity in recovery. By contrast, women lose all vestige of their normative femininity during drug addiction in the stories. As a consequence, they have no subjective foundation, that is, apart from their addict identity, on which to construct an emergent moral and feminine non-addict identity in recovery. What is more, their emergent non-addict identity in recovery is fashioned, not by themselves, but under the tutelage of the moral man or the patriarchal institution that supports and guides them in their recovery from drug addiction.

Stigma, marginalisation and palliation

Cultural stigma repeatedly surfaces in the Chinese stories of drug addiction. It most clearly is evident in the stereotypical use of negative labels to degrade the personhood of the Chinese drug addict, as discussed in the initial section of this chapter. The use of these labels linguistically signifies and discursively affirms the cultural, political and institutional construction of drug addicts as 'marginal beings' [边缘人] in the Chinese stories of drug addiction. This disempowers and disenfranchises the drug addicts such that, in most cases, they only can be rescued from their drug addiction by moral men or the (patriarchal) state and its affiliated institutions.

116 *Conclusion*

Chinese cultural stigma weighs most heavily on the woman drug addict (Zhou 1999). This is borne out in the Chinese stories by the woman drug addict's inability to retain a vestige of normative femininity when drug-addicted. This forever marks her as a marginal being, whose claims of meritorious behaviour from before, during or after drug addiction lack credibility. This, in turn, seals her mortal fate, unless a moral man or patriarchal institution rescues her from her drug addiction. The male drug addict, by contrast, can more readily atone for the moral transgressions that he commits when drug-addicted. He does so by retaining a semblance of normative masculinity when drug-addicted. This makes his meritorious conduct from before or after drug addiction more plausible. As a result, the Chinese stories of drug addiction can overcome cultural stigma to some extent and palliate the male drug addict through his displays of heteronormative fraternity, family-centeredness, everydayness, business acumen and masculine righteousness from before, during and after drug addiction. The Chinese stories, however, cannot palliate an emasculated male drug addict. He remains a marginal being, who is destined to suffer the same mortal fate as the unsupported woman drug addict.

The filmic stories from all three geographical regions and the life stories from mainland China and Taiwan discursively validate this stigma against drug addicts in Chinese culture. This may be because, as Kleinman *et al.* (2011, p. 255) observe in mainland China, 'using humiliation and stigmatization to socially punish the [Chinese] misdoer is believed to be a powerful tactic for warning other people not to engage in socially defined misconduct, such as . . . illicit drug use'. The Hong Kong life stories, however, often contest this stigma. This is accomplished by constructing drug addicts as essentially good human beings, who momentarily have veered off-track in their lives. The culturally stigmatised addict identity [道友] that society assigns to them for life is countered in these life stories by the everyday 'student' identity [學員] that they take on during drug rehabilitation. In these stories, the drug rehabilitative facility constitutes a place of learning, where drug addicts are taught to believe in and value themselves, and to formulate and achieve their personal goals. Taking on a student identity while in drug rehabilitation discursively normalises them. Everyone is a student at some stage of their lives. In this way, the Hong Kong life stories are able to discursively empower a highly stigmatised group in the community, in contrast to the filmic stories from the three geographical regions and the life stories from mainland China and Taiwan, which discursively disempower drug addicts in line with the prevailing meta-narrative in Chinese culture. This cultural meta-narrative presents drug addiction as morally transgressive and something to be feared.

'Preferred' stories of the drug rehabilitation facility

The Chinese stories of drug addiction that are analysed in Chapter 3 are shaped in ways that bear out the story of drug addiction that the rehabilitation facility

Conclusion 117

in which they are told 'prefers' (Ramsay 2013, p. 13). At the same time, they engage or contest prevailing cultural and political discourses. It is likely that the preferred story of drug addiction would become apparent to drug addicts as life stories are 'told and retold' by others during drug rehabilitation activities (Ramsay 2013, p. 13). Drug rehabilitation facilities somewhat differ across mainland China, Taiwan and Hong Kong. Mainland Chinese facilities are secular, due to the mainland Chinese state's ongoing suspicions about organised religion, which date back to the Communist takeover in 1949. Private facilities add to a vast network of government-run facilities across mainland China (see Chapter 2), but their therapeutic reasoning is not grounded in spiritual teaching. It would remain highly unlikely that a Communist mainland Chinese government would allow a religious organisation to undertake as sensitive a social and political endeavour as drug rehabilitation in the foreseeable future.

The situation in Taiwan, however, is quite different. This can be traced to the long history of Christianity in Taiwan, which dates back to the seventeenth century (Kuo 2008; Lo 2011). This has brought about an indigenisation of Christianity in Taiwan, although the Taiwanese stories of drug addiction reveal a degree of scepticism and suspicion toward Christianity in Taiwan, at least amongst some of the population. Christian organisations are the dominant providers of non-penal drug rehabilitation services in Taiwan. They offer free-of-charge drug rehabilitation programs, where therapeutic reasoning is grounded in Christian teachings. Hong Kong, like Taiwan, has a network of Christian-run drug rehabilitation facilities. Hong Kong also has an extensive network of secular facilities. These Christian and secular drug rehabilitation facilities in Hong Kong espouse charitable missions that reflect the long and largely unbroken history of the provision of social welfare services in Hong Kong (Jones 1990).

The stories of drug addiction that are told in the Daytop drug rehabilitation facility in mainland China describe the transformation of the drug addicts [瘾君子; 隐君子], from sullied, shameless, abnormal, marginal selves, who they usually had been since a young age, to completely new, normal, drug-free, moral selves in recovery [操守]. This stark transformation can only be brought about under the stewardship of the Daytop therapeutic community, which is led by a 'mighty' [伟大] patriarch, Director Yang. The Daytop community, of which they become 'members' [成员], refashions them into their new selves in recovery. Following this, they can return to society and live a normal and productive life, as good socialist citizens do in contemporary mainland Chinese society. Moreover, their newfound morality and normality [正常人] are gendered in line with Chinese cultural norms, as outlined earlier in this chapter. The Daytop community prescribes that the new man will be righteous and readily employable, and will get married and have a child. The new woman, on the other hand, will be frugal, refocus on her home life, and be a good wife and mother. As a result, the stories told in the Daytop facility bear out 'the working logic of the [Daytop] treatment

118   Conclusion

system' (Järvinen & Andersen 2009, p. 865), while upholding Chinese political and cultural scripts.

In like manner, the stories of drug addiction that are told in the Operation Dawn drug rehabilitation facilities in Taiwan bear out Christian schema while maintaining Chinese cultural affinity. The Taiwanese drug addicts are 'big sinners' [大罪人] who face violent deaths and 'eternal damnation in Hell' [萬劫不復的無底坑], in line with Christian teachings. Meanwhile, they sin by contravening gender norms in Chinese culture. Women are bad daughters, wives and mothers, who are of dubious sexual repute. Men, on the other hand, are unrighteous [不義] in their dealings with other men and their parents. The drug addicts are saved by being 'reborn' [脫胎換骨] as drug-free, moral human beings [做人] in Operation Dawn. Their newfound Christian selves are filial [孝] and productively contribute to their families [禮]. This helps to restore their families' moral face [臉], which has been lost during drug addiction. As such, their new, drug-free selves are moral in both Christian and Confucian terms.

Institutional discourse, however, shapes the stories of drug addiction that are told in the Christian CZSC and secular SARDA drug rehabilitation facilities in Hong Kong in a distinctly different way. The Hong Kong drug addicts are not fundamentally sullied and flawed human beings, who are refashioned into completely new drug-free, moral human beings through their spell in a drug rehabilitation facility (Daytop and Operation Dawn). Instead, they are fundamentally good human beings, who momentarily have deviated off-track due to certain negative external influences and circumstances. CZSC and SARDA restore them to their true, good inner-selves, by casting them as ordinary 'students' [學員], who can look forward to rewarding, autonomous, drug-free lives in recovery. The personal integrity that will accompany their lives in recovery [操守] will be fortified by the newfound senses of self-worth, self-fulfilment and self-confidence that they have developed while in the CZSC and SARDA facilities. This occurs regardless of the age or gender of the drug addicts, whether or not their drug rehabilitation facility functions as a properly constituted school (CZSC), and whether their drug rehabilitation facility is nominally Christian (CZSC) or secular (SARDA). It is likely that such an account of drug addiction draws on the discursive schema of social work services in Hong Kong, which espouses liberal notions of client-centeredness and client-empowerment (Jones 1990; Lo 2011). The Hong Kong stories do not surrender the autonomy of the drug addict to absolute control by the (patriarchal) rehabilitative authority, as the mainland Chinese stories (the Daytop therapeutic community) and the Taiwanese stories (the Operation Dawn Christian community) do. The Hong Kong stories also do not gender the drug addict in disempowering ways that invoke Chinese cultural stereotypes. Moreover, they do not yield to the stigmatic language that commonly marks drug addiction in Chinese culture, especially in Hong Kong. As such, these Hong Kong life stories are told in ways that

Conclusion 119

appreciably resist cultural discourse, in contrast to the mainland Chinese and Taiwanese counterparts.

Chinese versus Western stories of drug addiction

There are a number of similarities and differences between the analytic findings of this book and the findings of the research that has examined Western stories of drug addiction, as outlined in Chapter 1. The Chinese stories of drug addiction, like their Western counterparts, construct drug addiction as abnormal, bad, imprisoning, phoney and dirty. They likewise construct non-addiction in recovery as normal, good, liberating, genuine and clean. The Chinese and Western stories, however, differ in that recovery from drug addiction in the latter tends to be contingent on the '[a]rticulation of a new guiding value', which can motivate, sustain and empower the drug addict in recovery (Hänninen & Koski-Jännes 1999, p. 1,847). By contrast, the guiding value in recovery in the Chinese stories is often neither new nor empowering, but informed, in normative ways, by prevailing cultural or political discourse.

The Chinese and Western stories of drug addiction discursively draw on similar directional and spatial metaphors. Drug addicts commonly descend into addiction and rise up into non-addiction in recovery. They are on the inside when undertaking drug rehabilitation and go out when they relapse. Remaining in a drug rehabilitation program and ascending into recovery often constitute a battle in the Chinese and Western stories. This battle is discursively congruent with a wider political war on drugs, which the mainland Chinese authorities continue to cast as the 'people's war against drugs' [人民禁毒战争] (Liang & Lu 2013, p. 315. See also Chapters 2 & 4). The Chinese stories, however, differ from their Western counterparts in the vocabulary used to denote non-addiction in recovery. Drug addicts become 'clean' in recovery in Anglophone Western stories (Weinberg 2000), while they gain 'personal integrity' [操守] in the Chinese stories. Cleanliness is a concrete, external, physical state of being that most people can attain through a fairly straightforward and familiar course of action. Personal integrity, on the other hand, is an abstract, inner, moral state of being that most people only gain through a relatively complex and reflective learning process. The Chinese expression [操守] that denotes being drug-free in recovery, by implicit opposition, points to the essential connection between drug addiction and a loss of morality in Chinese culture. This reflects the cultural status of drug addiction as an exemplar of immorality, as borne out in the Chinese stories (see earlier in this chapter).

Both Chinese and Western stories of drug addiction gender drug addiction. The woman drug addict loses her normative femininity during drug addiction, by neglecting or debasing her role as a mother or wife (Addenbrooke 2011; Friedling 1996; Hirschman 1995; Muzak 2008). This makes plain 'the double alterity' of being a drug addict and a woman (Infantino 1999, p. 93). The Chinese stories,

120   *Conclusion*

however, differ from Western stories in that women rarely are empowered in their recovery from drug addiction, an exception being women in the Hong Kong life stories. While women in Western stories may fashion 'identities more congruent with their political beliefs and more inclusive of their gender-specific needs', women in the Chinese stories rarely do so (Aston 2009, p. 624). Moreover, while Western women may recover from their drug addiction with the guidance and support of other women, Chinese women only do so with the guidance and support of a moral man or patriarchal institution. Meanwhile, men in the Chinese stories invariably are normatively masculine in their recovery from drug addiction. This contrasts with Western stories, where men can take on normatively feminine traits, such as actively connecting with and emotionally sharing with others (Hänninen & Koski-Jännes 1999).

This difference in the gendering of the Chinese and Western stories may stem from a greater resonance of traditional patriarchal values and gender roles in contemporary Chinese societies (Croll 1995; Guo 2010; Louie 2002; Pearson & Liu 2002; Roberts 2010). It also may stem from drug addiction being an exemplar of immorality (see earlier in this chapter), in a Chinese culture where women drug addicts are 'the most shameless human beings on the earth' (Zhou 1999, p. 119). This may make it impossible for a woman drug addict to rehabilitate and recover from drug addiction, in stories of this type, without the guidance and support of a moral man or patriarchal institution. Alternatively, the difference in the gendering of the Chinese and Western stories may stem from the latter's greater biomedicalisation of drug addiction (Anderson, Swan & Lane 2010; Muzak 2007; Weinberg 2000). This facilitates community formation during drug rehabilitation and recovery, since drug addiction, like any illness, is 'a tangible and distinct condition that signifies as an obviously serious problem' that warrants social connection and support (Muzak 2008, p. 102). Accordingly, it would be unremarkable if, in the process of overcoming their 'illness', drug-addicted men and women in Western stories form social attachments with other men and women in ways that may countermand gender norms or empower.

The mainland Chinese and Hong Kong *life* stories, by contrast, do not biomedicalise drug addiction. Drug addicts in these stories do not invoke an illness identity. This likely is because biomedicalising drug addiction may attract the intense stigma that illness akin to mental illness draws in Chinese culture (Ramsay 2008, 2013). This stigma extends beyond the sufferers and onto their family members, since such illness is believed to run through family lines in Chinese culture. As a consequence, if drug addicts were to biomedicalise their drug addiction, they would risk adding to the stigmatic burden that they already shoulder due to their moral transgression in being a drug addict. This means that, unlike their Western counterparts, they cannot be subjectively empowered by 'the "gift" of a new [illness] identity' that the biomedical explanatory model offers to them (Aston 2009, p. 619). Nor can they absolve their moral censure by placing the blame for their drug addiction on illness. Instead, just like the non-white minorities and the poor in Western stories, the blame for their drug addiction lies in personal or familial 'vice' and 'character defect' (Muzak 2007, pp. 256–257). Notwithstanding this, the Taiwanese life stories commonly invoke the biomedical explanatory model. This may be because the drug addicts in these stories have been born again into new, drug-free lives as Christians. This washes away their past moral and patho-physiological taints (see Chapter 3). Meanwhile, the *filmic* stories of drug addiction from all three geographical regions also invoke the biomedical explanatory model. This may be because these stories tend to be told by outsiders, who would remain unaffected by any stigmatic taint that biomedicalising drug addiction may bring upon drug addicts and their family members.

The Chinese stories also can be differentiated from their Western counterparts by the predominance of linear life trajectories in drug addiction. By contrast, both linear and non-linear life trajectories characterise Western stories (see Chapter 1). In a linear trajectory, drug addicts may progress from a normal, everyday life from before addiction, into a debased life as a drug addict during addiction, and onto a drug-free, moral life in recovery. Distinct identities and moral traits that often are normatively gendered characterise each temporal stage of this linear life trajectory. Meanwhile, in the non-linear life trajectory, drug addicts may simultaneously take on addict and non-addict identities, as they successfully maintain the appearance of an everyday life while profoundly addicted to illicit drugs. The woman drug addict, for example may be able to capably take care of her children when they are at home, and then give herself over to her drug addiction when they go off to school. A constant tension between addict and non-addict identities that is aggravated by an endless cycle of quitting and relapse characterises this non-linear life trajectory in drug addiction (McIntosh & McKeganey 2000; Murdoch 1999). The absence of this non-linear life trajectory in the Chinese stories of drug addiction may stem from Chinese cultural scripts requiring an unequivocal resolution to the moral quandary of drug addiction. This is apparent in the Chinese stories of drug addiction, where the life trajectories of drug addicts invariably culminate in death, madness or long-term incarceration, in line with the prevailing meta-narrative in Chinese culture, or in an enduring drug-free life in recovery, when they have gained the support and guidance of a moral man or patriarchal institution.

Political discourse appears to shape the mainland Chinese stories of drug addiction in ways that make them stand apart from their Taiwanese, Hong Kong and Western counterparts. Some of the mainland Chinese life stories are marked by familiar political language, in equating drug addiction and recovery to a 'long-term struggle' [作斗争], and non-addiction in recovery to 'liberation' [解放]. These stories also draw on familiar political imagery, in likening the battle against drug addiction to the determined efforts of the Communist forces during the anti-Japanese war and the civil war. Such imagery continues to characterise

122   *Conclusion*

contemporary political pronouncements about the sovereignty of mainland China's off-shore territory.

Meanwhile, all of the mainland Chinese life stories and filmic stories appear to be politically correct, in presenting drug addiction as primarily an affliction of those who mix in bourgeois and business circles. Very few of the mainland Chinese drug addicts are members of the former model political classes of worker, peasant and soldier [工农兵]. These stories also pay tribute to the meritorious socialist citizen, the model socialist cadre, the leadership of the mainland Chinese state, as well as valued state institutions such as the People's Liberation Army and the police force. Moreover, the mainland Chinese stories appear to meet the political agenda of the mainland Chinese state by their discursive emphasis on punishment [惩罚]. As stated in Chapter 1, there is strict enforcement of the laws that criminalise illicit drug use and trafficking in mainland China (see also the concluding section of this chapter). Possibly by political design, all of the drug addicts in the mainland Chinese stories are beneficially incarcerated at some stage of their drug-using lives, or they are killed in a way that invokes a familiar criminal-justice ritual in mainland China, namely, the burning of illicit drug pyres.

Clinical implications

The analytic findings of the book and their similarity to and difference from the findings of the research that has been conducted into Western stories of drug addiction may be of value to people whose professional and personal responsibilities bring them into contact with Chinese people who are addicted to illicit drugs. This would especially be the case where this contact is cross-cultural in nature, as could occur in multicultural societies such as Australia, Canada and the United States. The status of drug addiction as an exemplar of immorality in Chinese culture is a case in point. Health professionals may benefit from an awareness of how and why drug addiction is so maligned in Chinese societies. Drug addiction constitutes moral transgression in Western and Chinese societies. This moral transgression, however, seems to take on a greater weight and a different form in Chinese culture. Chinese drug addicts betray their families and the wider society in the most fundamental of ways (Kleinman *et al.* 2011). They abrogate their culturally prescribed roles and duties, and do not contribute to the greater good. Women drug addicts, in particular, stand out as utterly shameless, highly sexualised beings, who neglect or debase their roles as dutiful mothers, wives or daughters. They are so morally impoverished by their drug addiction that they only can achieve redemption through death or through the kind and generous efforts of moral men or patriarchal institutions. Even then, it remains highly unlikely that they ever could be accepted by Chinese society as normal people [正常人].

Taïeb *et al.* (2008, p. 994) state that a drug addict will draw on the 'popular and professional' stories of drug addiction that are encountered in daily life, in

Conclusion 123

order 'to organize his or her life, to give it intelligibility, and to attempt to become "coauthor as to its meaning"'. Citing Ricoeur, they add that 'this appropriation can take on a multitude of forms, from the pitfall of servile imitation, . . . to all the stages of fascination, to suspicion, to rejection, to the search for a just distance with regard to such models of identification' (Taïeb *et al.* 2008, p. 994). People whose professional and personal responsibilities bring them into contact with Chinese drug addicts may therefore benefit from an awareness of the popular and professional stories of drug addiction that are commonplace in Chinese societies. This may help them to appreciate the societal and structural pressures on Chinese drug addicts to conform to certain stereotypes and life trajectories. This may also enable them to recognise where and how Chinese drug addicts appropriate elements of these stories into their own stories. The woman drug addict, for example may repeatedly confess her failures as a mother, wife or daughter. Alternatively, she may go to great pains to point out that, unlike other women drug addicts who she knows, she is not sexually promiscuous or deviant. Meanwhile, the male drug addict may repeatedly confess his unrighteousness and his failure to provide for his family. Alternatively, he may repeatedly draw attention to his *wen* and *wu* masculine traits, his everydayness, and his unswerving respect for authority. People whose professional and personal responsibilities bring them into contact with Chinese drug addicts also may benefit from an awareness that the popular and professional stories of drug addiction – and, so, the stories told by their drug-addicted clients or loved ones – can vary depending on their geographical community of origin, namely mainland China, Taiwan and Hong Kong. Moreover, they subsequently can use this knowledge to empower their clients or loved ones, by exposing them to a greater selection of Chinese stories told from inside or outside of their geographical community of origin (Taïeb *et al.* 2008).

The aetiology of drug addiction that is alluded to in the Chinese stories may be of particular interest to clinicians who work with Chinese drug addicts. A number of causal factors are presented in the stories. These, at times, differ across geographical regions. In the mainland Chinese stories, Wen's drug addiction is caused by his heteronormative fraternity and his desire to expand his business enterprise. Wang's drug addiction stems from a bit of harmless fun with some women friends, just after she had divorced her husband. The Daytop clients become drug-addicted because of deep-seated personal flaws and shortcomings from a very young age. Meanwhile, Jia's and Pei Pei's drug addictions can be attributed to their narcissistic, bourgeois lifestyles. In the Taiwanese stories, the Operation Dawn clients become drug-addicted because they are sinners, as all people are in Christian schema. Ah Jie's drug addiction can be attributed to his emasculated character, while Pickle's drug addiction stems from parental neglect and abuse. In the Hong Kong stories, clients of the CZSC and SARDA facilities become drug-addicted due to family troubles or after being led astray by peers. Ah Hou's, Ah Him's and Lemon Tea's drug addictions, like Pickle's, stem from family neglect and abuse.

124　*Conclusion*

Additionally, Ah Him, like Ah Jie, is an emasculated character. Ah San, meanwhile, is a lesbian.

Family trouble, neglect and abuse, therefore, often present as causal factors in the Hong Kong and Taiwanese stories of drug addiction. By contrast, families tend to be blameless, and often are commendable, in the mainland Chinese stories. The aetiology of drug addiction in these stories is located more in the individual, stemming from deep-seated character flaws or imprudent lifestyle choices. Where the aetiology of drug addiction is individualised in the Hong Kong and Taiwanese stories, the sexuality of the drug addict often is in question: the male drug addict is emasculated and the woman drug addict is homosexual. As has been noted in this chapter and Chapters 2–4, the storytellers from all three geographical regions shy away from a biomedical aetiology for drug addiction, unless they are born-again Christians or are telling the story from outside of the experience of drug addiction. This likely is due to the intense stigma that illness akin to mental illness attracts in Chinese culture (Ramsay 2008, 2013).

Finally, people whose professional and personal responsibilities bring them into contact with Chinese drug addicts may benefit from an awareness of the intense stigma against drug addiction in Chinese culture. The analysis that is undertaken in this book suggests that a number of social and political factors can contribute to this stigma. Clinicians may be able to take these factors into account and devise an effective therapeutic regimen for lessening the impact of cultural stigma on the Chinese client. This regimen may differ from that commonly employed for non-Chinese clients. For example biomedicalising drug addiction may be counterproductive and only amplify the cultural stigma felt by a Chinese client. The Hong Kong life stories of drug addiction that are analysed in Chapter 3 may offer a starting point for developing such a therapeutic regimen that effectively destigmatises drug addiction while empowering the Chinese drug addict.

Epilogue

On 24 January 2015, *The New York Times* published a news article on mainland China's latest nationwide campaign against illicit drugs. The report claims that the current clampdown is in response to a marked increase in drug addiction in mainland Chinese cities. It puts the number of mainland Chinese drug addicts at present 'at roughly 13 million', much greater than the National Narcotics Control Commission's most recent figure of 2.76 million (Levin 2015). The report adds that while heroin remains the most commonly used illicit drug of addiction in mainland China's vast rural areas, methamphetamine may be overtaking heroin in the urban areas.

The clampdown began in October 2014 and by January the following year had netted '[a]round 180,000 drug users', of which 'more than 55,000 [had been] sent to government-run rehabilitation centers' (Levin 2015). A prominent victim of the clampdown was Jaycee Chan, the son of Chinese film star Jackie Chan [成龍].

Conclusion 125

Jackie Chan immediately publicly condemned his son for his illicit drug use and crime. He lamented that his son's actions had brought great dishonour to the Chan family name. Jaycee Chan, in turn, publicly expressed his profound remorse for his wrongdoing, following his release from detention on 13 February 2015. He acknowledged that he had shamed his family and offended broader society.

Jaycee Chan's widely publicised story of drug addiction emulates many elements of the mainland Chinese stories that are analysed in this book. Jaycee was living a bourgeois lifestyle amongst mainland China's artistic elites. He fundamentally betrayed his family by succumbing to drug addiction – quintessentially immoral conduct that is 'threatening to individuals, families and the nation' (Dikötter, Laamann & Zhou 2004, p. 112). In the apparent absence of his moral (and normatively masculine) father's support and guidance, Jaycee eventually was arrested and incarcerated. On his release from prison, he was openly contrite and promised to return to society and live a moral, drug-free life.

This book has demonstrated the value of examining stories of drug addiction that are told from inside the experience (life stories) as well as outside of it (filmic stories) (Ramsay 2013; Taïeb *et al.* 2008; Viano 2002). What may be silenced in one narrative form can be voiced in the other. Filmic stories, for example often more readily engage 'the prevailing meta-narrative that circulates in a cultural community . . . aspects of which may remain hidden from view in life stories told by those inside the experience' (Ramsay 2013, p. 61. See also Hersey 2005; Hirschman 1992, 1995). This prevailing meta-narrative in Chinese culture presents drug addiction as morally transgressive and something to be feared. The book concludes that drug addiction is feared because it inevitably leads to violence and death, or to mental illness, a fate worse than death in Chinese culture (Ramsay 2008, 2013).

The book's analytic findings support Davies's (1997a, p. 9) claim that drug addiction is not just a state of being but also 'a way of thinking' and 'a way of talking', that is, a discursive 'construct' (see also Hänninen & Koski-Jännes 1999; Hughes 2007). The contemporary Chinese life stories and filmic stories that are analysed in the book, as stated in the outset of this chapter, do not merely 'inform' about drug addiction but 'perform' drug addiction (Davies 1997a). Future research may seek to further examine how these discursive processes of informing and performing manifest in contemporary Chinese mass media reports and literary stories about drug addiction, as well as in contemporary Chinese accounts of drug addiction that are elicited during interview. In this way, a greater understanding can be gained about a pervasive social phenomenon that is central to the Chinese historical narrative and continues to command the attention of contemporary Chinese societies across the globe.

Note

1 Sadly, in real life, Jia eventually relapsed into drug addiction and suicided in his forties.

126 *Conclusion*

References

Addenbrooke, M. 2011. *Survivors of addiction: narratives of recovery.* New York, NY: Routledge.

Anderson, T., Swan, H. and Lane, D.C. 2010. Institutional fads and the medicalization of drug addiction. *Sociology Compass*, 4 (7), 476–494.

Aston, S. 2009. Identities under construction: women hailed as addicts. *Health: An Interdisciplinary Journal for the Social Study of Health, Illness and Medicine*, 13 (6), 611–628.

Bakken, B. 2000. *The exemplary society: human improvement, social control, and the dangers of modernity in China.* Oxford: Oxford University Press.

Brady, A. 2002. Regimenting the public mind: the modernization of propaganda in the PRC. *International Journal*, 57 (4), 563–578.

Brady, A. 2008. *Marketing dictatorship: propaganda and thought work in contemporary China.* Lanham, MD: Rowman & Littlefield.

Brady, A. 2009. Mass persuasion as a means of legitimation and China's popular authoritarianism. *American Behavioral Scientist*, 53 (3), 434–457.

Brady, A. 2012. State Confucianism, Chineseness, and tradition in CCP propaganda. In A. Brady (ed.) *China's thought management* (pp. 57–75). London: Routledge.

Croll, E. 1995. *Changing identities of Chinese women: rhetoric, experience and self-perception in twentieth century China.* Hong Kong: Hong Kong University Press.

Davies, J.B. 1997a. *Drugspeak: the analysis of drug discourse.* Amsterdam: Harwood Academic.

Dikötter, F., Laamann, L. and Zhou, X. 2004. *Narcotic culture: a history of drugs in China.* London: C. Hurst.

Friedling, M. 1996. Feminisms and the Jewish mother syndrome: identity, autobiography, and the rhetoric of addiction. *Discourse*, 19 (1), 105–130.

Gibson, B., Acquah, S. and Robinson, P.G. 2004. Entangled identities and psychotropic substance use. *Sociology of Health and Illness*, 26 (5), 597–616.

Guo, Y. 2010. China's celebrity mothers: female virtues, patriotism and social harmony. In L. Edwards and E. Jeffreys (eds) *Celebrity in China* (pp. 45–66). Hong Kong: Hong Kong University Press.

Hänninen, V. and Koski-Jännes, A. 1999. Narratives of recovery from addictive behaviours. *Addiction*, 94 (12), 1837–1848.

Harding, G. 1986. Constructing addiction as a moral failing. *Sociology of Health and Illness*, 8 (1), 75–85.

Hersey, C. 2005. Script(ing) treatment: representations of recovery from addiction in Hollywood film. *Contemporary Drug Problems*, 32, 467–493.

Hirschman, E.C. 1992. Mundane addiction: the cinematic depiction of cocaine consumption. *Advances in Consumer Research*, 19, 424–428.

Hirschman, E.C. 1995. The cinematic depiction of drug addiction: a semiotic account. *Semiotica*, 104 (1/2), 119–164.

Hughes, K. 2007. Migrating identities: the relational constitution of drug use and addiction. *Sociology of Heath and Illness*, 29 (5), 673–691.

Infantino, S.C. 1999. Female addiction and sacrifice: literary tradition or user's manual? In J. Lilienfeld and J. Oxford (eds) *The languages of addiction* (pp. 91–102). New York, NY: St. Martin's Press.

Järvinen, M. and Andersen, D. 2009. Creating problematic identities: the making of the chronic addict. *Substance Use and Misuse*, 44, 865–885.

Jones, C. 1990. *Promoting prosperity: the Hong Kong way of social policy.* Hong Kong: Chinese University Press.

Kleinman, A., Yan, Y., Jun, J., Lee, S., Zhang, E., Pan, T., Wu, F. and Guo, J. 2011. *Deep China: the moral life of the person: what anthropology and psychiatry tell us about China today*. Berkeley: University of California Press.

Kuo, C.T. 2008. *Religion and democracy in Taiwan*. Albany, NY: SUNY Press.

Levin, D. 2015, January 24. Despite a crackdown, use of illegal drugs in China continues unabated. *The New York Times*. Retrieved from www.nytimes.com/2015/01/25/world/despite-a-crackdown-use-of-illegal-drugs-in-china-continues-unabated.html 24 February 2015.

Liang, B. and Lu, H. 2013. Discourses of drug problems and drug control in China: reports in the *People's Daily*, 1946–2009. *China Information*, 27 (3), 301–326.

Lo, L.K. 2011. Taiwan, Hong Kong, Macao. In P.C. Phan (ed.) *Christianities in Asia* (pp. 173–183). Malden, MA: Wiley-Blackwell.

Louie, K. 2002. *Theorising Chinese masculinity: society and gender in China*. Cambridge, UK: Cambridge University Press.

Lu, H., Miethe, T.D. and Liang, B. 2009. *China's drug practices and policies: regulating controlled substances in a global context*. Farnham, UK: Ashgate.

McIntosh, J. and McKeganey, N. 2000. Addicts' narratives of recovery from drug use: constructing a non-addict identity. *Social Science and Medicine*, 50, 1501–1510.

Murdoch, R.O. 1999. Working and "drugging" in the city: economics and substance use in a sample of working addicts. *Substance Use and Misuse*, 34 (14), 2115–2133.

Muzak, J. 2007. "They say the disease is responsible": social identity and the disease concept of drug addiction. In V. Raoul, C. Canam, A.D. Henderson and C. Paterson (eds), *Unfitting stories: narrative approaches to disease, disability, and trauma* (pp. 255–264). Waterloo, ON: Wilfrid Laurier University Press.

Muzak, J. 2008. "Addiction got me what I needed": depression and drug addiction in Elizabeth Wurtzel's memoirs. In H. Clark (ed.) *Depression and narrative: telling the dark* (pp. 97–109). Albany, NY: SUNY Press.

Pearson, V. and Liu, M. 2002. Ling's death: an ethnography of a Chinese woman's suicide. *Suicide and Life – Threatening Behaviour*, 32 (4), 347–358.

Ramsay, G. 2008. *Shaping minds: a discourse analysis of Chinese-language community mental health literature*. Amsterdam: John Benjamins.

Ramsay, G. 2013. *Mental illness, dementia and family in China*. London: Routledge.

Roberts, R.A. 2010. *Maoist model theatre: the semiotics of gender and sexuality in the Chinese Cultural Revolution (1966–1976)*. Leiden: Brill.

Taïeb, O., Révah-Lévy, A., Moro, M.R. and Baubet, T. 2008. Is Ricoeur's notion of narrative identity useful in understanding recovery in drug addicts? *Qualitative Health Research*, 18 (7), 990–1000.

Viano, M. 2002. An intoxicated screen: reflections on film and drugs. In J.F. Brodie and M. Redfield (eds) *High anxieties: cultural studies in addiction* (pp. 134–158). Berkeley: University of California Press.

Weinberg, D. 2000. "Out there": the ecology of addiction in drug abuse treatment discourse. *Social Problems*, 47 (4), 606–621.

Zhou, Y. 1999. *Anti-drug crusades in twentieth-century China: nationalism, history, and state building*. Lanham, MD: Rowman and Littlefield.

Index

addict *see* drug addict
addiction *see* drug addiction
agency 8
amphetamine *see* drugs
anti-drug campaigns 4, 33, 85; *see also* 'people's war against drugs'
Anti-Drug Law of the People's Republic of China (2008) 36–7, 43

biogenetics 55
'biographical disruption' 6, 28
biomedicalisation 6, 9–10, 29, 39, 43, 55–6, 78–9, 120–4

Chairman Mao *see* Mao, Zedong
Chan, Jaycee 124–5
China: attitudes to drug addiction 39, 43, 54–6, 68, 78–9, 108, 112, 115–24; family responsibility in 10, 24, 28–9, 31, 36, 55, 58–61, 78, 99, 105, 111–12; filmic stories from 74–86; health service provision in 9; life stories from 50–6; psychiatric practice and 79–84; rehabilitation in 59, 69; womanhood in 30–1, 84–5; *see also* femininity; gender; stigma
Chinese culture: and addiction i, 29–34; family caregiving 78, 99
Christianity 12, 56–69, 117–18, 123–4
clinical application 122–4
Communism: drug addiction and 1–5, 12, 22; drug addiction as allegory 121; rehabilitation facilities 117
Community Health Organisation for Intervention, Care and Empowerment (CHOICE) 62
compliance 9, 30, 78
concealment *see* shame; stigma

Confucian tradition 22, 30, 60, 118
criminality 64, 80, 85, 98, 99, 107, 111–12, 122, 124–5; *see also* re-education-through-labour; rehabilitation as punishment
Cultural Revolution 30, 35, 40, 51
culture–definition 11

Dawn on the Black Seas: Rebirth Testimonies of Friends in Drug Rehabilitation 56–61
Daytop Drug Rehabilitation Village 12, 50–6, 68–9, 113–18
diagnosis 76, 79
disempowerment 13, 55–6, 106–8; *see also* empowerment
drug addiction: attitudes towards 39, 43, 54–6, 68, 78–9, 108, 112, 115–24; cultural constructions of i, 1, 8, 11, 78, 111; definition of 11; ethnic minorities 2, 9, 27, 121; family caregivers and caregiving and 24, 27–31, 52, 60, 78, 82–4, 95, 104–7, 121; in filmic stories 11–13, 73–110; hereditary potential and 29, 55; humanities research and 11–13; treatment for 8–9, 62–3, 83, 96, 99; *see also* biomedicalisation; China; gender; Hong Kong; 'preferred' story; recovery; rehabilitation
drug addicts 2–3, 7–10, 106; *see also* drug addiction
drug dealers *see* drugs
Drug Prohibition: The State of the Art 62–7
drugs: amphetamine/methamphetamine 2, 22, 57, 59, 61, 64–5, 91–2, 95, 99, 101–2, 124; heroin 3–4, 34–44, 53, 59, 64, 65, 68, 80–6, 106, 112, 124; ketamine 2, 64,

130   *Index*

65, 95–8, 100–3; marijuana 86–90, 101; opium 2–4, 23–32, 85; production and supply of 4, 80–1, 95, 98, 103
Drum Beat 62–7

empowerment 8, 9, 44, 67–9, 116–24; *see also* disempowerment
'exemplarity' 21–2, 40–5, 50, 114
explanatory models of illness 120–1

face 23–30, 43–4, 52–6, 61, 68, 98, 100–1, 112, 118
family 24–9, 36–7, 45, 55, 58, 61–7, 74–80, 89–90, 111–16, 124–5; betrayal of 80, 86, 106
"felt stigma" 61; *see also* stigma
femininity 8, 31, 44, 115–16
fiction: addiction in 73
filial piety 30–1, 57–8, 64, 68, 78, 84, 86, 93, 106, 112, 118
film *see* filmic stories
filmic stories 73–100; drug addiction in 73–4, 84–6, 89–90, 93–4, 98–9, 103–5; psychosis in 76, 79

gender norms: addiction and 8, 12, 21–46, 84–6, 89, 94; *see also* masculinity; femininity
gendered language 85
ghost authoring 49

hallucinations 76, 97–8
Happily Sharing, Seventeen Years of Age 94, 100–5
He Is Not Lonely 94–100
Heaven and Hell 23–34
Help Me Eros 86–90
heroin *see* drugs
heteronormative fraternity 114, 116, 123
homosexuality 38–41, 58, 60, 104–7, 124
Hong Kong 1–2, 4, 49–50; British colonial rule 1, 4, 12, 49; filmic stories from 94–105, 112; life stories from 62–9, 114, 116–18; rehabilitation in 117–18

identity: addiction and 7–8, 41, 44–5, 54–5, 66–7, 79, 112, 115–16; gender and 30, 41; illness and 9–10, 34, 41, 55–6, 60, 78; sexuality and 103–4, 113, 124
institutional narrative 53, 59; *see also* rehabilitation facilities

Jump Ashin! 86, 90–4

ketamine *see* drugs

language use 5, 10, 36, 43, 85, 106, 112
legislation 4, 23, 43–4, 107, 122
life events: ordering of 11, 107–8, 111
life stories *see* China, Hong Kong, Taiwan
loss of 'face' *see* face

magic realism 86
Mao, Zedong 1, 4, 22, 26, 30
marginality 13, 52, 55, 61, 66, 73–4, 104–7, 115–17
marijuana *see* drugs
masculinity 28, 30, 42, 90, 93, 98–9, 105–6, 113; recovery and 114–15
mental illness 55, 60–1, 77–9, 96, 99, 112, 120, 124
meta-narrative 73–4, 80, 85–6, 90, 99, 104–5, 116, 121
metaphor 10–11, 119
methamphetamine *see* drugs
moral exemplar 12, 22, 50
moral transgression 74, 78, 80, 84, 86, 103, 105–6, 116, 122

narrative 6, 11; community and 56; corpus 49; discourse and 10, 21, 49; format 51, 57; institutional use of 53, 59; *see also* meta-narrative
narrative processes 13, 32, 107–8

open door reform 1, 21, 30, 40
Operation Dawn 12, 56–69, 113–14, 118, 123
opium *see* drugs
Out From the Margins 50–6, 59, 61

palliation 73–4, 115–16
People's Liberation Army 26, 32, 82, 107, 115, 122
'people's war against drugs' 33, 42, 85, 119; *see also* anti-drug campaigns
'preferred' story 12, 50, 68, 117; *see also* narrative
propaganda 22; *see also* preferred stories
psychiatric treatment 79–80
psychosis 60–1, 79, 99, 106–7; as spirit possession 58, 60–1
punishment 9, 38, 52, 77, 85, 107, 116, 122

Quitting 74–80, 105

recidivism: punishment for *see* re-education-through-labour recovery 6–10, 114; in filmic stories 73–4, 78, 80, 82, 84–6, 94, 98–9, 103–5; in life stories 26–30, 33–4, 39, 41–5, 58, 113; masculinity and 114–15

re-education-through-labour 37–42, 45, 52, 114

reform and opening up *see* open door reform

rehabilitation 36, 50; facilities for 12, 37, 41, 50, 116; in filmic stories 74, 78, 80–1, 83, 85–6, 94, 98–100, 103–7; in life stories 50–69; punishment and 36–7, 52, 77, 122; *see also* Daytop; Operation Dawn; Society for the Aid and Rehabilitation of Drug Abusers (SARDA); therapeutic community; Zheng Sheng College

relapse 9–10, 32, 82, 115, 119, 121

religion 59, 117

Republican-era China 3–4, 25

SARDA *see* Society for the Aid and Rehabilitation of Drug Abusers

sense-making 107–8

setting 5

shame 10, 24–6, 29, 36, 80, 103, 112, 125; *see also* face; silencing; stigma

silencing 68, 125; *see also* face; shame; stigma

Society for the Aid and Rehabilitation of Drug Abusers (SARDA) 12, 62–9

stereotyping 54, 66, 68, 108, 115, 118, 123

stigma 43–4, 54–6, 66–8, 79, 104, 108, 111–12, 115–16, 118, 120–1, 124; *see also* face; 'felt' stigma; shame; silencing

Struggle Spirit 34–44, 85, 105, 106

subjectivity 11

suicide 58, 74, 81, 84–6, 89, 103–4, 106, 115

Sun, Yat-sen 25, 30, 113; *see also* Republican-era China

Taiwan 59; Christianity in 59, 61; filmic stories from 86–94, 105–7, 112; Japanese colonial rule 1, 4, 59; life stories from 56–62, 68–9; rehabilitation in 59–62, 117

television serial *see* filmic stories

temporality 12, 21, 65, 103

therapeutic community 50, 53, 55–6, 63, 68, 117, 118

transgression *see* moral transgression

Tung Wah 67

violence 51, 58, 68, 78–80, 85, 90, 93, 125

The War of Two 74, 80–6, 90, 105, 106, 107

We are Good Zheng Sheng Kids 62–7

We Love Zheng Sheng Kids 62–7

womanhood 30–1, 40, 42, 84–5

Young People, Treasure Your Youth! 56–61

Zheng Sheng College 12, 62, 96–7, 99, 106